A MAN MAY FISH

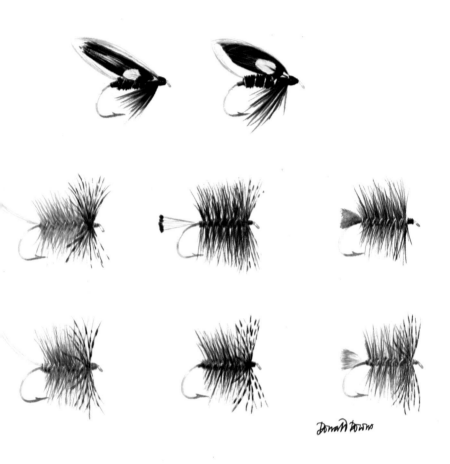

Flies tied by the author. Top row: the Kingsmill. Rows 2 and 3, the Bumbles. (left to right) Golden Olive, the Claret, the Bruiser, the Fiery Brown, Grey Ghost and Magenta. These flies have been painted by Donald Downs from those on display in the Fly Fishers Club.

The Hon. T. C. Kingsmill Moore, LLD

A MAN MAY FISH

By

T. C. Kingsmill Moore

("Saracen")

with a foreword by
Hugh Falkus
and an introduction by
Conrad Voss Bark

COLIN SMYTHE
Gerrards Cross, Bucks.

First published in 1960
Second, revised and enlarged edition published by
Colin Smythe Limited, Gerrards Cross, Buckinghamshire
in 1979
reprinted in 1983

British Library Cataloguing in Publication Data

Moore, T. C. Kingsmill
   A man may fish. – 2nd ed.
   1. Trout fishing – Ireland
   I. Title
   799.1'7'55   SH688.16

   ISBN 0–86140–024–0
   ISBN 0–86140–025–9 Special ed.

Printed in Great Britain.
Set by Watford Typesetters Limited and printed and bound
by Billing & Sons Ltd., Worcester

TO THE MEMORY OF MY WIFE

who made so many fears groundless,
so many dreams a reality.

FOREWORD

Hugh Falkus

In 1975, in my book *Sea Trout Fishing,* I wrote of *A Man May Fish* (then long out of print) that 'It is in my top-twenty list of best angling books and I urge the publishers to bring out a re-print; better, to persuade the author to enlarge it and bring out a second edition'.

I am delighted that these words helped to get this new edition published, and that K.M. was able to add so much new material before he died, for it is by far the best book on Irish sea trout fishing I have ever read.

INTRODUCTION

Conrad Voss Bark

T. C. Kingsmill Moore was a most distinguished judge of the Irish High Court and of the Supreme Court and he had played a leading part in Irish political life as a member of the Senate, yet it was once said of him that his real profession was fishing. He liked that story and admitted there might be a little truth in it.

He fished and wandered along most of the great rivers and loughs of Ireland for more than 50 years so that few men knew them more intimately than he did; yet he never fished passively, accepting the traditional fly patterns and methods without question. He was continually questioning, continually experimenting, never satisfied until he had found the answers to the problem of fly design and presentation that he sought. This book is a record of those journeyings, of his experiments, of the new fly patterns he created and of the ways that they were fished. The book, in one very true sense, is an angler's progress; and yet it is so much more.

I first read *A Man May Fish* many years ago and fell in love with it, and the reason why I found it so entrancing is this: Kingsmill Moore may well be writing about fishing but when he does so he has that rare gift of being able at the same time to illuminate Ireland, and in particular the people of Ireland whom he loved. He uses his subject as a key to open his readers' minds to wider horizons. He has an astonishing ability too, as a writer, to create living people. His portrait of Jamesie is a minor masterpiece. No other ghillie in fly fishing literature that I know of comes anywhere near the reality of Jamesie. I read about him year after year and always with a great warmth and affection. That is the quality about Kingsmill Moore himself that I like most: his warmth and affection for the life of Galway and

Connemara and the wild places and the people who live there. He has it at his finger tips. Moreover, there are times when his words have a terrifying magic:

> As the night deepens the river takes command. Its voice mounts, filling the valley, rising to the rim of the hills, no longer one voice but a hundred. Time and place are dissolving; the centuries have lost their meaning; timelessness is all. One foot is crossing the invisible frontier which bounds the land of the old gods . . .

Any sea trout fisherman who has fished at night will know the truth and the quality of that writing. I do not know anyone who has given a better description of what it feels like to be alone in a river after dark. That is just a taste of the pleasure that is to come to you if you are reading this book for the first time.

Kingsmill Moore was born in Dublin in March 1893 and he died in Dublin in February 1979 at the age of 85. He went to school at Marlborough, in England, and returned to Dublin to take a degree at Trinity and he kept in close touch with the university all his life. During the First World War, from 1917–1918, he was in the Royal Flying Corps in France and Flanders. He became a barrister in his return to Dublin and during the Civil War, from 1922–1923, was also for a short period the war correspondent of *The Irish Times*. Then followed political work and his election to the Senate. He played a considerable part in the rebuilding of Irish life after the bitterness of the war. In 1947 he was appointed a judge of the High Court and, in 1951, a judge of the Supreme Court, retiring in 1965. His personal life was happy. He was married to a charming woman known to everyone as Alex – she did not like her birth names – and they had a son and a daughter. It was his wife, his great companion, who persuaded him to write this book. He did so, at first rather diffidently, and was then delighted at the way it was received. He revised the text and wrote two new chapters for this second edition shortly before he died.

June 1979

PREFACE

No one but a master or a fool is dogmatic about fishing, and I have no pretensions to be the one nor wish to appear the other. Reservations continually repeated can, however, become exasperating. May I ask, then, that conclusions which appear to be stated too positively should be read as if introduced by the words – "As far as my limited experience goes and as a provisional hypothesis . . ."?

Personal experience is bound to be incomplete, and so, misleading. Kelson is supposed to have said that no one should open his mouth about salmon fishing till he had landed three thousand fish, and I have no reason to doubt that he observed his dictum; but that did not save him from expressing opinions which no modern fisherman takes seriously. As my own score is still not quite five hundred I have heeded his warning to the extent that I deal only incidentally with salmon.

What fishing has meant, and means, to me may be summarized in a plea and a protest. A protest against the itch to make records, the urge to extract every possible fish in any way that is not illegal, the desire to go one better than the next man; a plea that fishing should be not so much a pursuit as a pastime, calling for concentration sufficient to put all worries out of mind, yet not such concentration as to be in itself exhausting. It was not his skill but his approach that made Walton the father of anglers.

PREFACE TO THE SECOND EDITION

The first edition of this book has been out of print for many years but I still get frequent queries as to where a second-hand copy can possibly be obtained. A new edition would seem to be justified.

Much water has flown under anglers' bridges since the first edition. Nylon has completely superseded gut, involving new knots and methods of making up a cast, greenheart and split cane are going out of fashion for rods in favour of new materials, the tube fly has made inroads on the salmon rivers and the old Redditch scale for hooks has returned to oust the new scale introduced at the turn of the century. These changes have necessitated some minor alterations in the original text. I have also added two new chapters and an appendix.

The suggestions as to fly tying have met with approval. Conrad Voss Bark in his *Fishing for Lake Trout* goes so far as to say that they mark a significant stage in the dressing of lake flies and has adopted my ideas of mixed hackling for his nymphs.

Patterns advocated in the first edition seem also to have stood the test. The Kingsmill, Claret Bumble, Golden Olive Bumble and Bruiser have become standards on some lakes and I have had pleasant letters from correspondents previously unknown, telling of their success in places as far removed as Iceland, the Shetlands and Germany. Most surprising was a letter from an angler who seemed always to get his limit with the Kingsmill on Two Lakes, a fishery which I would have thought quite unsuited to that pattern. I notice too that Mr. Veniard in his *Further Guide to Fly Dressing* gives Mr. Westmoreland's selection of three flies for river, lake and sea trout, and of the three flies two are the Kingsmill and the Claret Bumble. As Veniard's book was published within four years of my first edition the two patterns mentioned were not long in winning their spurs.

Fishing has changed sadly during the seventy years of an

angling life in the course of which I fished 32 Irish lakes and 36 Irish rivers, some for only a day or two, others for periods which, when added together, amount to many months. When I was a boy first class fishing was to be had free or for a trifling sum. Owners of highly preserved waters often were willing to give leave for a day or two and boatmen could be had for five shillings a day. Now the cost of any fishing which could be reckoned as first class has gone to heights which only the rich can afford and as the price has gone up so has the quality gone down. Stretches of brown trout rivers have been ruined by pollution, the extent of drift net fishing with nylon nets threatens the extinction of salmon and even white trout are only half as numerous as they were. I was fortunate to have been born in 1893.

With spring salmon fishing, which played so large a part in my angling life, I am still unable to deal, though the fault is not mine. I was lucky enough to acquire an old half-derelict water mill on the Slaney and converted it at small expense to a week-end cottage, using the ancient water wheel to provide electricity. With the mill went just under half a mile of fishing on the right bank and I rented an adjacent stretch of about the same length. For over 25 years nearly every Saturday and Sunday in the months of March, April and May, saw me on the river. My water was far from first class – my best season was 37 salmon including a thirty pounder – but it contained a number of lively streams in which fish took well during the spring run. Twice it gave me seven in a day and on several occasions five or six. I kept meticulous records of each day's fishing; height, colour and temperature of water; temperature of air and behaviour of barometer; force and direction of wind; nature of weather and type of sky; patterns and sizes of fly; fish seen, risen, lost and caught. Anything of interest or of an unusual character was noted down. My hope was that when all these records were collated and analysed some worthwhile general conclusions might emerge.

Then came the great flood, unprecedented for nearly 200 years. It knocked down bridges which had stood since the 18th century and fell with its full fury on my old house filling it up to the ceilings of the ground floor rooms, laying flat part of the back wall and sweeping furniture, books and all the records of my fishing down to the sea. One chair was recovered, caught high up in the branches of an elm five miles down stream.

The house was repaired, the furniture replaced. Then came the salmon disease sweeping up the Slaney like the Black Death. Every reach was full of dead or dying salmon. In the short pool at my gate seven fish lay dead on the bottom. It was too much. I sold my house and fishing, and never fished the Slaney again.

ACKNOWLEDGMENTS

My thanks are due to the proprietors of the *Irish Times* for permission to reprint "A Shannon Fisherman", which first appeared in that paper, to the Committee of the Fly Fishers Club for leave to reproduce the appendix, which first appeared in the *Flyfishers' Journal,* and to Mr. Frank W. Lane for leave to reproduce the wonderful photograph of leaping salmon taken by Mr. Ronald Thompson: to the late Brigadier W. N. Stokes for allowing me to choose from his collection the beautiful landscape photographs to which his name is attached, and to Mr. J. R. Harris for putting his fishing photographs at my disposal. To Mrs. David Wilson and Miss Irish Bardon is due the credit of managing to decipher my abominable handwriting and render it into legible typescript.

All my fishing friends, in one way or another, by example, precept and conversation, have contributed to the contents of this book, but I should like to mention specially Mr. J. R. Harris, the most expert fly-fisherman and fly-dresser I know, Mr. E. C. Micks, an ideal fishing companion, and Mr. Oliver Gogarty, whose wit and good humour ensured that no day could ever be dull and who so often went out of his way to save my wearied limbs.

It is hard to single out particular names from the many fishery owners who at one time or another have made me free of their waters, but I must mention Sherry and Molly Shepherd, Sir Edward and Lady Stracey, Lord Killanin, Mr. Noel Huggard, Sir Charles Harmon, Alec Wallace, Mrs. Manning Robertson and Mrs. L. G. Humphreys.

Lastly I should emphasize that this book would never have appeared but for the continual encouragement, help and constructive criticism of my wife, who, from suggesting the title to the final revision of the proofs, has done most of the work and nurtured many of the ideas.

CONTENTS

LIST OF ILLUSTRATIONS

A SHANNON FISHERMAN
(Ernest Phelps, K.C.)

They talk of Master Ernest still beside the Shannon shores,
Leaning upon their idle spades, and over closed half-doors;
And tales go round of distant lies that he alone could reach,
Of Lame Man's Rock, and Counsellor's Throw,
                                    and Fifty-Pounder Beach.

From Back of Leap to Fork of Weir, from Landscape to Doonass,
By Cock, and Cloon, and Commodore, they watched for him to
      pass.
True, constant, tireless as his own stout Castleconnell rod,
He bore each ill that fate assigned, served man,
                                    and worshipped God.

The waters where he plied his craft are gone, as he is gone,
Shrunken, dispirited and maimed, the Shannon stumbles on:
But through the gates of memory the great, grey waters roll
And – "Master Ernest's in a fish, down by the Dancing Hole!"

PART I

INTRODUCTORY AND GENERAL

1

ENTERED APPRENTICE

It may have been fortunate that fishing was not made too easy. Boys who are born with an enthusiastic father and the Test at the bottom of the garden have been known to react and end up by train-watching. As my father and grandfathers were clergymen and headmasters without any interest in field sports, as no lake or river was anywhere near my home, and as the library contained no book on angling, not even Walton, there was nothing to put fishing into my head. Nevertheless to the dismay of my elders the fishing germ made its way early into my system, and all my childish phantasies were centred on fish. The old family doctor, who kept up tradition by never abandoning the frock coat and top hat and always arriving in his brougham, comforted my mother by the assurance that, though fishing was an incurable disease, he had never known it to be fatal.

Odd things began to happen to keep my interest alive. My dear little German governess in the course of a tearful parting pressed into my hands an envelope containing two dozen white trout flies and a lady friend of my father presented me with a pig-skin fly book so elegant that to this day I have never used it. There was the gypsy who appeared from nowhere when, bent over a bridge, I was absorbed in a fingerling trout, and foretold success for me because I was "born under Pisces". He followed up his prophesy by some practical advice on the use of the dock grub, which he called "a whitey kind of worm" and insisted was most killing if dug at the full moon. Next came the gardener's find. Returning home slightly sober on a Saturday night he stumbled over something which, on examination, turned out to be a fly book filled with all the patterns then popular. Though I had still no means of using them, they became a "fingering collection" and in future years caught fish. Some I still keep, as examples of the way they tied flies when Victoria was on the throne.

What might have been a disaster turned out a blessing. My father, worn down at last, presented me on my eighth birthday with a "fishing outfit". What he in his innocence brought home was a stout bottom rod, some thirty yards of thin spinning line, and a toy brass reel without a check. No one, however expert, could have cast a fly ten yards with such a rig, but the fly had to be got to the fish somehow and so, at the threshold of my fishing, I learned to experiment. Our forefathers with their hazel rods and hair lines had faced the same problem, and I found out the same answers, discovering on the way some minor tactics which came in useful even when I had acquired proper equipment. The very lightness of the line, which made it impossible to cast, allowed it to be floated out on a strong breeze with a fly, natural or artificial, at the end; and so I got my first lesson in dapping. I found that in wooded streams if the rod was poked through the branches and the fly, at the end of only a few feet of line, was danced on the surface, trout took it readily. That, though I did not know it, was dibbing. A third trick has no name nor have I seen it described. It consisted in unreeling slowly till the stream had carried out twenty yards of line and then letting the fly swing in the current. One might expect the fly to hang inertly, but actually it darts and dithers in the most life-like way. A small silver bodied fly is best, for you are imitating a tiny fry, and the most profitable places are deep runs on the outside of a curve where the river has undercut the bank. On a bleak March day when there is no sign of fly or fish this trick may save a blank. On just such a day in an Aberdeenshire burn it was the only method which was of any use. A device of desperation, some fishermen's consciences revolt against it – a form of scrupulosity to which I was always immune.

Fishing literature burst upon me when I went to Marlborough, for in the school library were all the standard works of the day, the Badminton volumes, Stewart's *Practical Angler,* (still after a hundred years the best book for a boy) the earlier volumes of Halford, that high priest of chalk stream eclecticism, and, most delightful of all angling books, Sir Edward Grey's *Fly Fishing.*

Not four hundred yards from where I sat reading, the Kennet glided under White Horse hill, and from Preshute and Duck bridges trout were on view. This land of chalk stream and meadows was strange country to me, and though boys were not allowed to fish, no one could bandage my eyes. Up and down stream I wandered. It was the hey-day of the water meadows, when carriers were kept clean and sluices in repair. Nowhere is life more teeming than in a water meadow when June is high, the air heavy with the scent of elder, water mint, and sweet cicely, sedges and withy beds quivering with warblers and buntings, back waters a continual bustle of coot, dabchick, and water hen. I lay on my face and saw the bright beetles and all the scurrying insects of the grass roots crawl under me, stood waist deep in the water to dip out the hiding nymphs, watched them turn into duns and then, shedding their last film, into the crystal of the spinner. The wild duck led her string of ducklings down stream and never noticed me, the trout sucked in a dun or swirled more energetically after an escaping sedge within a few yards of where I sat motionless. It was a lesson in "Study to be quiet".

On the wall of my study still hangs a rod case holding the remnants of a rod, its bottom joint a mass of splinters. It was my first rod, a two piece green-heart, bought for a guinea from Ogdens of Cheltenham when I was 14. For 10 years it was my constant companion catching my first four pound trout and my first salmon. As perfect a rod as I ever handled, it is so full of memories that I cannot bear to throw the remnants away. How came it by its present condition? An acquaintance (not even a friend) borrowed it from my rooms without permission and returned it in fragments. He explained that, on his way to the river, one of the struts supporting the hood of his motor car had given way so that he had to use my rod as a substitute. "It proved quite unequal to the task" he said in a tone of complaint. I had my revenge however for, a week afterwards I removed his motor bicycle and rode off on it for a very successful fishing holiday.

Fishing was reserved for the holidays when, a suitable rod having at last been acquired, I roamed the countryside on a bicycle, stopping at any bridge over a likely stream and casting my fly where I fancied. Only once was I questioned. I had un-limbered to fish a deep pool in Donegal where first a white trout of a pound, and then one of over two pounds, came to me. As I was landing the second fish a bailiff approached and asked me for my licence. Of course I had not got one, and I said quite truthfully that I had come to fish for brown trout. He smiled. He had heard that one before. But all he said was "There's another good pool round the corner" and left. Forty years later he gave evidence before me in a fishery case. I had no recollection of him and asked if there was a good run of white trout in a certain river. "Faith and there is, and your lordship wouldn't be long in whipping them out" was his disconcerting answer. He had recognised the poacher turned gamekeeper. He did not omit to tell counsel, nor have counsel allowed me to forget.

A threat of tuberculosis took me from the chalk stream to a Deeside sanatorium and a very different fishing country. It was near the end of the long drought of 1911, and the Dee looked more like a graveyard than a river, with stones sticking up everywhere and hardly any water visible. Below the falls of its tributary the Feugh the salmon lay thick, discoloured and listless, with white patches of fungus spreading over head and flank. There, on the bridge above the falls, when the drought at last broke, I was lucky enough to see for the first time one of the most exciting sights fishing can offer, the coming of a great flood.

Inch by difficult inch the river began to rise, spreading a film over dry rocks, turning trickles to rivulets and rivulets to cascades. In the pool below all was agitation. Excited by the taste of fresh water the salmon were showing, jumping and swirling, making ready to go. Now the note of the fall had deepened and the pool was starting to fill, lessening the height a fish would have to jump, giving him greater depth from which to gain impetus. A curtain of water was arching over the lip of the rock, and a salmon whose leap had not cleared the full height, might yet by desperate swimming win through the last few inches. One got up, then another, then three at once. The water rose and rose, and soon there was a steady procession of writhing, splashing bodies, till at last the falls were drowned and the fish could go through unseen. When the flood receded every fish was gone, and far away in the hills the redds were being prepared.

February came and the Dee ran clear, not yet at spring level, for the winter had been hard and much water was still locked away in snow and ice in the mountains. An old man, white bearded, came along, wielding a heavy salmon rod, fishing only the nearer water and leaving the further lies to his ghillie. He fished carefully and with obvious mastery. Presently from the high bank I saw the turn of a fish, the line straighten, and the rod go up with a slow lift very unlike the instantaneous strike which mountain trout had taught me. It was the first salmon I had seen hooked, and I was much more excited than the fisherman to whom the fight was routine. The fish was gaffed and the old man sat down, a little exhausted. I drew near delicately, for he had the look of a Hebrew prophet with whom it would not be wise to take liberties. All went well. "Nice fish," he said, "sea lice! There's generally a fish in that near eddy, but people miss it by casting too far out." He was in a mood for talking and showed me his flies – long Dee strip wings, venomous Spey patterns and the more standard tyings. I asked his name. "Andrew Lang." "Not *the* Andrew Lang – I mean the man who wrote the Fairy Books and translated Homer and wrote the poem about the Odyssey – and the pavilion cat?" He smiled for the first time. "I must acknowledge them all." He got up a little stiffly. "I have to be getting back. Time was when I could have fished as long a day as Stewart himself. Now I get tired too soon. Good luck. Never neglect the nearer water." It may have been his last salmon, for he died that year.

I was to have an experience of the Dee before I left it. The head of the sanatorium owned a stretch and gave me leave to fish for trout. In borrowed waders, much too short for me, I made my way into the strong stream where the March Browns were fluttering like brown snow fall, fishing up stream as Stewart had taught me. Among all those myriads my imitation had no chance of being singled out. Nowadays I would put on a completely contrasting pattern and fish it downstream with deliberate drag to attract attention, but then I merely pushed further and further out, casting madly among the madly rising trout. The shingle started to wash from under my feet. I took a hasty step back, was spancelled by the short waders, and the Dee had me. Two hundred yards further down I grasped a rock and was able to make my way to the bank my rod still undamaged. I emptied my waders and fished out the day. "Well, if you can do that," said the Chief, as he completed his examination, "I think we can restore you to circulation."

My apprenticeship was at an end. I could cast tolerably, fish an up-stream worm, knew a little of riverside entomology, and made most of my own tackle. I felt that I could meet others as a fellow craftsman.

2

WHY DO FISH TAKE?
AN EXCURSUS INTO PSYCHOLOGY

Angling is differentiated from other forms of fish-catching because in angling the initiative is with the fish. Unless we can intrigue or exasperate the fish into taking our hook into its mouth we go home empty-creeled. What every angler desires to know is why a fish takes, and how to make it take more frequently.

All non-anglers and most anglers would regard the answer as being so obvious that the question is not worth asking. "Fish take," they say, "because they are hungry and we have surrounded our hook with something which is good to eat, or at least looks good." To anglers for the so-called coarse fish this answer is true and sufficient. In dealing with trout it is partially true, for sea trout less true, and for salmon, whose feeding in fresh water is minimal or non-existent, it is not true at all.

The scientists are not helpful. In anything which can be explored by test tubes or microscope, or where controlled experiments can be devised, they overwhelm us with facts. Anatomists tell us how fish are constructed, physiologists explain how their organs work, and physicists draw diagrams to illustrate the optical limitations of their vision; but the answer to our question is to be found in the mind and temperament of fish. Fish psychology awaits its Freud. A conversation with a zoologist usually ends abruptly with an accusation of anthropomorphism. This makes the day for him, for he has convicted us of a major scientific heresy expiable only at the stake. The word acts as a kind of "I spy strangers", putting a closure on a debate which may be getting a little out of his depth. Failing controlled experiments (which may come in time) what is left to us? Free observation, interpretation, and that *a priori* reasoning which is now so unpopular even among epistemologists.

Compared with bird watchers, fish watchers are at a great disadvantage, for reflection, refraction, and turbid water combine to conceal fish from our eyes. To see fish you must either get under the water or high above it. Under-water chambers have been constructed, but their range of utility is limited. High wooden towers were built over some Irish pools to watch the entry of fish and guide the netsmen, but we cannot line a river with such contraptions. The ordinary fisherman has to make do with bridges, cliffs, high banks and trees. Helped by polarized glasses it is astonishing how much can be seen, especially if large fish such as salmon are under observation.

Ears are useless, for the fish are mute, but sensitive hands can tell a lot about the mood of the fish, distinguishing the mere brush on the gut of a mildly interested salmon coming to have a look, from the tentative lipping of curiosity, or the fierce onslaught of the killer.

When we have made such observations as we can, the next difficulty is that of interpretation. We see fish behaving in a way which in a human being would indicate anger, fear, or curiosity; but those are words which have come into existence to describe human emotions, and the brain and nervous system of a fish are so different from ours that we are not justified in ascribing to fish such emotions as we feel.

I refuse to be too much daunted by the anthropomorphic bogey. Why should not the capacity to feel emotions have developed gradually in the evolutionary process because of their utility in the struggle for survival? Fish are in the same evolutionary phylum as ourselves. Is there any reason to deny them primitive emotions resembling our own though less perfected, a kind of proto-fear, proto-anger, proto-curiosity? the introduction of a Greek prefix seems to have a mollifying effect on scientists. Having made the gesture we may, for brevity, drop the prefix.

No advanced form of life can have survived unless it possesses in a high degree the three fundamental urges, the urge to eat, the urge to escape being eaten, and the urge to reproduce. Though all of those urges have been utilized to catch fish by net, trap, or snare, only the first concerns the angler and his use of it is such as to require no comment. I did know an old angler who attempted to use the reproductive urge by soaking his fly in the eggs or milt of the first fish he caught, hoping to attract the opposite sex, but his mediaeval methods did not seem to be particularly successful.

The urge to eat has played such a large part in angling that it has tended to obscure the other reasons why fish take our lures. Modern man uses his mouth only for eating (apart from talking and kissing which have no interest for fish) and he assumes that when a fish takes something into its mouth the reason is that he wants to eat. This overlooks the cardinal anatomical fact that a fish *has no hands*. Everything which a man does with his hands, or other animals with their paws, a fish must do with its mouth if it does it at all. The mouth is the only available organ for attack, defence, or exploration. Now we are on the right track.

Supplementary to the primary urges and aids to their realization are the emotions, and of these secondary urges ferocity, fear, and curiosity are of importance to the angler, for all three stimulate a fish into using its mouth. Ferocity has an almost infinite survival value. Even among the peaceful ruminants it is necessary to secure a mate. When the disparity between hunter and hunted is not too great, its presence may save one from starvation and the other from sudden death. There are stories of stoats being daunted by unusually fierce rabbits and I have myself watched a dispirited-looking stoat running over a field followed at a distance of about twelve yards by a large rabbit. It certainly looked as if the rabbit was seeing him off. Ferocity can become so ingrained as to be an end in itself, and a rogue dog among sheep or a fox in a hen house will kill for the sheer gusto of killing. So also will a fish.

No one hesitates to ascribe ferocity to a shark or a pike, but trout and salmon are regarded as gentlemen and invested with the old school tie. A pike could take lessons from the trout. Three times have I caught trout with victims of nearly a third of their weight protruding from their mouths, a six ounce trout with a two ounce cray fish, a pound trout with a six ounce brother, and a three pounder with a fish of nearly three-quarters of a pound. In each case the lower third of the prey was partially digested, while the upper portion was in perfect condition. Those trout could not possibly have been hungry, yet, in spite of their gagged condition, they attacked and even managed to get my fly inside their mouths from sheer desire to kill. It is well known that animals will attack anything which appears to be wounded, sick, or behaving in an unusual way. I have seen peaceful ducks savage an injured hen. There is no particular difficulty in fishing a live bait for salmon in a quiet pool, as is done successfully for pike, or even in mounting a dead fish in a way to give it a natural motion; yet the consensus of angling opinion shows that the most successful baits are the spoon, the spinning minnow, the plug, all of which have an unnatural motion suggesting a creature which is injured and out of control.

Fear can work both for and against the angler. Too often have I seen a fish lunge forward with gaping mouth and then, catching sight of me, put on all his brakes and fade away. A large prawn in low water may drive every salmon out of a pool. But something dangerous, appearing unexpectedly, can cause a panic ferocity. A familiar instance is the cat who, if it sees a dog coming, will make for a tree, but if surprised, will turn at bay and then use the moment of consternation to escape. If for any reason a salmon does not see a fly till it is within a few inches of its eye, it will snap at it as a dog does at a wasp. This I have seen to occur when the fly had been drawn up unnoticed from behind the fish. In rocky rivers the angler's minnow must often be concealed till it is almost on top of the fish, and a really savage take is common in such circumstances. Running fish, if they take at all, usually do so with a sideways snap which results in foul hooking or a bad hold. I once followed a group of slowly running salmon from pool to pool for nearly half a mile catching three (one foul hooked) and losing six from light hooking. The explanation seems to me that these fish, intent on their upward journey, did not see my fly till it was almost touching them and then responded in the panic way which I have described.

One curious incident I am inclined to attribute to this kind of fear-ferocity. In a lake where it was customary to put back all fish of less than a pound, I had carefully unhooked and slipped back into the water a fish of about fourteen ounces. It wriggled out of my hand, swam away about two feet, and then whipped round and returned in an extremity of ingratitude, to bite my finger hard.

Finally comes curiosity, including in that term the urge to explore and experiment. Curiosity is proverbially a danger – "Curiosity killed the cat". All the same, the cat tribe in one form or another has distributed itself over the globe and seems in no danger of extinction. Curiosity may bring danger to the individual (as the angler hopes), but it is as necessary as ferocity for the survival of the species, and so has become a kind of built-in trait. Environment is never static, sometimes changing rapidly, sometimes slowly, and corresponding adaptations which involve experiment must be made by the creatures of the environment.

Take the case of a stew-fed trout turned out into the open river. He has to experiment and learn new methods of feeding in a few days or he dies. A different and long-term problem faced the fishes when the wet Ordovician period was succeeded by the dry conditions of the Devonian. They had to develop lungs, though they had several hundred thousand years to make the change. They did it – the African lung fish is a modern example of this adaptation – but it is difficult to think of any method of evolution by which the change could have been brought about without some experimental air-sipping.

Trout keep a careful eye on all the debris which floats down the river and, if not satisfied, they test it by mouth. I have seen them lip bits of leaves, paper, cigarette butt, milk curds, anything that was not too large; and an inventory of things found in their stomachs would fill the page. I have been able from a post of vantage to observe a fly or prawn fished over a group of salmon by a fellow angler. One of the fish shows signs of curiosity. His tail moves faster. He rises a few inches in the water. You tell the angler to keep on repeating the same cast. Each time the fish gets more curious, he comes up higher, drives forward to meet the object of his interest, and finally perhaps on the fourth or fifth presentation makes up his mind to take. He may on the other hand get bored and relapse into inertia.

A fish which takes from curiosity usually takes quietly, for he is exploring rather than killing. A small prawn or a bunch of worms may be caught and rolled between the lips so delicately that the angler does not know it has been taken, unless some one is there to tell him. If he does know he must not strike, for the hold is so light that the hook will come away. Sooner or later the fish by a kind of reflex action will swallow, and then it is time to hit. By contrast a salmon intent on killing may take the prawn with a wrench that nearly pulls the rod into the water. The line between what will interest or annoy a fish into taking and what will send him away in alarm is often fine. It varies with the height, temperature, and colour of the water; the freshness of the fish, and the number of lures it has recently seen; the light, the presentation. A correct appreciation of this line is the secret of success whenever we are trying to catch fish by methods other than the simulation of their ordinary food. This chapter is not meant as an argument for raking the Test with large wet flies (though Colonel Hawker seems to have done this with success) but there are times, places, and fish which require a more catholic approach to the problem of capture than would be suitable in a highly stocked and preserved chalk stream. The angler, like the fish, should always be experimenting, always trying to approach as near as he can to the critical line without crossing it.

3

SOME PROBLEMS OF VISION AND COLOUR

All that we know about the vision of fishes in the sense in which scientists use the word "knowledge" is to be found in *The Vertebrate Eye* by G. L. Walls, a book which every fisherman should consult. Scientists are not supposed to speculate. It is their business to devise experiments in which, by isolating one factor of a problem after another, they can arrive at positive and demonstrable conclusions. This chapter does little more than pose questions and speculate on possible answers.

The anatomical construction of a fish's eye shows that it is short sighted, but I suspect that we incline to exaggerate the extent of its short-sightedness. The archer fish brings down its prey from a height of six feet by squirting a jet of water at it, which implies considerable acuity of vision, and a couple of incidents in my own experience suggest that trout can see objects at a greater distance and higher in the air than we are inclined to suppose.

Standing on a bridge over the Slaney I was watching a trout some two to three feet under water when the ash of my cigarette fell off. It had about sixteen feet to fall before it touched the surface, but even a cigarette ash when unbroken does not take long to fall that distance on a calm day. The trout came up and took the ash accurately as it touched the stream. To give the fish time to rise through that depth of water while the ash was falling it must have spotted the ash the moment it was detached. It certainly rose to the ash, for there was nothing in the way of life on the water, which was directly under my eye.

The other incident took place on Lough Mask. The day was thundery and there was a flat calm. I was sitting with my rod between my knees, the tail fly just in the water and the bottom dropper hanging six inches above it. Suddenly, without the slightest apparent disturbance of the surface, a big head and shoulders came vertically into the air, opened its jaws, closed them on the dropper and sank down vertically, still without any disturbance. It turned out to be a three pounder, and if a fish of that size had used its tail anywhere within two feet of the surface there would have been a big and visible swirl. That trout must have spotted the fly five feet or more under water, have swum straight upwards for several feet, and then allowed its impetus to carry it on without further exertion. It was a most uncanny performance.

For long it was a question whether fish could see colour. Dr. Wall describes experiments which prove at least that some fish see some colours. But it seems to me unlikely that fish have the same range of colour vison as we have. There are at least three mystery colours, claret, gentian blue and bright orange, which seem to have an attraction for them not accountable by the occurrence of these colours in their natural food. Claret and Mallard must go very near heading the list of successful lake flies. In my experience claret (not necessarily combined with Mallard) comes second only to golden olive for brown lake trout, and second only to black for white trout. In nature I know of only one insect which displays claret – the Claret Dun. It is a rather dark purple-claret, quite unlike the more brilliant colours usually favoured by fishermen, and is an insect of acid waters and local distribution; while claret artificials serve equally well in alkaline waters and indeed anywhere in our island.

A deep blue is to be found in nature in the Blue-bottle and the elytra of the Sailor beetle, but these insects do not figure to any extent in a trout's menu. Yet, under different names, an artificial with a body of dark gentian blue floss and a black hackle is a most killing fly in Ireland, England and Scotland. When I was a boy more flies of this pattern were sold in Dublin tackle shops than of any other, and they were fished from the beginning to the end of the season.

Orange – true orange – occurs in ichneumon flies and the wing cases of several beetles; there is a touch of dull orange in many nymphs; and there is the dead-beech-leaf colour of a number of spinners. Orange floss darkens to a mahogany when wet, and so might approximate to some of the duller oranges of nature. But orange quill, orange seal's fur, and orange hackles preserve a

brilliant intensity which, to my eyes, exceeds anything in the
natural food. No colour seems to be more popular with fly
dressers. Apart from Orange Dun and Orange Quill, pure orange
has been combined with the following feathers to make well
known flies – Partridge, Light Woodcock, Dark Woodcock, Light
Snipe, Dark Snipe, Dotterel, Grouse, Bustard, Wren and Curlew.
Theakston, a Yorkshire fisherman in the middle of the last
century, gives careful descriptions of some ninety naturals and
their dressings, and in nearly half of his dressings orange or
copper-coloured silk is a feature. A brilliant orange hackle is
employed in some successful May fly dressings, though there is
no orange in a May fly. Certainly the limited occurrence of orange
in nature bears no proportion to its popularity in artificials.

Fishermen are realists, and they would not continue to use
these colours unless success justified their use. The conclusion is
irresistible. Either these colours have some aesthetic appeal to
trout, which appears unlikely, or trout do not see them as we see
them, but find in them some resemblance to the colours of natural
insects which appear quite different to us. Anyone who troubles
to go through the most approved representative dressings of
naturals which he knows well, will find that the orthodox dressings
tend to a colour which is nearer the red end of the spectrum than
is the colour of the natural. A watery skim-milk colour is
imitated by cream, cream by primrose, primrose by yellow, yellow
by buttercup, buttercup by orange. In lake flies he will find great
use made of a scarlet which has no counterpart in any natural.

A possible explanation is that the infra-red rays invisible to our
eyes may have a visible colour to trout. This was suggested to me
when I was trying to discover the best material for a black body.
I tied bodies of black quill, black wool, black seal's fur, black
silk, black cotton, and black ostrich herl. The silk and the ostrich
herl, especially the latter, were out on their own when it came
to catching fish. Now black is black because it absorbs all colours
and reflects none. I could not account for the varying success of
different black materials till it occurred to me that not all blacks
absorb infra-red rays. Some reflect it, at least partially. Manufacturers of black cloth for use in the tropics are careful to use a
black dye which reflects as much infra-red as possible, for this
makes the cloth cooler to wear. I retied all my bodies on plain
hooks, and got a scientific friend to photograph them on plates
sensitive to infra-red rays and by a light rich in infra-red. Only

the black silk and the ostrich herl came out as true blacks, the others being various shades of grey. This meant that if a trout's vision comprised infra-red, and if, for instance, a black beetle did *not* reflect infra-red, only my two successful blacks could be mistaken for the beetle. I then made similar experiments with other colours. The photographs showed that colours similar to the eye varied enormously in the amount of infra-red reflected, especially in the blue range. A darker blue might appear much more brilliant in the photograph than a light blue.

These experiments are quite inconclusive. To draw any worthwhile inference, it would be necessary to photograph on plates sensitive to infra-red, many dozens of natural insects and on the same plates their most approved representative dressings, together with dressings which seemed to the eye more exact. Even then it would be difficult to prove anything. But if trout can see an infra-red colour, and if natural flies reflect infra-red in any degree, they would not appear to the trout in the colour that we see them; and some of the success of patterns, which to our eyes are not near the colour of the natural they represent, might be explained.

Salmon flies do not represent anything. If certain colours are uniformly more successful it must be because they attract the fish in their own right. Anyone who takes the trouble to examine the patterns most popular for fresh-run salmon will be struck with the prevalence of blue and yellow. Blue Doctor, Spring Blue, Suir Blue, Lee Blue, Boyne Blue, Glenicmurrin Blue – the list is endless. For many years I have taken nearly eighty per cent of my early spring salmon on a very simple fly which I devised and which goes by the name of "The Yalla haired Girl", or, among my more literary friends, as "Counsel's Doxy". It has a wing of pale yellow bucktail, a body of yellow floss butted in the larger sizes with black ostrich herl, and a long gentian-blue hackle. Nothing could be simpler – or more effective. But as soon as the salmon have been up a little time, and begin to colour, the fly loses its attraction. There is a shift in preference towards the red end of the scale, and orange takes the place of yellow, claret of blue. I do not say that I have never taken a fresh run salmon on a claret fly, or a coloured salmon on a blue fly, but the occasions are very, very rare. A similar change in preference occurs in sea trout. When they are completely fresh run, Blue and Teal is a successful fly; then, as they lose some of their freshness, magenta is preferred and finally claret. Fishing those three colours on the same cast in a lake which held fish of varying degrees of freshness, I have found a remarkable correspondence between the fly selected and the advance in coloration of the fish. At the end of the season, both with brown and white trout, there comes a sudden preference for flies with some scarlet in their make up, which I vaguely connect with the approach of spawning and the arousing of sexual combativeness.

Finally there appear to be mystery materials as well as mystery colours. Hare's ear, blue jay, and black ostrich herl seem to have queer attraction for fish. The old Irish fly tyers always used black short ostrich to butt the tail and again at the head. It has been suggested that this was to hide untidy work, but if you unpick an old fly you will see that this is not so. As far back as the Book of St. Alban's this material is recommended, and despite its fragility and other disadvantages it is still largely used. I believe it has some virtue of its own – perhaps its absorption of infra-red.

Hare's ear fur is used with success to imitate bodies with no apparent resemblance to it in colour, and jay feathers, whether you use the blue for hackles or the cinnamon and black for wings, seem more effective in attracting fish than similar feathers from other birds.

4

LOST FISH AND THEIR LESSONS

Unless a fish has been exceptionally big or exceptional difficulties lay in the way of his capture the details of how it was done fade rapidly from memory. Angling literature is sprinkled with purple passages telling of desperate encounters and nineteenth century illustrations show anglers in positions more suited to a tug-of-war than the playing of a salmon but, if one is to be candid, after a short experience the handling of a hooked trout or salmon becomes almost routine. The resources open to a fish in his efforts to escape are limited, the proper responses of the angler familiar and automatic. Only rarely does anything occur of a type to leave an imprint on the mind.

With a lost fish it is very different. That momentary sick feeling when the rod springs straight and you know the fish has gone seems to act as a fixative. The whole scene is engraved with the incisiveness of a dry point. There is the drift of white anemones lining the far bank, there is the charm of long-tailed tits tumbling through the bushes and the dipper doing his dot-carry-one on the boulder in mid-stream. The self-searching which always follows a lost fish fixes more firmly in the memory incidents which would otherwise be forgotten. Was this done amiss or that neglected? Was it skill that was deficient or judgment that went wrong?

The reasons why fish are lost may be legion but broadly they fall into two types, failure of tackle and failure of the hook to retain its hold. For the first the angler is nearly always responsible. The cast may not have been sufficiently tested, the knots not tied with sufficient skill and care or perhaps there was just an attack of mutton-fistedness. For the second the angler may be blameless. Yet in both cases there is often a debatable area. The cast may have been cut on a sharp edged rock, but should not the

21

angler have foreseen the danger and taken steps in time to steer
the fish away from the peril? The hold on the fish's mouth may
have been light but could not the angler have made sure that it
would be firmer?

Undoubtedly with salmon an unsatisfactory hold of the hook
may be the result of too early a strike. This occurs most frequently
when the salmon can be seen coming under water at the fly. The
temptation to strike is often irresistible and even if the fly is not
pulled away from the fish the hook only penetrates the lip or the
skin covering the palate instead of lodging solidly in the tough
tissues at the angle of the jaws. Orthodox instruction is to hold
several yards of line loose in the left hand and, when the rise or
movement of the fish is seen, to let this line run out, at the same
time swinging the rod downstream and towards the bank. Then,
if all goes well, the pressure of the water on the loose lines eases
the fly back in the fish's mouth till it catches in the angle of the
jaw and, as the fish swims away, it hooks itself. Yes, but what is
the fish doing in the considerable period before the line tightens.
If it does not like the feel or the taste of the fly it has plenty of
time to spit it out. When the line does straighten there may be
no fish at the end.

Outstandingly the finest salmon fisherman I have known would
have nothing to do with orthodoxy. His advice was this. If a fish
shows his body when he rises, wait till he has disappeared or
perhaps a second longer and then strike hard. If he does not
show his body but the only indication is a disturbance of the
water, wait a second and again strike hard. He argued that a
minimal delay was sufficient to allow the fish to turn down. When
he did so either he had the fly in his mouth or he had not. If he
had not, a quick hard strike could do no harm: if he had, and if
your hooks were kept sharp the hard strike should ensure a good
hold. The advice to strike hard requires some modification. Owing
to an accident my mentor had lost the use of his left arm and
fished a light single-handed rod. For salmon fishers using a
double-handed rod the advice would be "hold firmly".

It is easy to pick holes in my mentor's advice but by following
it I landed a greater proportion of rises than before and, with
modifications, it enabled me to hook a fish in a lie which had
previously defeated me. Owing to the configuration of the bank
this particular lie could only be covered when the fly was "on the
dangle". In this position a fly will rise many fish but it is almost

impossible to hook them properly. I tried the orthodox method of releasing line without any success. Then I experimented with another method. I held my rod high and almost vertical so that the line ran from the top ring to the water in a marked curve. When a fish rose I watched the line. If it remained in a curve it meant that the fish had not taken the fly; if on the other hand it straightened after a short delay this meant that the fish had gone down with the fly in its mouth and I struck firmly. The new recipe was not infallible but it enabled me to take a number of salmon from a lie which up to this had not given me a fish. The delay between the rise and the straightening of the line, due to the slack curve, was sufficient to let the fish get the fly firmly in its mouth.

Looking back through the long gallery of memory I have picked out the tales of six lost fish. In three cases I am still uncertain whether I could have done anything to avert the loss; in the other three the loss was my own fault but the circumstances were unusual and I did not appreciate them in time. They may easily recur and my experience may serve as a warning.

*

The Owencarrow flowing through a boggy valley in Donegal is a sluggish stream at best, but to-day after a dry spell the long pool below the railway bridge was as motionless as a canal. No sign of wind ruffled its surface, the sun was a brazen shield in a clear sky and the whole world seemed in a trance. The only human being in sight was the driver of an ass-cart who was asleep over the reins. Even the smoke from the cottage on the hillside barely oozed from the chimney. I was a boy just turned fourteen who had come out to handsel his first proper fly rod, a two piece greenheart which had cost the princely sum of one guinea. I was dejected for despite reducing my tail fly to a 00 Stewart Black Spider on a 4x point, I had not caught even one of the diminutive brown trout which that acid water breeds and was reduced to practising my casting by trying to put my fly on a solitary leaf circling slowly in an eddy near the far bank.

Suddenly the pool seemed to erupt, my rod was bent and I was into my first salmon. As so often happens in Ireland when you hook a fish the countryside, which seemed so empty, sprouted humanity. Two men, who had been footing turf unobserved in a hollow, let out a yell which woke the ass-cart driver. He whipped up his ass into a canter and the clatter of wheels aroused a couple of road workers who had been taking a siesta in the ditch. From the cottage emerged a very old man who hobbled and stumbled down hill followed by a very young boy.

That fish was a gentleman. He played me gently up and down the middle stretches of the pool, jumped once to show his size, about 8 lbs., and then sat on the bottom for a rest. Advice was plentiful. "Hould him". "Let him go". The old man eyed my diminutive net. "Ye'll niver lift him with that wee bag. Sean, do you run up to the house and fetch the hook that is in the thatch". (If anyone else does not know what a gaff is doing hidden in the thatch he is ignorant of rural Ireland).

That last remark was too much for the salmon. He detached himself from the bottom and started to swim slowly and purposively down to the tail of the pool where I saw with apprehension a large patch of water lilies. With my tackle I was powerless to stop him. On and on he went straight into the centre of the patch. There was a large swirl, half a dozen leaves were pulled under the surface and my cast came back to me broken at the point. "Ye had a right to hould him out of that" helpfully remarked the ass-cart driver.

Could that fish have been landed? I have caught salmon in lakes on 3x when fishing for white trout on a windless day, but then I was able to work them away from the shore into open water; and I have caught them on 2x in an unencumbered river. Perhaps if I had sprinted downstream ahead of the fish and applied pressure from below he might have turned back into safer water. But even then all he had to do was to sit on the bottom in a deep place and 4x would not have been strong enough to lift him.

*

When I tell my friends that I have hooked and played two salmon at the same time, when fishing only one fly, they look at me dubiously. Yet it ha ppened!

It was April, the best month for the Slaney, though the river was lower than usual and so I was fishing a grilse rod and light gut. The long sharp about a quarter of a mile below Clohamon bridge was almost too thin to hold fish but half way down, one of about 12 lbs took and made off down stream. This suited me, for the sharp had some troublesome rocks but ended in a deep clean pool ideal for playing a fish. All went well, the pool was reached and soon the fish was reasonably under control and near my bank. However, he was not yet finished and made a run straight across the pool diving deep as he did so. When he surfaced there were not one but two fish on my line. About 3 yards above the cast the second salmon, much the same size as the first, was firmly attached. For about 3 minutes the two fish threshed around the pool and all the time the second fish kept slipping further and further down the line. Finally, when it had almost reached the cast, the line broke.

My host, a renowned angler, whose record 51 pounder may still be seen in a Dublin fishing tackle shop, had watched the whole proceeding. "What on earth happened" he said. "I have no idea" I replied. Together we examined the line. From the point where the second fish had first been attached to where it was broken the line was scratched and scored, at two points nearly severed. Independently we came to the same conclusion. Fish number two must have been hooked on a natural or artificial minnow some time before and had broken away with a treble still in its mouth. The first fish, diving deep, had brought the line across the treble and it had jammed behind the barb. As the fish struggled it pulled the treble down the line, the barb scoring and tearing in its course, till finally it cut right through. That was a loss for which I do not blame myself.

To catch two salmon at the same time when fishing a dropper is rare but not unknown. To hook two good sea trout simultaneously when fishing a lake is quite usual. The best tactic, I think, is to hold the fish lightly and let them play each other to exhaustion. R. H. Harris disagrees with this and thinks it better to hold both fish hard. Let the boatman net the dropper fish, bringing the net only just inboard of the gunwale. While he unhooks the fish the angler holds the lower part of the cast in his hand so as to prevent the second fish from going under the keel. The fish will by this be too weak to break the gut even with a direct pull when its companion has been unhooked it can be netted with ease.

*

My water on the Slaney ran through a valley reputed to be peopled by fairies and my best pool was named the Fairy Seat. A high diagonal weir keyed on a boulder (which was probably the Seat) sent the stream slanting across to hit against the far bank and run parallel with it over a nest of rocks which gave ideal lies. Standing on one identical spot I once hooked and landed in rapid succession four spring fish with not more than three or four casts intervening between landing one and hooking the next. My upstream neighbour, who was not devoid of jealousy, was watching through field glasses and her remarks were retailed gleefully to me next day by her companion. "Good, Kingie is in a fish". "My God, the judge has got another". "The bloody fellow has hooked a third". "This is too much, the bastard has a fourth".

Some straggling alders fringed part of my bank, their roots in the water, and a favourite trick of a hooked fish was to run into my side and try to get shelter under their roots. To avoid this meant extending the rod over the water at the full length of an arm while keeping a finger on the reel plate. One day a biggish fish of about 18 lbs was particularly determined in his attempts, boring and chugging inwards for a good two minutes before he suddenly changed his mind and made out to midstream. The reel unaccountably jammed, the rod point was pulled down to the water and the fish was gone.

The reel was a first class production by a famous maker. When I tried the handle it moved easily both ways. Dismantled it showed no grit or any obstruction between the plates. Tackle dealers to whom I showed it could offer no explanation though one advised using tallow instead of oil as a lubricant explaining that if a reel got hot thin oil would leak away leaving a dry plate. The reel continued in use and behaved perfectly. Two years later came the explanation. A fish hooked in the same place behaved in the same way, a rapid run from the far side, a persistent attempt to get into the alder roots and then a sudden reversal of direction. Again the line refused to run but this time I spotted the reason and a quick tug set all to rights. The initial run into my side had necessitated frenzied reeling in to keep in touch with the result that the line got wound rather loosely on the drum. When the fish kept boring in the line had slipped under a couple of loose coils and jammed. This mishap is not so rare. When a fish runs rapidly towards you it is standard practice to retreat as fast as you can while reeling in, so as to be able to keep tension on the coils; but the presence of the alders and the necessity to stay near the edge so as to prevent refuge in their roots had made retreat impossible.

*

Clearing the banks is an annual chore on any salmon river. There are errant branches to be cut back, bushes to be trimmed, the ubiquitous briars to be slashed with a bill-hook. When all this is finished you are left with heaps of debris which ought to be burned, but there is the river and the temptation to pitch the lot into the stream can be too strong. If the river is in high flood and the dumping takes place well before the start of the fishing season, not much harm will be done though some trails of bramble are sure to festoon themselves on rocks there to remain till the next flood sends them again on their journey to the estuary. Those who decant their trimmings when the season has got under way deserve death, preferably an unpleasant one, or so I thought when, in the pool next above the Fairy Seat, I saw a mattress of floating debris about four yards long and extending six or seven feet out from the bank. Of course I should have spent a few minutes hoicking out the bigger bits with my gaff, but I am by nature lazy and remembered that fish hooked in that pool nearly always battled it out in midstream. Not so the big one with whom I connected some thirty yards lower down. He elected to run into my bank and then forged steadily up stream not two feet from the edge, on and on till he reached the raft of debris. The water next the bank was a good eight feet deep, so that there was no difficulty in sinking the point of the rod far enough down to prevent the line from getting fouled as he swam inexorably up under the raft and on till he had nearly reached the weir. I hoped that he would veer out across stream allowing me to swing the line, still deep in the water, clear of the obstacles. Instead he sat down to rest. I knew exactly where he was, behind a sunken boulder where he would find easy water, and I knew that he would stay there so long as there was no strain on him. I would have time to disintegrate that evil mass of flotsam.

Though the water was deep a narrow six inch ledge of rock ran about two feet below the surface giving a precarious foothold. Pulling a few yards of line from the reel I allowed it to hang loose in the water so that there would be no strain on the fish. I put my rod lengthwise on the bank and lowered myself down on to the ledge to begin a game of giant spillikins. It was easier than

I had expected. Teetering somewhat, I managed to identify the key branches, lever them free with my gaff and, in an excess of virtue, toss them up onto the bank instead of letting them float down river. Soon the whole mass of leaves and weeds started to revolve, to disintegrate, and to slip harmlessly away. The salmon had not stirred for the line, lying loose in an area where there was practically no current, did not incommode him. With difficulty I climbed the steep bank, regained my rod, retreated a few steps to straighten the line and very gently felt for him. Good, a responsive wiggle showing that he was still on. Once real pressure was applied he was almost certain to bolt across stream so I made sure that the line was not round a button and the reel handle was free. There he goes – but, but, once again the line refuses to run, the rod is pulled straight and the gut parts. This time the cause was obvious. A curl of line had wrapped round the top and had jammed under the end ring. Perhaps one of the branches when thrown out had twitched the loose line round the top, perhaps, elated with my success on getting rid of the raft, I had been careless in picking up the rod.

This mishap is not uncommon with beginners who allow the line to droop slackly at the end of their back cast and I have seen it happen even with an expert angler who had laid down his rod in the boat with a certain amount of line loose on the thwart. It is a possibility which should be kept in mind.

*

A series of steep rapids sent a strong stream down the centre of the pool. From the right bank at intervals of about twenty yards three small gnarled reefs stretched out like rheumatic fingers to the edge of the stream, forming quiet bays of water. Off the point of the top reef a good fish rose but did not touch. I changed my number 1 for a number 3 and tried again with the same result. Now a number 6, and again a rise but no pull. Finally he took a number 7 and was off to the head of the stream making for the rocks. With the stream to help me I was able to frustrate him though he persisted in his efforts for a good five minutes. Then he tried another and more dangerous tactic, angling his body across the stream and allowing the full force of the water to bear him down. When a big fish does this in a strong current it is almost impossible to pull his head round if he is opposite or slightly below you. His body acts like a paravane.

What you must do is to sprint down so as to get well below him when you will have the force of the current to help, not hinder you, in forcing his head round to your bank. In doing this you inevitably lose ground and so, when I had him faced round and out of the current, he was opposite the lowest of the three little bays. Further down I could not let him go because of a tree growing on the bank. He must be landed in the bay, and into the bay I brought him, for the moment submissive. I could see his size, somewhere between 18 and 20 pounds, and could see also that he was only hooked in the lip. At the sight of me he turned and made off again for the stream: apprehensive of that weak hold I dared not check him too roughly but did slow him before he reached the stream and brought him back to the edge of the bay, a little further down. He repeated the performance and was again eased back, by now within a few yards of the lowest reef. I tried to walk him up but he resisted and made to go round the point of the reef on which he would probably have cut the cast. This time he had to be held. He struggled fiercely but I held on till suddenly the hold gave and the fly sailed over my head into a gorse bush.

What are you to do with a lightly hooked fish which shows you that he is lightly hooked by splattering on the surface. If you hold him gently the combat will be long and the strain from different angles will enlarge the hole so that the hook may drop out. If you put on too much pressure you will tear the hook away. If there is plenty of room I think the best plan is to keep a light but very even strain, playing him off the top joint and holding the rod so that the line is at right angles to it. This does not mean holding the rod high, which is dangerous, for it encourages splashing on the top of the water. You can attain the proper angle with the rod held low and well back over the bank. Others advise getting well below the fish, so that your line is parallel to his body, and then giving a strong strike. If all goes well the hook is pulled deeper, or perhaps pulled right out of its fragile hold to lodge more firmly in the angle of the jaw. I have known this to succeed but it is risky.

*

And finally a contretemps with a white trout. High in the upland of Iar Connaught lies a small lake which communicates with the main river by a bog stream often less than a foot wide and half buried under coarse grass. White trout find their way up this runnel and into the lake which is mostly unfishable because of a growth of rushes spearing up from the bottom, sometimes dense sometimes sparse, but always sufficiently close together to prevent any working of a fly. At one spot however a canal of open water, about 12 yards wide, stretches out from the shore and then turns sharply to the left. In shape this clear area is that of an inverted capital L the long arm being about 35 yards and the short arm about 15. At the shore end a big granite boulder, about six feet high but climbable, provides a casting platform. Usually a white trout or two could be picked up here, mostly herling not exceeding a pound in weight. But this fish was no herling. It took some ten yards from shore and without a second's delay shot off for the far end of the canal. A biggish white trout is away the moment he is hooked and the first twenty yards of his dash is just one electric streak. My fish made straight for the rushes that rose like a wall at the far end of the open water canal. If he reached them he was safe. If I tried to stop him too brusquely there was the probability of a break. Very gentle checking slowed him perceptibly but he showed no sign of stopping. When he was two yards from the rushes I took a chance and clamped my finger on the reel plate. Only two yards to go! He fought relentlessly to gain his asylum while I held on not giving an inch. It must have been two minutes or more before the strain suddenly relaxed and I was able to recover a few yards of line. But now he was off up the shorter left arm of the open water putting a long stretch of rush studded water between us. Owing to the height of the boulder on which I was standing it was possible to keep line and cast above the rushes which were not very tall, but there seemed no way by which to bring him back into the main canal. I examined the area of rushes. Yes, there was one place where they grew more sparsely. A tired fish might, with luck, be skull-hauled head above water through the obstacles and back into the long arm, but the problem was how to keep him in open water till he was sufficiently exhausted to make the experiment worth trying. If he chose to run towards me and into the near rushes he would be free in a few seconds. Luck was with me for, by keeping a steady strain I ensured that he would pull against the strain and towards the further fringes of the rushes. A series of short spurts varied by jumps further wearied him. Now he was opposite the sparse area of rushes and the attempt must be made.

The first stage was to get his head above water which meant lowering my rod top as much as possible without fouling the line and then raising it to its full extension with my hand high above my head. Good, he was showing on the surface. Now it was a question of stripping in the line so rapidly that he became bewildered and for the moment ceased resistance, all the while steering him away from the denser growth. More than once the dropper touched projecting spikes but did not take hold and now, at last, he was in the main arm and completely under control. I could see him clearly, a fresh run fish of between three and four pounds. At the base of my boulder crouched the ghillie, a young man of 18 already an expert boatman and trained to net a fish by keeping the net well sunk in the water till the fish was drawn over it. I glanced down. There was the net a foot below the surface. In came the fish unresisting in a steady glide till at the last moment he saw me, checked and made to turn back. It was too much for my ghillie who took a step into the water and scooped wildly. The fish balanced on the edge of the net half in and half out, fell back catching the dropper in the rushes, and was gone.

The lesson is to net your fish yourself and this normally I would have done, but for the difficulty of climbing down from the six foot high boulder with a fish at the end of the line. The second lesson is never, never, allow your ghillie to scoop at a fish. Some boatmen are expert at landing a fish in this way but it is always more risky than allowing the angler to draw the fish well over the net and then raise it steadily.

PART II

———◆———

BROWN TROUT IN RIVER AND LAKE

5

THE LITTLE FISH

We all have a soft spot for them, these page-boys of the hills, in their livery of saffron and umber with garnet buttons down the sides. Surely it was a piece of impudence no longer than his hand that Schubert has sent lilting down the centuries! To justify the capture of creatures so lovely, and of such negligible food value, is not easy; yet they provide an indispensable part of an angler's education. I never met a really competent fisherman who had not learned his rudiments at the fins of little trout, and, if any one finds himself passing through a period of clumsiness, let him try a refresher course on streams that pick their course through heather and granite. These mountainy urchins teach the things which cannot be learned from books and are yet fundamental to all good fishing – observation, alertness, delicacy, and unconscious co-ordination of hand and eye, mind and muscle. With them, rise, take, and rejection follow so closely one on the other that, unless the response is equally quick, there is no fish on the end of the line.

How rapid can be their reactions was borne in on me one hot July day when I was fishing a burn with up-stream worm. Shoulder-high boulders obstructed the bed and made it easy to fish from concealment. Peeping over their tops I could see nothing but empty pools, but, as soon as the worm was lobbed round the rock and started to trickle down the pool, a fingerling would shoot out from under a stone like a squeezed orange pip, grab the worm, and make back for its holt. Before it had gone a couple of feet, often after a few inches, something – hook, gut or drag – roused suspicion and the worm was dropped. The time between taking and rejecting rarely exceeded half a second. As the fish were really too small to take home I had not been striking, but now I began to experiment, and I found that I got the best results by starting my strike just *before* the fish took the worm. The fractional delay which always intervenes between resolve and result, coupled with the delay in response due to the whippiness of the rod, ensured that the line tightened just at the right moment to enable one of the hooks of the Stewart tackle to find a hold.

It is the same story if you are fishing fly. A pool with high banks, masked at the top by scrub projecting like eyebrows, will allow you to see everything that goes on. As the flies settle on to the surface, and sometimes just before they touch it, one or more trout become detached from the bottom and shoot up to inspect. A proportion turn back before they reach the fly and those who do take spit it out in an instant. I have watched similar performances in a pool full of small herling. Again it is best to attempt the strike just before the trout reaches the fly, but if the fish are of any size, say a pound or over, the strike has to be delayed, for the take is both more determined and more deliberate.

Fish of the upland reaches are hungry and adventurous, ready to have a go at anything that looks like food, and it is not necessary to be wise in entomology or exercise a nice choice of pattern. The essentials are concealment and a knowledge of the places where keepable fish are likely to be found. Concealment usually involves wading, and fishing very much up-stream. Recognition of the places where the better trout lie comes with experience. Bigger fish always take the best places and drive away rivals, but what are the best places? Those where the fish can get the most food with the least effort. If a trout can lie in comparatively slow water, with a more rapid stream bringing the food along within range of vision, he has attained his object. An ease between two streams, eddies behind or in front of stones, the tail of a run, the belt of slacker water which often intervenes between current and bank, are favourable spots which can easily be picked out. There are also underwater currents and resting places with no apparent clue to their existence which some fishermen can divine by an instinct which they are unable to explain.

To time his strike correctly a good wet-fly fisherman must be able to detect, and act on, the slightest clue. An infinitesimal humping of the surface, a fraction of lag in the down stream progress of the nylon, a sub-surface glint so evanescent as to be no more than a suspicion, these are all the warnings likely to be given. As often as not an experienced fisherman can give no reason as to why he struck other than "I just knew that a fish was there."

The worst of little trout is that they are so little. No nice verbal evasions – "breakfast fish," "jolly little mouthfuls," and so on, can conceal the fact. When you can see without being seen, strike without knowing why, and guess correctly where the best fish lie, they have taught you all they can; it is time to move on to the lower reaches and the lake, the sea trout and the salmon. Your self esteem will be flattered though your enjoyment may be no greater. I have been lucky enough more than once to catch seven spring salmon on fly in a day, but I doubt if I got as much pleasure as from days when, in the grey dawn, I stole out of a still sleeping university to catch the steam tram that crawled into the Wicklow hills. Looking like a joint production of Emmet and Heath Robinson it clanked its way the fifteen miles to Blessington, showering hot cinders on the road, stampeding the cattle on the long meadow and rousing the countryside with dolorific hoots. It took two hours to complete the journey, but on arrival there were two rivers to fish, from their junction just above the town to their sources on the hilly horizon. Dipper and kingfisher shot up and down stream like flying shuttles, herons swung away in slow climbing turns, curlews cried their desolate timeless call, and longtailed tits played follow-my-leader through the bushes. There was the certainty of a few fish, the hope of half-pounders, the bare possibility of a pounder. There was wind and sun – and youth.

In our fishing progress there is a vast deal to learn, but nothing which the little fish teach has to be unlearned, except the lightning strike. Big fish take slower than small, salmon slower than trout, and the tightening of the line must be delayed correspondingly. In western waters the next fish may be anything from a half-pound herling to a salmon, and if you are to time your strike correctly the diagnosis must be made at the earliest possible moment and from the smallest variations of swirl and underwater glint. Even the most expert will make mistakes, but fishermen who have learned the trick of instant observation by a novitiate among mountain trout soon get the hang of the difference in rises, while those who have made reputations on Test and Dee often remain unteachable.

After the upper waters come the middle reaches. Most Irish

mountains are of granite, quartzite or sandstone, overlaid with peat, and this combination produces an acid water unfavourable to insect life and to the growth of fish. Lower down, the streams may pass through belts of limestone, limestone drift or calcareous boulder-clay, which neutralize much of the acidity; the land becomes richer and more cultivated; trees and bushes line the banks. All of these changes increase the number and variety of the insects. Fish are of better average size and more particular. Rivers are wider and slower, and fishing methods must be adapted. Some knowledge of entomology is useful, and patterns have to be chosen with an eye to the natural. There are quiet pools and glades where the dry fly is more successful than the wet. Except in the pure limestone streams of the central plain, trout are still on the small side, and a quarter-pound fish is keepable, but there will be some much bigger. Even in the Slaney, which starts as a very acid river, I have known trout to be taken up to four pounds and I have heard a story that one of six and a half pounds was caught on my own water by some one who did not have leave to fish. Obvious difficulties lie in verifying the story and I do not believe it. Probably the fish was a coloured salmon.

Most Irish anglers prefer to fish down-stream in the middle reaches, but this is, I think, a mistake. Up-stream should still be the usual rule, but up-stream with a difference. In the head waters the fly has to be cast nearly straight up, it is rare to cast more than twice from the same place, and you may have to travel long stretches where it is not worth your while to put a fly on the water, for there is no spot likely to hold a takeable trout. In the middle waters half a mile of river will be as much as you can fish thoroughly in a day; faced with a broad stream any part of which may hold trout, you may have to make ten or more casts without moving. The first will be straight up under the near bank, the next a yard or two further out, and so on till the flies are dropping under the far bank. Each cast is a little less up-stream, a little more across than its predecessor, till, if the river is twenty yards or more wide, the final casts will be almost directly across. It is a mistake to cast a yard further than is necessary and careful wading may make it possible to cover the whole river without putting out more than a dozen yards of line, but deep water may enforce long casting and this at once raises the problem of drag. The aim must be to allow the flies to come down like inert things, neither faster nor slower than the stream and above all without being pulled across it. With a short line this is only a question of raising the top of the rod at the correct pace; with a long line the grip of intervening currents and eddies makes this procedure insufficient. Some modern wet-fly fishermen have borrowed a hint from salmon anglers. They grease all except the last yard or two of their line and defeat the drag by small well-timed "mends". "Mending" a line means lifting it off the water and putting it down in a fresh place without moving the fly. With a long two-handed salmon rod this is difficult to do, but with a trout rod it is easy. Suppose a fast current, intervening between rod and fly, has started to put a down-stream belly into the line. This curve has to be reversed and put up-stream. Hold the rod out with a straight arm at shoulder level, parallel with the water, and imagine there is a blackboard just in front of the point and facing you. Now with a fairly stiff arm try to trace a circle about four feet in diameter on the blackboard with the point. Do this smoothly and slowly. You will find that the line comes up from the water and is put down again with an up-stream belly which will defeat the drag till the fly has travelled down another two or three yards. This is less tiring than casting afresh for every foot or two of the flies travel, which may be the only alternative. Mending the line is also effective in delaying drag when fishing down-stream.

Up-stream fishing must not be allowed to become a thoughtless fetish. If there is a strong down-stream wind, to persist in up-stream casting when tired can easily cause a strain of wrist or elbow, and it is not called for, as the wind ruffles the still pools and so gives a measure of concealment to the angler. In a wide river the water is covered more rapidly and effectively by the down-stream method, and, here also, concealment is secured by the greater length of cast. When fishing with sedges in the evening the drag of down-stream fishing is no disadvantage, as drag simulates the scuttling and fussing of the natural insect. Drag is unimportant also if your aim is to make the fly represent not a weak insect which can only float down with the current, but a small fry which can swim against it. Some anglers have what seems to me an illogical objection to using a fly in this way. Why it should be more sportsmanlike to catch a fish by imitating an insect than by imitating some other form of life I never understood. On a cold day in early spring, a silver-bodied fly worked deep under your own bank may be your only chance. In some of the smaller limestone rivers the growth of weed is so rapid that fly fishing is confined to the early months, and the big trout which they contain, although in perfect condition, are slow to rise to a small natural, but can be tempted by a good sized fly (No. 12 O.S.) fished down-stream and well below the surface. A Dublin surgeon, marooned in county Meath by the 1916 rising, put in his time usefully with this method. The first day he caught eight trout weighing sixteen pounds and the second day, from the same stretch, sixteen trout weighing eight pounds, a curious contrast.

Another unorthodox procedure – this time up-stream with a short line – is to make the dropper dance up and down, now in the air, now just touching the water. This is not so unnatural as it sounds, for it imitates the movement of the egg-laying spinner, with which trout are perfectly familiar. Once when weeding my rock garden my attention was called to a pool by a perfect turmoil among the trout, and on going down to look I found it was caused by a column of spinners making their way up-stream, ovipositing as they went. It was not difficult to locate the position of several fish and to watch their movements. Any spinner which touched the water within a radius of three feet of where the trout was lying had an uninsurable prospect of life. To meet the fly at the instant when the fly touched the water (and the touch is only momentary) the fish must have been watching its movement in the air and have started to meet the fly as soon as it began to dip.

Lastly there is night fishing, where everything must be sacrificed to safety and simplicity. One fly, a strong cast, a reasonably short line, heavily nailed boots and down-stream fishing are the rule, for it is easy to get a tangle or a bad slip. Heavy fish are taken and occasional heavy baskets are made in this way. When the new reservoir was constructed at Poulaphouca, anglers fishing the mouths of the rivers had some exceptional nights. The tales of regular slaughter to be made in this way can, however, be grossly exaggerated. I never got more than half a dozen fish of very moderate size by fishing at night. Nor did I greatly care. The value of night fishing is as a sedative to fretted nerves and a tired brain. A sedative, yet something more, a portal of escape from the instancy of the present. As the night deepens the river takes command. Its voice mounts, filling the valley, rising to the rim of the hills, no longer one voice but a hundred. Time and place are dissolving; the centuries have lost their meaning; timelessness is all. One foot is crossing the invisible frontier which bounds the land of the old gods. Then comes the whistle of an otter, the bark of a fox – and you are back in the world of sentiency. Almost you fear to turn lest, black upon the moonblanched sand, there should be the hoof marks of a goat.

6

FORM AND FASHION IN WET FLIES

The Large Dark Olive of spring (Baetis rhodani) is to be found on nearly every river. On the table in front of me lie four famous patterns, each designed to represent this natural. The nearest is Waterhen Bloa, which comes from the North Country school of fly dressing; next is Blue Upright from the West Country; the third is a Greenwell's Glory, tied in the fashion popular along the Border and in the Scottish lowlands; and the fourth, Blue Dun, is the traditional tie which goes back at least as far as Cotton. In general colour all four patterns have a resemblance to each other and to the natural, which is a slatey-blue olive, colder or warmer in colour according to temperature and locality, but in construction they are utterly different. The differences in body materials are not significant. All bodies are made in the same way, by wrapping something round the hook shank, and though West Country may have a leaning to quills and herls and the northern schools to silk and dubbed fur, the four materials are used by all four schools. But look at the other parts of the flies. Can they have had the same model? North Country and West Country both dispense with wings and rely on hackle alone, but the hackle of Waterhen Bloa (taken from the undercoverts of a moorhen) is sparse, soft, mobile and of a rather cloudy appearance; while that of Blue Upright (taken from a gamecock) is a sweep's brush of stiff, dark, shining fibres.

The Greenwell and Blue Dun have wings as well as hackles, but what different wings! Greenwell has a simple rolled pad, sticking straight up like a Bermuda mainsail; and Blue Dun has two wings made of slips of feather, sloping back at an angle of forty-five degrees. The variations between the two schools would be just as marked if any other natural fly had been selected as

42

the insipration for the artificials, say one of those bits of gauzy nothingness known as the Pale Wateries. Again we may ignore the bodies. North Country tried first the soft hackle from under the wing of a cheeper grouse, and then went one better with a feather from the dotterel, so filmy and unsubstantial that the only way I can use it is by twisting feather and silk together and then winding them both at once as Stewart advised. West Country sticks to a zareba of cock hackle, this time of a brassy or a watery colour; the Border has its little upright wing, made usually from the secondaries of a chaffinch, with a ginger hackle; and Traditional has developed Ginger Quill. Always the signature tunes are the same, soft hackle, stiff hackle, upright wing, sloping wings.

These differences are no accident. The dressing of each fly is as detailed and precise as a doctor's prescription. The feather for Waterhen-Bloa has to be taken from a particular row, which is supposed to be more hyaline than the others, and even the eyes of the natural are sometimes imitated by a turn of magpie herl. The experience of generations of expert fishermen and fly dressers has gone into determining these constructions. Why then are the schools so widely varying in their ideals and what type of fly are we to adopt? The latter question is the easier to answer, for reasons which will be later apparent. If you are fishing up-stream use a North Country soft hackle at point, a Border upright wing as centre dropper, and a West Country stiff hackle as top dropper. If you are fishing down stick to the sloping wings of the Traditional fly.

The first question involves for its answer a rather lengthy digression into the dynamics of flowing water, for each style attempts to evolve a fly which, in water of a certain type and fished in a certain way, will simulate as nearly as possible the movements and behaviour of a natural carried down by the stream.

Let us have a look at the river. The somnolent pool above the mill has a few medium olives, which appear at first sight as if they are moving down on a conveyor belt. There are half a dozen of them in a tight convoy, with a May fly like an escort cruiser on the port bow. Now they are starting to straggle, and two of them disappear in underwater explosions. The May fly drops back as if to shelter them – and now she has gone too. What caused those irregular movements? There are no more duns, but foam flakes from the weir higher up will do as indicators. They are dispersing where the convoy dispersed, and one is falling back as did the May fly. From a point of vantage we can see the cause, a deep sunken rock causing an invisible boil. Now that our eyes are alert we can see also that the analogy of the conveyor belt will not do. The foam flakes show us half a dozen different belts moving at different rates, sometimes sliding transversely across, sometimes curling back on their tracks. The variations are not rapid. This is dry-fly water and a good fisherman could damp them out for the necessary few feet by casting a loose line. But what about wet-fly water?

Below the mill is a typical wet-fly run of rapid water, over a bed full of sunken rocks and pot holes. The main features are easy to take in, a couple of eases in the centre, three streams of varying pace, and a back eddy. To discover the minor complexities we will have to call in aid a few handfuls of confetti. The different colours and shapes allow us to follow the fortunes of individual pieces. Scatter a narrow belt about two yards long across a stream and watch the progress of the fragments. Here there is no question of belts of water, or ropes, or even strands. Every square inch of surface seems to have an independent movement of its own. The little paper fragments interweave, shuttle, bunch, hesitate, separate, shoot forward. One scrap pursues an even course, another progresses in a series of spurts and halts. Two pieces may start almost touching and in seconds they are yards apart. Of another touching pair one may soon be found leading the procession down-stream, while the other curls by a devious route into a backwater.

So far we have only watched the surface. What is happening underneath? This requires markers of slightly greater specific gravity than water. Small weeds from my garden with a certain amount of soil left on the roots served the purpose. The tale was the same. They were sucked down, boiled up, swirled round, buffeted here and there in inextricable confusion. Not infrequently the water below the surface was moving in a direction contrary to the surface stream.

In this turmoil of three-dimensional motion your flies and cast are submerged. Every fly, every inch of the cast, is subjected to different pressures and movements. Some of the pressures may neutralize each other, the cast is so thin as to offer little water resistance, and both tail fly and droppers have a certain freedom to move with the water, but sooner or later all will be subjected to forces which prevent their moving freely at the pace and in the direction of the square inch of water which surrounds them. They will behave as if they were moving under their own impulse and not merely being carried down.

There is nothing necessarily unnatural in this. Though duns and spinners, drowned or floating, are carried down inert by the current, nymphs, shrimps, sedges and fry have a will and motion of their own; and if the wet-fly, when tweaked through the water, behaves in the manner of any of these organisms and does not cause unnatural eddy or disturbance, no harm is done. The various schools have in different ways attempted to secure the double object that the artificial, when moving inertly with the water, shall resemble some natural in appearance and, when it is forced to move contrary to the movement of the water, shall do so in a way which some organism adopts.

The North Country soft-hackled patterns fished at point are my favourites. These are often loosely called spiders, but anyone who closely examines the colours and materials will have no doubt that they are meant to represent drowned duns or spinners. As drowned flies are invisible under water to our eyes, we do not appreciate the toll that is taken by weirs and rapids. An accident brought it to my notice. On the calm reach there was a good hatch of a small dark olive which I wanted to identify, but, as the banks were steep and difficult, I thought it would be easier to dip one out from a jetty in the rough stream. Between the smooth water and the jetty there were two low weirs and some rapids. I could not find a single fly on the surface, though sundry gleams and swirls showed that the trout were busy feeding on something just below it. In a back eddy I found what I was looking for, several drowned duns, their bruised limp wings very like the soft hackles of the North Country dressing. Not a fly had survived the weirs. It is right to say that conditions on that day were exceptional. There was a slight film on the water, which had enabled foam to build up to a height of three feet against the sluice gates, and such a film always makes it more difficult for duns to take wing.

The North Country dressing is at its best in wide rippling streams below weirs, fished moderately up-stream. At point it has the chance of moving freely with the water for an appreciable time, its soft hackles spread out at right angles to the hook like the wings of a drowned fly. Sooner or later there will come a pull from some part of the line or cast, moving in water of a different velocity. What happens? The soft hackles fold back, partially encasing the body and offering no resistance to the water, and the fly gives a little dart, like some of the swimming nymphs. It has contrived a double debt to pay. Nymph patterns bearing a greater resemblance to the natural have been produced and are no doubt necessary in chalk streams, but in rough water, at times when there was no hatch of fly, so that they could not be mistaken for drowned duns, I found that the North Country hackle was taken at least as well as more specific imitations of nymphs. Even fished down-stream this type of fly has its uses, for the hackles, folded back by water pressure, develop a life-like flicker and cause no disturbing eddy. I think it is then taken for some swimming creature.

The West Country dressing works quite differently. It has no mobility, but great sparkle and brilliancy, and imitates these qualities in the newly hatched dun or alighted spinner. It is the wet-fly fisherman's dry-fly, meant to be fished on the top of the water. The construction, with the body often of quill and the hackles of stiff cock, prevent it from becoming waterlogged. With or without a drop of oil it will go very near floating. Fished at top dropper it can be made to dance on the water. I have never fished the West Country streams but friends who have, among them Eric Taverner, confirm the view which I had previously formed, that this type of fly was designed to be fished in narrow rough waters, very much up-stream, with a short line and frequent casts. I like if possible to keep this type of fly on the surface or in the surface film, and hope that when drag develops it may be taken for wind-drag (insects can be blown along the water) or the struggles of some creature which can struggle. In a very rough stream, where even a North Country Pattern might float down unobserved, surface drag may even act as an advertisement. I never use it down-stream. Fished down-stream it drags like a sea anchor.

The Traditional dressing with its small soft hackle, narrow entry at the head, and sloping wings, is meant for down-stream fishing. If the wings were more upright it would resemble one of the ephemeroptera more closely; if they were more sloping it would be better streamlined and drag even less. It is a compromise which works well enough in skilful hands provided that the line is not allowed to come further down-stream than an angle of forty-five degrees to the bank before a new cast is made. After this angle is reached, the fly, if near the surface, makes a wake like a water-rat. It may however, in the circumstances already mentioned, be brought further round if it is fished deep and made to imitate fry. When intended to be used in this way the wings should be made more slanting.

Lastly comes the Border or Lowland dressing. In general shape, with its single upright wing and short hackle, this type is more like a natural dun, just hatched, than any other type; and so long as it is moving freely this may give it an advantage. How long can this be? Sooner or later, particularly if fished at middle dropper where I prefer it, there is going to be a pull from some part of the rest of gut or line. What happens? That little pad, vertical to the hook, is the reverse of streamlined. In mathematical terms it exerts a strong turning moment, and makes the fly give a little bob or curtsey. No natural fly does this. No fry does it. But there is one form of under-water life which is not streamlined and which has a movement not so dissimilar, the fresh water shrimp. I venture a rash guess that this dressing may owe part of its success to the fact that, when subjected to the inevitable tweaks, twitches and pulls from the rest of the tackle in a rough stream, it does behave in a way which resembles a shrimp.

There are other schools with their own peculiarities. Every expert fly dresser signs his work as legibly – often more legibly – than his cheques. Most of the advances in fly dressing have been made by talented amateurs, and when the pattern gets into the hands of the professional, whose girls, however expert in the mechanics of their work, are not practical anglers, the character of the original can insensibly be lost. Much of the effectiveness of the North Country dressings is due to the sparseness of the hackle but the teeth of a few trout can reduce such a fly to nothing. This does not matter if you can run up half a dozen in a few minutes (these patterns are very quickly tied) but an angler who has to pay money for them wants something more durable and so the shops often tie much too bulky a hackle. I have been shown flies which I was told were some of my own lake patterns. If I had not been told I would certainly not have guessed.

7

THE CHOICE OF PATTERNS

Pretty fables have a long life. There are still people who picture the expert as a person who, on arriving at the river, identifies the natural on which the trout are feeding, sits down on the bank, and proceeds to tie an imitation which will deceive the very elect of fish. It is quite possible to tie flies on the bank, though, with a wind blowing and rank herbage to hide anything that drops, there could hardly be a worse place. It is also possible to construct a fly which will kill trout from the most haphazard materials – a dead grass stalk will wind into an attractive body, and there are always odd bits of feather lying about which can be manipulated into top hamper. But any fisherman of experience should already have with him patterns which bear more resemblance to the flies he is likely to meet than anything he can put together from the miscellaneous jetsam of the countryside, and if he is to carry sufficient materials to imitate all the rare flies that occasionally attract a trout, he will need to drag round a small portmanteau.

Leonard West in his book *The Trout Fly* illustrates in colour over a hundred natural flies and their specific dressings. Roger Woolley gives over four hundred dressings of river flies, though his work includes alternative dressings of the same naturals. If we add the dressing suggested by Halford, Dunne, Ronalds, Theakston, Lunn, Harris and the rest, the number will exceed eight hundred, and an angler who provided himself with the full complement would not have finished his selection before the rise was over. It is a relief to recall that Stewart was content with six patterns, all general, and that some successful anglers use a cast of the same three flies from one end of the season to another.

It can rarely be necessary to carry more than a dozen, or a

dozen and a half, patterns at one time. The selection will vary somewhat according to the type of river and the time of year. An Irish angler will not need the Grannom, for it is unknown in Ireland, and for most rivers he will dispense with the March Brown, which is not widely distributed. When fishing a moorland stream there is nothing to be gained by taking imitations of flies whose nymphs only live in alkaline mud. Sedges will not be needed before June, or ants before the end of July. Hawthorn, Alder, and Bracken Clock have a limited season of a few weeks. Particular flies can be added or discarded at any time. What we must have is a nucleus of patterns which will cover the whole season on any typical wet-fly river.

Artificial flies are classified conveniently as (1) "specific", which attempt to represent one particular natural, or one particular stage of a particular natural; (2) "general," which aim at being a reasonable simulation of a number of insects bearing a resemblance to each other; and (3) "fancy," which in their make-up are sufficiently life-like not to alarm a trout, and sufficiently unusual to arouse his curiosity or combativeness.

The three classes shade into each other. Wickham's Fancy, as its name denotes, was a child of the imagination, and as a fancy fly is still an excellent pattern, but it has turned out to be serviceable as a specific imitation of the Lake Olive and, dressed large, of certain sedges. Red Quill started life as an imitation of a Red Spinner dressed as a dry-fly, but has proved itself an excellent general pattern, wet or dry. Even stranger have been the mutations of Greenwell's Glory. According to the account written by the Canon when he was ninety-six (more than half a century after the fly was invented) one day, when fishing his home waters, he found a fly hitherto unknown to him monopolising the attention of the fish. He studied it, determined on the best method of imitation, got the famous James Wright to dress it for him, and in the next two days nearly emptied the river. How the Canon, already a fisherman of great skill and experience, when fishing a familiar river could be totally unfamiliar with a fly which hatched in quantity is difficult to explain – the more so as the original dressing must be an imitation either of a large dark olive with a body lighter than usual, or a medium olive with a body rather darker than usual. Such variations are known to all anglers. However this may be, starting as a specific imitation, Greenwell soon became the best known of all general wet flies.

Now, with minor alterations in the shade of body and wing, Greenwell has reverted to providing specific representations of nearly all the olives and even of the Pale Wateries.

How are we to choose our nucleus of maids-of-all-work? There can be no such thing as "The Twelve Best Patterns". Out of the mass of patterns which have been tested by time and proved by the experience of expert fishermen, there would be no difficulty in selecting four lists, each of a dozen flies, with no pattern in common; and yet each list would reasonably cover the requirements of the ordinary angler. Everyone is influenced in his choice by his own style of fishing, the type of river which he generally frequents, the school of fly tying which most appeals to him, and the chances of his individual experience. To expect general agreement is impossible.

Why then attempt to compile a list which cannot be authoritative? It can, at worst, avoid being misleading. It can act as a general guide to the inexperienced, and among the experienced provoke sufficient controversy to enliven conversation. It can introduce some method into the choice of a fly, and curb the excesses of the "I-must-have-that" brigade. In suggesting the assortment which follows I have had in view the middle reaches of a typical wet-fly river such as the Slaney.

The first two flies to appear after the season opens are a small type of stone fly and the Large Dark Olive. I say "a small type of stone fly" for the species varies considerably from river to river. February Red, the commonest in parts of England, is unknown in Ireland. The Early Brown is common to both countries, but this fisherman's name covers, at least three species. Fortunately these species resemble each other so closely that there is no need for anyone to become an entomologist. All have bodies of a general reddish brown, and semi-translucent wings, horn-coloured, and liberally marked with dark brown nervures. The pattern which on the whole I found most successful was Woodcock and Orange, but almost equally good was Orange Partridge. The balance is tipped in favour of the latter by the other uses to which it can be put. It is an excellent nymph-suggesting pattern, and, at a pinch, will serve to represent the male Blue Winged Olive Dun. True, the orange floss (which turns reddish orange when wet) is noticeably more vivid than either the nymphs or the dun, but it seems to work all the better for this. Partridge and orange, then, is our first fly.

The Large Dark Olive (Baetis rhodani) which usually starts to hatch about 11 a.m. in March, is so universal and so popular with the trout as to have given rise to innumerable dressings. For a point fly there is no dressing to equal Waterhen Bloa. The orthodox body for this fly is water vole or blue mole, spun thinly on a yellow tying silk, so that the yellow shews through the fur, taking away some of the coldness of the blue.

On the rivers I have fished, as the season began to advance, the natural fly was warmer in colour than the artificial. Though I have no great belief in a trout's general acuity of colour vision, in the olive range they can be particular, so I hit on the device of dying some mole fur in picric acid which made it a shade of dull green-olive. Mixed with the blue, it provided every shade of the natural Large Dark Olive, and used unmixed it was the colour of the female dun of the Blue Winged Olive – again a dual purpose fly.

For hackle, instead of the orthodox waterhen, I experimented with some dark medium blue hen which came into my possession from the cabinet of a dead Yorkshire angler. He was somewhat of a connoisseur. Whenever he came across hackles of exceptional quality, he stripped all the weak fibres from the base, and then mounted them in rows by inserting the stalks between two strips of stiff paper gummed together. Each strip bore a record of the date and place where the hackles were obtained. Mine were "Dark medium blue hen, Wensleydale 1843". His vintage blue-dun hackles made a perfect combination with my picric-dyed mole fur.

For a winged pattern there is a choice between Greenwell's Glory and Rough Olive. It is unnecessary to carry both. Either pattern, with modifications, can be made to cover the whole gamut of olives from Iron Blue to Pale Watery. The body of Rough Olive is made from herl taken from a primary wing feather of the heron. These feathers shade from deep slate blue to the faintest French grey. Dyed in picric, they give a range from an olive so dark as to be almost black, to the pale yellowish green, the colour of chlorine gas, which is to be found in some of the pale wateries. The wings can be chosen from coot, hen blackbird, dark starling, light starling or tern, according to whether you are trying to represent Iron Blue, Dark Olive, Medium Olive, Blue Winged Olive or Pale Watery. Hackles are olive hen, dyed in various shades.

An almost identical range can be obtained in Greenwell. The original tie has a waxed yellow tying-silk body, ribbed with gold wire, dark furnace hen hackle, and wings from the secondaries of a female blackbird. According to the wax used – cobbler's wax, harness-maker's wax or colourless wax – the body can be given any of the shades of olive. For a pale watery it is best to use unwaxed primrose floss which has a greenish tinge when wet. Hackles vary from dark furnace through light furnace to ginger, and the range of wings is the same as that suggested for Rough Olive. Both these flies are Protean. Of the two I prefer the Greenwell, for the gold wire ribbing seems to have a special attraction. The Greenwell compartment in my box carried a number of varieties. Small and dark for Iron Blue and the small dark olive, of much the same size, which appears on the Slaney; small and light for Pale-Watery; large and dark for Dark Spring Olive; large and medium dark for Medium Olive and female Blue Winged Olive. A very useful and comprehensive fly.

Overlapping in season with the Dark Spring Olive, and usually hatching a little later in the day, comes the Medium Olive (it may be Baetis Tenax, Baetis vernus or Baetis rhodani; for the name is a fisherman's term and not a scientist's) distinguishable by its warmer colour and somewhat smaller size. Now is the time to change the point fly to another North Country dressing, Light Snipe and Yellow. This pattern is said to have originated as a representation of a Pale Watery, for which purpose it is inferior to Dotterel and Yellow. For me it has taken more trout than any other fly when not-too-dark olives are about. To tie it is a matter of seconds: yellow tying silk lightly waxed, and the pale cloudy hackle from under a snipe's wing. With the silk unwaxed and in a smaller size it serves its original purpose as a Pale Watery.

For a winged fly there is a suitable Greenwell, and Gold Ribbed Hare's Ear. For over a century and a half the Hare's Ear has been a favourite in England, Scotland and Ireland. Stewart chose it as one of his three winged patterns. Usually it is tied with a wing from a starling secondary, sometimes from a woodcock's feather, and if used as a top dropper, is probably best with the hackle fibre wing popularised by Roger Woolley. The brown-grey of hare's ear is not a close imitation of the natural, but in practice it works.

One bleak forenoon, without any warning, the water will be covered with scraps of darkness; the trout will become demented, and you will know that the Iron Blue has arrived. You will fish with frenzy, catch three or four while the rise is on, and kick yourself for not catching more. I have never met a man pleased with himself after an Iron Blue hatch.

Once I was fishing a Meath river when an immense hatch came about. I collected a couple on a Dark Snipe and Purple and two more on a small dark Greenwell. As the hatch ceased I gathered about two dozen flies, put them in match boxes, and took them home for close examination under a hand glass. All the wings were the same, a dark iron grey; the bodies varied, some being a dark elephant grey with grey legs, and others having a distinct tinge of olive in the grey both of body and legs. I laid myself out to imitate them. "Imitation" is a word I avoid, preferring "simulation" or "representation". By imitation I mean reproducing as closely as possible the exact colour, shape and size of the natural as it appears to our eyes. By "simulation" or "representation" I mean something which is sufficient to satisfy, or at least not to antagonise, the trout. The test of imitation is appearance; of simulation or representation, success. In my experience the most successful patterns often those which do not seem to be the most exact imitations, the reason I suspect, being a difference between the colour vision of man and trout.

I matched the elephant grey body exactly with a shade of heron herl, and the more olive body with mole's fur mixed with a little of the same fur dyed in picric. The legs were pretty accurately reproduced by jackdaw's throat hackle, and a furnace hen which had been given a dose of an olive dye. There remained the wings. For these I wanted a tom-tit's tail, and there were plenty of tom-tits in the garden, usually up to no good. It is however impossible to shoot a bird with whom one is on a social footing. My favourite cat, who thought such squeamishness nauseating, went out and in ten minutes returned with a dead tit. He did the same on another day when I was starting to tie a batch of Greenwells, and found I had no hen blackbird. I started to make-do with coot, when there was a shadow in the window, a plop on the floor, and a hen blackbird laid at my feet. It is fair to say that he was unusually intelligent, even for a cat.

Tom-tit's tail is not the easiest of feathers to manipulate, but for once all went well. Some of the wings were dreams, and I finished with four or five flies which, when examined in my study and subsequently compared with the naturals by the water side, seemed to me just about as good imitations as could be achieved. Next I looked up all the dressings of the Iron Blue I could find in the books, from the oldest to the newest, and tied specimens of them all. I was, if I may use the expression, after the Iron Blue's blood. If there was a satisfactory dressing I was going to find it.

There were some good hatches of the Iron Blue that year and all the patterns had their chance. None was a complete failure, but none was really successful. The best were the Snipe and Purple and the small dark Greenwell, and my imitations were nearly at the bottom of the list. So, with purple tying silk and a feather from the outside of the shoulder of a snipe's wing, you can tie the only extra fly which is necessary for a rise of Iron Blue.

As summer sets in, the Blue Winged Olive appears on most rivers. I associate it with calm evenings and the dry rather than the wet fly. Partridge and Orange for the male, Waterhen Bloa dressed with mole dyed in picric for the female, and a large Greenwell with dark starling or waterhen wing will be adequate for wet-fly work without increasing the number of patterns in your box.

The Pale Wateries are also flies of summer. A number of different flies are grouped under this name. Baetis scambus is like a Small Dark Olive and is well represented by a small Greenwell. Centroptilon luteolum, called the Little Sky Blue Dun, and Procloeon rufulum called the Pale Evening Dun have bodies of a milky or pale yellow-green-colour. Light Snipe and Yellow, Dotterel and Yellow, or a pale Tup's Indispensable are all good representations.

The spinners can be dealt with in a general and unscientific manner. Dry-fly fishermen may find it necessary to have different patterns for each sex of each of the Ephemeroptera, but in the rougher and swifter water, where the wet fly is likely to be used, it is sufficient to divide the spinners into two main classes – those whose bodies are of the colour of a dead beech leaf, and those whose bodies are the colour of Chateau Yquem. Orange Partridge and Pheasant Tail will look after the first class, and a pale Tup the second. Another successful pattern for the second class has a body of pale greenish-yellow seal's fur, with a hackle of pale honey dun, or blue dun.

In high summer there are no large rises of the Ephemerids

during the day time, but under the trees and in quiet stretches you may find the trout smutting steadily on small black two winged flies, either the Black Gnat (Bibio johannis) or one of the forms of Reed Smut (Simulium). There are innumerable dressings, none of them very successful, for smutting trout are as difficult to catch as they are impossible to put down. You can spend an interesting, exasperating and unprofitable few hours trying out various patterns before you sink away to fish the rough water with a fancy fly. One of the best dressings for smutting fish is a small wingless pattern of a fancy fly – William's Favourite.

Small dark sedges will generally be on the water in the afternoons and Skues Little Red Sedge with a dark hare's ear body and wing and hackle of landrail will meet all needs. In the evenings and far into the warm night, the medium sedges will be matching, running on the water and drifting down spent. As the number of species runs into hundreds, strict economy is necessary. In Ireland the artificial patterns are known as the "Rails" and the "Woodcocks", from the feathers of which their wings are made. The Rails, with wings from the secondaries or primaries of the corn crake, imitate the cinnamon sedges, and the Woodcock imitate these with a brown mottled wing. Various coloured bodies are used, but with a green fur body for your Rail, and yellow fur for the Woodcock, and the standard pattern of Alder in case there are some dark sedges, failure will not be due to lack of a proper pattern.

Beetles of many kinds find their way into the water and are eagerly taken. One beetle pattern should be enough, and it had better be a representation of the natural which hatches in the greatest numbers. This in my experience is the Bracken Clock or Coch-y-bondhu. I have seen lawns by the Slaney shimmering and heaving with these beetles in June. They lay their eggs in grass, and these hatch into disgusting grey-white grubs which feed on the grass roots. By September, lawns and pasture fields are no more than a brown felt which strips away under foot. The rooks come and gorge themselves, tearing into the earth with their pick-axe bills but hardly reducing the numbers. I have picked over 150 grubs from a single square foot of lawn, and in some years the pasture fields over several miles beside the river were devastated. Fortunately such wholesale visitations are rare. The best pattern is a body of bronze peacock herl with a red landrail hackle.

Fancy flies are a delicate subject. Their use is opposed by two types of fishermen, the old fashioned purist who will not tolerate the use of anything except an imitation, good or bad, of the fly on which the trout is feeding, and the ultra-scientific, who dislike the use of anything for whose success they cannot find a satisfactory explanation.

No one has a right to quarrel with the restrictions which a club or the private owner of a fishery chooses to impose. Most sporting prohibitions are artificial, but so long as the supply of fish and game is limited, there is a lot to be said for confining the methods of fishing and shooting to those which require most skill, and in which, for that reason, the greatest pleasure is to be derived from success. No one wants to see thread line fishing or night lines on the Test, or to allow pheasants to be shot when they are roosting. Even the practice of fishing a large minnow-suggesting wet-fly down-stream in early spring, can with reason be reprehended in preserved water. But, on the ordinary wet-fly stream, there are times when the use of a small fancy fly is necessary and unobjectionable. There may be no fly hatching, there may be a hatch of which the trout are taking no notice. They may be gorged, or bored, or suffering from a dose of accidie. Why not try to arouse, excite, stimulate them by something a little out of the ordinary?

All the same the use of fancy patterns is probably overdone. Recently I was given the opportunity of visiting the workrooms and examining the stock of a wholesale supplier of trout flies, who tied patterns to the order of retailers all over Great Britain and Ireland. Rather over sixty per cent. of the patterns were fancy, the remainder being equally divided between general flies and recognizably specific imitations. Any fly, no matter how bizarre, will catch some trout at some time, but the same hopefulness which induced the men of the middle ages to spend their days in pursuit of the Philosopher's Stone, or the Elixir of Life, inspires anglers to search for the fly of all flies which will bring them success anywhere and at all times. I know of one fisherman who admitted, half in shame, half in pride, that he had over five hundred different patterns in his study.

I used to carry three fancy patterns – Wickham's Fancy, William's Favourite and Blue Body Black Hackle. Wickham is too well known to need comment. William's Favourite I used for many years without knowing its name. Casting an indolent eye over the patterns displayed in a tackle shop, I was attracted by a quiet combination of black floss, ribbed silver, black hackle and starling wing, called I think Lee's Fancy. I took a couple, and found them effective. By substituting silver wire for the original flat tinsel, and leaving out the wing, there was as good a representation of smuts as any other – again a dual purpose fly. Years afterwards I discovered, in Mr. Courtney William's book on trout flies, that the pattern had been invented by his father. It is a magnificent all-round fancy fly.

Blue Body Black Hackle is an Irish name for a fly which has been used by generations of fishermen. In my youth no Wicklow fisherman made up a cast without it. In Scotland it is known as Cairn's Fancy, in the north of England it is identical with one of the dressings of Broughton's Point, and without any name attached it was one of Stewart's winged flies. Starling wing, black hackle and a body of dark gentian blue – sometimes a purple claret – ribbed with flat silver, it will kill from the first day of the season to the last on any mountain stream. Dressed larger, and called the Blue Bottle, it killed well on mountain lakes.

Let us see how our list is now composed. Five north country soft hackled patterns – Orange Partridge, Waterhen Bloa, Light Snipe and Yellow, Dark Snipe and Purple, Bracken Clock. Two west country with stiff hackles – Pheasant Tail and Tup's Indispensable. Two general winged flies – Hare's Ear and either Rough Olive in variety or Greenwell's Glory in variety. Four sedge patterns – Little Red Sedge, Rail and Green, Woodcock and Yellow, and Alder (treated as a sedge). Three fancy flies – Wickham, William's Favourite, Blue Body Black Hackle. Sixteen in all. Do we require any more? There are the land bred flies, Hawthorn, Cow Dung, Oak Fly, Alder, House Fly and Ants. They do get into the water, and they are taken by trout, but with the exception of the Ants never in sufficient quantity to bring on a rise. A few Ants should be in the box if you are fishing in late summer, for, although a fall occurs only on two or three days in the season, you will feel cheated if you are out on one of these days and have not one of the standard imitations. The other land flies may be ignored, though one or two of each will not take up much room in a compartment. Lastly if you have sufficent hardihood, hide away in a corner tied on No. 12 hooks

a Silver Partridge and an Invicta, for that blustery March day
when neither fly nor fish is showing. Fish them deep and down-
stream – but only use them as a last resort. Some people will
exclaim at the omissions in this list. I have already explained
why the March Brown and the Grannom are not there. The Great
Stone fly – Theakston's "Imperial Empress" – I have never seen
in Ireland. But what about the May-Fly which abounds in our
lakes and limestone rivers?

The odd May-Fly which floats, a stray and a lonely thing, on
the surface of an acid water may be ignored by the angler as it
usually is by the trout, but if you are going to fish a river where
there is a real May-Fly hatch it must be taken seriously. There
can be no question of getting away with a couple of artificials
crammed into a compartment. It is a matter of a separate box
and a large one. You will need patterns to simulate both male
and female dun spinner and spent spinner. The May-Fly is big
and variable, and the trout develop strange fancies for one pattern
or another. It is fished nearly always as a dry-fly, though a couple
of wet-fly patterns to serve as nymphs should be included.

I have neither the skill nor the experience to express any
opinion on dry-fly fishing, for it played little part in my fishing
life. Yet even the wet-fly fisherman on a wet-fly river is faced
with situations where wet should give way to dry. Unless he is
fishing what I may call a half and half river, he need not carry
a separate stock. The West Country patterns are practically dry-
flies in their own right, and need only a touch of flotant; the
winged patterns are turned into dry-flies by the use of stiffer cock
hackles. A dry Red Quill can find a place, and also a "bottle
brush" fly such as the "Robins" introduced by Roger Woolley.
Black Robin is nothing but a stiff black hackle wound palmer-
wise for the full length of the hook shank, and tipped with flat
gold tinsel. The hackles are cut short, and the fly floats well. It
may be taken for a beetle or one of the more corpulent diptera,
but it is safer to regard it as a fancy dry-fly. On those sluggish
August days when an odd trout rises irregularly every hundred
yards or so it will often tempt fish to a second and fatal rise.

The flies I have suggested cover the whole season and a wide
range of circumstances. On any day if you know your river you
need only carry about half a dozen patterns in an ordinary match
box. Particular rivers may have abundant hatches of a particular
fly, in which case it may be profitable and will certainly be

interesting to experiment with alternative dressings, and there are some flies of rare or local occurrence which I have not taken into account. But with the list given I should be satisfied to tackle any ordinary wet-fly river.

8

THE BIG HOUSE

". . . My son tells me that you are an ardent fisherman. We have a house on the shore of Lough Melvin which fishes well in April, and there will be some salmon in the Bundrowse. If you could spare a week or a fortnight of your Easter vacation to stay with us my wife and I would be very pleased."

This letter, the first of many phrased with the same careful courtesy, introduced me to the big lakes of the west and to a feature of Irish country life then rapidly passing away. At Bundoran a wizened coachman met me with an outside car which soon covered the hilly miles to where the Big House stood, surrounded on three sides by woodland and open on the fourth, where lawns and fields sloped to the water's edge. In spring the daffodils spread themselves in golden drifts down to the lake, in autumn the scarlet lobelia blazed a flare of colour between house and shrubberies. The house itself, built when the Georgian style was yielding to the Victorian, was large but architecturally undistinguished. Originally the walls of all the main rooms had been covered with French cartoons in grisaille, illustrating scenes from classical mythology. The many life-sized nudes were a little too explicit for Victorian taste, and pictures and furniture had been arranged to hide the more compromising details. When a later generation, bracing itself to acknowledge the facts of anatomy, removed the obstructions, it was too late. The discoloration was permanent.

Already the house was an anachronism, a manor house without an estate. For nearly a century, when Irish country life had been built on a structure of landlord and tenant, it had been the centre of interest for a barony, its stables full of carriages and horses, its garden a model, its owners men of learning and public spirit. Politics and literature have dealt harshly with the Irish landlord. Sad and mad and bad they may have been; too often they were absentees. But many of them were men of culture, bravery, and a high sense of public duty. Their libraries were good and sometimes remarkable. They planted world-famous gardens. They organised and endowed innumerable Irish charities, relieved distress, and helped and advised such tenants as were willing to accept their advice. Much of their time was spent in hunting and field sports, but these provided employment of the type that the Irish countryman likes, and made the big house a centre of interest and society. Above all, they supplied a personal relationship which made up for many abuses.

A good landlord was united to his tenantry by bonds part patriarchal, part feudal, and entirely human, which formed a not unsatisfactory pattern of life. Now all this had been changed, shattered irretrievably by a great reform which had enabled the tenants to become freeholders. The landlords lived on, financially not much worse off, still doing their duty on bench and synod, still spending much of their leisure in sport; but the ties which bound them and their families to the countryside were snapped. Old retainers still remained. The coachman who had met me was serving his fourth generation, the parlour maid had been nurse to my host, the gardener was trained by his grandfather. But the dust was settling; the Big House was dying at its roots.

My host, who had for some years been living a life of use and wont in which sport had ceased to play a part, his guns licensed but unfired, his rods idle in their cases, now roused himself to put his son and myself on the road of true orthodoxy. He was orthodox to a fault, his fishing methods not so much dated as out-dated, but I owe him a grounding in caution, in boatcraft, and in etiquette which was to help me in difficult times and places.

Each day began with a kind of drill. The boat must be examined to see that there were no seams strained, no nails projecting, and that under the peak there was a pair of spare rowlocks or, in the second boat, a bag of good thole-pins. The squire had lost a friend, drowned in a storm because only one spare thole pin had been carried. Next came ballasting, to be done afresh each day according to the conditions. For this purpose a supply of flat stones was kept in the boat house and more could be picked up round the shores, but he warned us that in lakes where there were no stones we would have to carry sand bags. In heavy weather the ballast had to be considerable so as to slow the drift and make the boat easier to row against a wind, and always it had to be carefully adjusted between bow and stern so that she would drift dead before the wind to the spot selected. There are occasions, as when fishing a shore which lies diagonally to the direction of the wind, when it is desirable to make a boat drift on a bias, and this can be done by a slight shift of ballast. More weight in the stern raises the bow, which catches the wind and is blown partially round, with the result that the boat runs by the head. More weight in the bow, and she runs by the stern. If you are fishing by yourself, correct ballasting saves a deal of rowing.

As befitted his position and generation, the squire set great store by etiquette. "Always remember there is another angler in the boat". He taught us to imagine that there was a high perpendicular sheet of glass fixed athwart the boat, and extending out for some distance from the sides. This marked out the areas proper to each rod, both in the forward and backward casts, and if flies did not trespass outside their own areas there could be no tangling. A simpler way to avoid any possible tangling is to use a switch cast, which ensures that the flies never cross the line of the boat and has the further advantage that the flies are longer in the water. The only time when experienced fishermen occasionally get their lines tangled is when fishing a dry-fly in the twilight, and when this happens it is well to remember how far sound travels over water.

Lines can get crossed through no fault of the anglers, if two big trout, hooked at the same time, make away on convergent courses. When this happens it is the business of the boatman to spin the boat round, so that the angler whose line is underneath is brought nearer to his fish, and his companion further from his. This uncrosses the lines. If the boat is too heavy for this manoeuvre, or the boatman unskilful, exchange rods, passing the one whose line is underneath below the other.

Consideration for the other angler also requires the direction of the boat's head to be changed frequently, especially when fishing a shore. Most anglers prefer to cast forehanded, with their arm free of the boat, and the cast nearer the shore is usually the better. I once asked the squire what he thought of a famous classical scholar who came from the neighbourhood. "Not much," he replied. "He always tried to take the inside cast."

"Fish like a cat" was a repeated adjuration. By this he meant that there was to be no clumping of heavy boots on the floor-boards, no careless dropping of tackle cases. We might shout and sing to our hearts' content, for fish did not hear noises in the air, but anything which caused under-water vibrations scared them. I doubt if such precautions are needed in a big wave, but when fishing quiet water under a windward shore they are essential, and the boatman as well as the angler must avoid any disturbance, slipping the boat along without ripple at bow or suck at stern and with the minimum of eddy from the oars. Old Pat Spellman, for nearly half a century head-keeper at Fermoyle, was a master at this kind of work. Anyone looking at the shallow bays becalmed under the high banks might well have written them off as unfishable, but Pat would prowl along in the deep looking for the best line of approach and having chosen it, would snake the boat in among the submerged rocks without a touch. The oars hardly seemed to move, but the boat glided forward as if the good spirit of the ancient mariner were under the keel. Pat would choose carefully the exact spot from which he wanted to start the drift and then, one oar shipped but the windward one in the water to wheedle the boat away from any obstructive rocks, we waited for the boat to move. Slowly the drift began, the water took a darkness, a pin ripple showed on the surface, the flick of little wavelets against the side became audible – and each rod was bent. By the time the fish were landed the water was too deep, and we picked our way back for a new drift.

Some of my best days with white trout have been made in this way. Fishermen are inclined to slight the windward shore. The lee shore, where the waves are big, is the easiest to fish, and there are few boatmen with the skill of old Pat, but the chief reason for the neglect is the belief that all the flies get blown across the lake to the lee shore. So they would be if there were no trout to intercept them; but why should the fish let this happen? Flies, with a few exceptions, are bred on land or in relatively shallow water. When the wind is light the land flies are dropped more plentifully near the sheltered shore, and the water-bred flies hatch out there. Trout lie off this shore, waiting for the wings of the wind to bring them their bounty, and if they are in feeding mood they do not let much pass.

The squire did not teach me anything new about ordinary wet-fly fishing. He was an adherent of the old school – long rod, light line, and work your flies – and I was to see a much abler exponent of this method when I went to Corrib, but he did teach me all that it was necessary to know about the lugubrious art of dapping.

The Victorians, for some reason, regarded dapping with great respect as a kind of arcane mystery, saying of an angler "He is a grand dapper" in much the same tone as we would say, "He is a wizard with the dry fly." Dapping has its place as a means whereby absolute novices can catch large trout, but it is, next to trolling, the dullest and least skilful of all methods. Dapping consists in fishing with the natural insect, the best known daps being the May-Fly, the Daddy, the Grasshopper, and that triumph of incongruity, a grasshopper flanked by two daddies. As the natural is too delicate to be cast it has to be drifted out on the wind, which means using a long rod and a light line of undressed silk, known as a blow line. Even the tools are unattractive. No one has ever caressed the unresponsive sixteen feet of a dapping rod or lost his temper over the merits of different types of blow line.

There are only two things to watch in dapping. First, to see that your dap, and only your dap, is in the water; and second, not to strike too soon. Perhaps I should add a third – not to fall asleep. The dap must skim over the surface at the same pace as the boat is drifting, and neither line nor gut must touch the water. This means that gut and line must be in the air slightly in advance of the dap. If you watch, end on, a boat with a competent dapper you will see that his line bulges out forward like a well set spinnaker. If the wind is light you may have to hold your rod at full length over your head, a back-breaking procedure. A couple of cigarette papers tied to the line, in the same way as paper tails are fixed to a kite, is a help to float it out in a faint breeze. If the wind is strong the rod must be held low or the dap will be whipped off the water.

There is nothing very difficult in learning to manage a dap. What is difficult, and quite beyond the control of many fishermen, is to restrain for a sufficient time the instinct to strike. If you strike too soon you will not hook your fish and the strike must be slower with the Daddy than the May-Fly, and with the Grasshopper than the Daddy. The most successful dapper with the Grasshopper that I have known was a Corrib boatman who waited what seemed an unbearable time (actually it was four to five seconds) before he tightened. The squire had a tip which sometimes works. When the fish rose the fisherman must start to sing loud and clear the first line of "God save the King," and strike only when he came to the word "King". This timing is correct for the May-Fly, but too short for the Grasshopper.

As may have appeared I am not enthusiastic about dapping, though I still remember a day on Sheelin with a rolling wave and not a trout under three pounds. For those who share my dislike, I advise the haphazard dry-fly, which on the many occasions when I tested it against the dap, did as well or better. By the haphazard dry fly (or dry flies, for a hackle pattern can be fished as a dropper) I mean a dry-fly cast hopefully on the face of the waters. No artificial fly can hope to be quite as good an imitation of the natural as the natural itself, but, in compensation, more water can be covered. The dap takes a narrow course straight down wind, and cannot be moved more than a foot or two sideways. If you want to cover a fish that has been seen to rise this can be done only by moving the boat. The haphazard dry-fly can be made to cover a wide arc, as it can be cast partially or entirely across wind. If a fish is seen to rise it becomes a purposive dry-fly, and if he is anywhere in range can be dropped on his nose, even if the rise is wide of the drift.

The patterns which I found most useful for this kind of work were not those which most closely resemble the natural. An element of the fancy seemed to attract trout more readily. Even when using the natural many boatmen like to impale a blossom of furze between the two May-flies, partly to give greater floating power but also because they believe the touch of brilliant yellow stimulates the fish into taking. Two patterns I found specially successful. The first was tied in the manner of Hammond's Champion, dyed whole wings of summer duck, detached body of yellow lamb's wool covered with yellow floss, a yellow hackle at shoulder, another tiny yellow hackle at tail, the whisks of fibres from the tail of a cock pheasant, and a ribbing of brown silk. The colour was Ming Yellow, much brighter than the somewhat greenish hue of the natural. The second was wingless. At the head was wound the lovely feather from a red-legged partridge, which is a combination of grey, brown, and lavender, and behind that a hackle of brilliant orange. The body was greenish yellow raffia, ribbed with gold wire, and the whisks as in the first pattern.

The Green Drake (our Irish name for the May-fly dun) may be thick on the surface and yet hardly a rising trout is to be seen. This is because the fish are taking the ascending nymph, which floats up past their noses and needs less effort to capture than a floating fly. Now is the time for a big wet pattern which may, if you like, be a copy of the natural nymph, though a big Golden Olive or Invicta seems just as good. I would also put in a good word for the Straddlebug, an old Lough Erne pattern, as ungainly in appearance as in name. Tied with a large hackle from the Egyptian goose, dyed yellow, and attached so that the natural curve of the fibres is forward, it resembles nothing except a baby octopus. When fished in short jerks, the soft feathers work backwards and forwards in a way that suggests a living thing of some kind, and the fish do not bother to enquire what. Though classed as a wet pattern of the May-fly, it is a shameless lure.

This disquisition on dapping and how to avoid it, has called in aid memories from many lakes other than Lough Melvin, where dapping is of little account. Melvin is essentially a wet-fly lake. It holds four varieties of trout, the ferox which can be caught only by trolling and so did not interest me, the ordinary brown, the gillaroo, and the sonaghan.

The sonaghan, which is not, as far as I know, found elsewhere, provides most of the sport. It is a sober looking fish, coloured in olive and iron grey with black spots; is rarely over a pound and a half in weight; lives in deeper water than any other trout except when it runs up the rivers to spawn, and seems to move in small shoals. Free rising, very strong for its weight, and red-fleshed, it can give a sparkling day, but the fishing is usually in short spurts, periods of inaction alternating with periods when both rods are engaged together. A complete contrast is the gillaroo which haunts rocky shores and takes best in rough weather, even in breaking waves. Though I never caught one over three and a half pounds they run larger. The gillaroo is the panther of the water, the loveliest of our fish. On a background of satin wood are scattered spots and blotches of red, orange, umber, and burnt sienna, so thickly as to touch and interfuse. Manley Hopkins must, I think, have had in mind a gillaroo when he wrote "Rose-moles all in stipple upon trout that swim."

There were saimon to be had in the bay at the far end of the lake where the river enters, and in the Bundrowse, where I caught my first spring fish and also disgraced myself by gaffing a kelt; and the squire usually managed to arrange for us a couple of days in August on the Erne, where I was taught to fish a single-hook prawn on a fly rod. This method was forbidden, but was winked at when the best of the season was over. The ghillie would ask you if you would like to try the "travelling fly", and out of his pocket would come a shrimp ready mounted. When your fly was removed and the shrimp attached he retired to keep watch for the bailiff and if you heard a whistle, off came the "travelling fly," and on went Rogan's Yellow Silk.

For four years my fishing centred round the Big House, ten days in spring and the same in August. The old retainers were dropping away. "I've seen what I've seen and I'll not see much more," said the coachman, now nearly ninety on the last occasion that he drove me to the station. On my next visit he was gone. Kate, the parlour maid, found her rheumatism too crippling, and the gardener retired on pension to a cottage. The squire had ceased to come out on the lake with us, and he was intellectually less alert. Over the port he had been eager to cross-question me on all the vexed problems of the day, with his unvaried courtesy treating my undergraduate opinions as if they were worth listening to. Now he avoided discussion. When things puzzled him he no longer sought an answer. He lived more and more in the past. A weary, slightly despairing look often came over his kindly face. I was too young to recognize the significance of these changes, signs that the organism could no longer adapt itself to its environment, the first, faint, far-borne notes of the trumpet of Azrael. Then at one stride came disaster. Father and then mother were dead; the son, always delicate, became incurably ill. The Big House had fallen. Another old Irish family had come to its end. Of the Big House itself only a few ruins now remain.

9

THE LAKE AND THE LURE

River fishing is a one-man pursuit, lake fishing a partnership. There may be a partnership of three, if the second rod is a friend with similar views, but the ideal is two: the angler and his boatman. The boatman supplies the knowledge of local conditions while the angler decides the method of fishing. It takes time to perfect such a partnership, for every angler has his own theories and methods, which necessitate the boat being handled in the way which suits his style, and the boatman must learn to do this without continual direction. Some boatmen will not learn and some try to dictate. The wise angler will accept suggestions from an intelligent boatman but he must never tolerate dictation.

I have had many fruitful partnerships but none so ideal as that with Miley Costello of Fermoyle. Speech was unnecessary, and indeed Miley seemed to have a mistrust of speech, doling out his rare remarks as if he was dispensing a dangerous medicine. It was a point of pride with him to be able to read the mind of his angler and take the appropriate action before he was told. Nothing escaped his observation. A turn of the head, a glance at the sky, a shift of position, the opening of a fly box, these gave him the clues to what was going on in my mind. Yet there must have been something more than quick observation. I would think "I wonder is the salmon which I saw move by the big rock last Saturday still in the same place?" and Miley would take up the oars and row me to the most favourable point for drifting the big rock. To fish with Miley was to have four eyes. Battling up against half a gale he would suddenly stop the boat and point out a direction for me to cast and as often as not the flies would be taken by a fish whose movement he had spotted despite the roughness of the wave. I can recall his making only one error,

68

and then the real fault was mine. While he was away gathering heather for the luncheon fire the wind died and I changed to a thin and rather worn cast, but kept on the same flies. I was so accustomed to Miley seeing everything that I forgot to tell him about the change when he came back. As soon as we started again after lunch, a big white trout took the tail fly and charged straight in towards the boat. The orthodox counter is for the boatman to pull half a stroke, allowing the fish's rush to take him past the stern and so avoiding the danger of a dropper catching on the keel. With any other angler Miley would have done this automatically, but he knew that with a cast of normal thickness I preferred to take in line with my hand and direct the fish by side pressure clear of the stern. The weak cast did not take the strain of so large a fish, and parted. Miley picked up the broken end, examined it and flushed. "To think I never noticed," was all he said.

In my early days on Lough Melvin there was little opportunity to experiment with different fishing methods, for the squire was set in his ways and the boatman, an old retainer, would obey nobody but his master. If he was not with us the boatman did what he liked, and my friend and I were too young to impose our wills. The result, happily as it turned out, was to direct our attention to the form and pattern of flies in an attempt to evolve some principles of selection from the kaleidoscopic variety offered by the catalogues.

I had plenty of material for experiment. At the end of each season W. J. Cummins used to sell off his surplus stock of lake flies at prices so modest that I had been able to acquire a good collection of the patterns then most in favour with English and Scottish fishermen. They filled one box. In another lay the Irish flies, the patterns fewer but representing the work of several different craftsmen including the famous Rogan of Ballyshannon.

The contrast between the two collections was marked. British taste in lake flies ran to a brilliancy of colour and a tailor-made precision of form – wings a sleek pad without a fibre astray, fur wound so tightly that the tinsel could not sink in but showed in prominent bracelets of gold and silver, bodies all in primary and secondary colours, shining like a handful of precious stones. (I use the adjectives "primary" "secondary" and "tertiary" in the meanings assigned to them by the old painters, and not in terms of spectroscopic analysis. Red, blue and yellow are primaries. The combination of any two of these primaries – purple, green, orange – are secondaries. The softer tones resulting from the combinations of three colours are tertiaries).

Compared with all this oriental splendour the Irish flies looked in their box a dull and scruffy assortment. Their wings were ragged and often separated, with strands all awry; the tinsel hardly visible, buried in the fur which had been loosely spun and then picked out with a needle. There was no primary colour and, with the exception of orange, no secondary. Instead there was an array of soft rich tertiaries, in tints of an autumn landscape. Thus, while the British collection had no olive, the Irish had four, Golden Olive, Green Olive, Brown Olive, and Sooty Olive. To the true claret of the Scottish "Mallard and Claret" Ireland added Fiery Claret, the colour of the inside of a blood orange, and Black Claret, which looked an actual black in the box but by transmitted light showed as maroon. Fiery Brown and two shades of grey, one silvery, the other with a hint of blue like a pale blue dun hackle, completed the characteristic Irish range.

When the flies were examined against a northern light the Irish assortment came into its own. British patterns, because of their opaque construction, lost their hues and became almost silhouettes; but with the Irish, the light found its way through the ragged wings, trickled in and out of the gleaming seal's fur, was reflected back from the hidden tinsel, and turned the whole body into a haze of colour.

Not every Irish fly justified this eulogy. Much depended on the particular craftsman, and I began to understand that there was as much art in tying those casual-looking creations as the dapper English patterns. Even more depended on the quality of the materials, especially the seal's fur. Rogan's seal's fur stood out for its shine and richness of colour. He did all his own dying and kept his secrets well, though I tried several times to extract them. The only advice he gave me was nothing new – to be sure to remove every scrap of grease before using the colour bath – but Ballyshannon gossip whispered that a necessary ingredient of his famous fiery brown was a bucket of jackass urine, kept till the sanitary inspector found it necessary to intervene.

The first practical step was to test the two sets of flies one against the other, an easy task with two rods both equally competent – or incompetent. One rod fished a cast of British flies, the other of Irish, and the casts were changed round at intervals. Very soon certain broad conclusions emerged. On their home waters the Irish flies were the more effective. At tail there was not much to choose, but as droppers the only English patterns which could compare with the Irish were those tied in the "Palmer" or "Bumble" fashion. Subsequent experience has confirmed these initial impressions. It is worth while to speculate a little on the reasons, for if the speculations are correct, they form the first guidance in the choice of pattern.

Irish flies, as has been noted, were the more translucent, British the more opaque, and in consequence the British looked at their best when seen by light reflected from them and the Irish by light which was transmitted through them. Droppers should be fished in or just under the surface in imitation of surface life, while the tail fly fishes a foot or so below the surface and must imitate some form of swimming life. Speaking broadly surface life is translucent and sub-surface life is opaque. There are exceptions. Some surface-moving life, such as shrimps or the early stages of perch fry, are fairly translucent; but the generalization is sufficiently accurate to provide one reason why droppers should be translucent and tail flies may be opaque. A second reason lies in the way the trout sees the flies. As the dropper is within an inch or so of the surface the trout sees it from beneath (and so by transmitted light) till the last moment. The tail fly he sees as often from the side or even from above (and so by light reflected from it and not by light coming through it). It is common sense to choose for each position the type of fly which looks at its most attractive in that position.

The success of the Palmers was particularly suggestive. Red and Black Palmers were as old as Cotton. Black Palmer had recently burst out into a red tail and, under the name of "The Zulu" had become very popular on both sides of St. George's channel. In Derbyshire this kind of dressing had been used in various colours and the flies went by the name of "Bumbles". The characteristic of this construction is that there are no wings and the hackle, usually a stiff cock, is wound from shoulder to tail. In the hand they give a misleading impression of bulkiness which disappears when they are examined against the light. No other form of tying is quite so translucent, and the hackles, especially dyed hackles, take on an internal fire and sparkle, shifting with every movement of the fly, which conveys an illusion of active life. Many of the

surface insects of the lake – the Daddy, the sedges, and some of
the diptera – indulge in a good deal of fluttering and movement,
and I suspect that the Bumble tie may suggest such motion. The
older writers refer to flies constructed in this way as "tied buzz",
apparently in the belief that they represented a fluttering insect.

Whether these explanations are true or false I am convinced
that flies built in this fashion are the best form of dropper, and
have been strangely neglected by anglers. In the next chapter I
describe some of my attempts to combine this old English form
of construction with the Irish principles of colour mixing. Underwater life (again with the exception of that unaccommodating
creature the shrimp) is swimming life, streamlined to make
passage through the water easier. Nothing could be less stream-
lined than a Bumble. To achieve even an approximation to
streamlining, hackles must be sparse and soft and the body must
be at least partially sheathed with smooth feathers – in other
words it must have wings, preferably tied low as in the old Spey
salmon flies. We reach the apparent paradox that to imitate the
winged life of the surface the artificial must dispense with wings,
while to imitate the wingless life under water wings must be
provided.

So much for form. The other questions often asked are – what
size should I use? Should I try to imitate natural flies or use
something which is frankly a fancy fly or lure? What colours
are best, and when should they be used?

To answer these questions we must try to put ourselves in the
trout's place. From his position near the bottom he can see
through that portion of the surface which is within his window.
The deeper he lies the larger his window and the greater the
chance that something edible may appear in it, but, if the surface
is disturbed, the less is his chance of seeing a small fly. If he does
see a small fly it may not be worth his while to make the exertion
of coming up through a number of feet of water to collect it, for
he will use up more energy in the effort than the tiny morsel can
supply. There will be better and more accessible feeding on the
bottom. On the other hand, if he comes nearer the surface so as
to spare himself the effort in swimming up for a fly, his window
will be so small that unless the insects are thick on the surface
he may miss them. In the open water of big lakes trout will not
come up even to take the natural unless it is very plentiful, or

unless it is an insect which will provide a good mouthful, such as the May-fly, the Daddy or one of the large sedges.

In small lakes – by which I mean lakes whose surface area is not more than about half a square mile – or in sheltered inlets in big lakes such as those which push deeply into the south east shore of Lough Mask, you will often find a large number of insects on the surface. The shallower water and gentler waves which permit a growth of weed and sedge favour water-bred insects. Trees, bushes and rich soil harbour the insects of the land. The surface is less disturbed and the trout can see their food more clearly. These are the conditions in which it pays to use imitative patterns, wet or dry. They need not be very good imitations. Hare's Ear, Greenwell, and Wickham will cover the Olives; Skues' Small Red Sedge is a generalized pattern which will embrace most small sedges; and in Mr. J. R. Harris's *Angler's Entomology* there are good dressings of Caenis and the Duck Flies. The lure type of fly, dressed reasonably small is also successful. It is a mistake to use too small a fly. Imitations of the smaller naturals should be dressed a size or two larger than the insects they represent, and No. 11 (O.S.) is about as small as is ever necessary for a lure.

Most of my lake fishing for brown trout has been on really big sheets of water such as Melvin, Mask, or Corrib, and I have never seen a good rise of trout to small insects. There may be a fall of ants in August, on some lakes the diminutive Caenis and the Duck flies have their seasons, and there is often a sprinkling of Lake Olives and other Olives; but speaking for myself I have never seen a good rise of trout to any of these in the open lake and have always done better by fishing very much larger patterns of the lure type than by using imitations of these small flies.

It is a different matter with the large natural flies. Here it does pay to use a colourable imitation though the most exact-looking imitation is not always the best. I have already mentioned two good patterns of May-fly. If you happen to strike an evening when the trout are feeding on the big sedges they will not refuse a large Invicta, or a large specimen of Kingsley's pattern of the Alder, though more exact dressings are given by Mr. J. R. Harris. The Daddy can be imitated more perfectly than any other fly. Make a body of natural raffia, tie in at the thorax six fibres of cock-pheasant tail with a couple of thumb knots in each to represent the joints of the legs, add two rusty blue dun hackle tips tied flat for the wings, then stick your finished fly in a curtain and watch the women of your household trying to brush it away. For flotation purposes, if you are going to fish dry, add a stiff rusty dun hackle. The wet pattern leaves out the wings and has a hen, or cockerel, hackle.

The most exciting experience which lake fishing has to offer is the mad rise which sometimes takes place in the twilight to the big sedges. Unfortunately it is very hard to hit it off. The last few days of June, July and very early August are the times, and the evening must be warm and calm. Even with perfect conditions there may be no rise, or it may be patchy and confined to a small area. Earlier in the evening an odd trout or so is usually to be found taking down medium sedges in sheltered inlets. It is best to fish him with a dry-fly but do not leave it squatting inertly on the water. Twitch it along the surface in little jerks of a couple of inches. This will attract the attention of the fish from a distance and it is a perfectly natural movement, for sedges fuss about like little power boats. Later on when the sun has set, the best method of fishing is neither wet nor dry but waterlogged. The fly, a large pattern with not too stiff a hackle, should furrow the skin of the water and make a big wave. "It pays to advertise." Above all use a strong cast – No. 26 nylon is not too heavy. A careless oversight in this resepect lost me what might have been a record.

I had been asked to a supper picinic on Lough Belvidere, and my host suggested that we might bring our rods on the off chance of finding a fish cruising for Silverhorns under the trees which line so much of the shore. Not very hopefully – it was August and the rise to the big sedges should have been over – I put a box of dry flies in my pocket. There was, I knew, a cast in the lid but I had forgotten that the cast had been made up for small Slaney trout and was 2x tapered to 4x.

No trout were rising under the trees so we rowed out to an island for supper and sat on gossiping while the sun sank below the horizon. Just as it did so my host pointed to a patch of the lake about a quarter of a mile away and said, "What on earth is that?" I looked. In a small area not more than three hundred yards square the trout were wallowing like pigs. In the rush, I had not even the sense to cut away the finer portions of my cast. When we arrived at the area of activity (it had shifted several hundred yards further away while we made our preparations) we found it criss-crossed in every direction by the lines of immense fish swimming under water, coming up now and then to slash at the scuttering sedges. Trout often take a moving sedge with a bang. These trout took like runaway railway trains. I was broken four times in rapid succession by fish not one of which looked to be under five pounds. When I tried to fish with a free reel the barb of the big hook did not go home and the fish kicked off. Still I never thought of cutting down my cast to the three feet which would have been quite sufficient in the growing dark. My companion, with a strong cast, was broken at least once but got a fish of over four pounds, while I did not land a single one. It was a quite ghastly bit of bungling.

The May-fly has a limited season, the sedges not only a limited season but a limited hour of the day, and the Daddy is never on the water in large numbers. For most of his time on big lakes the angler will see a surface devoid of life, or with only a sprinkling of flies which the trout are ignoring. They are feeding on the bottom if they are feeding at all. What is he to do? Fish a team of large flies with a vaguely naturalistic trend say a Woodcock and Hare's Ear, March Brown and Silver, and Greenwell? There is no reason why a fish should not come up to a sedge-like pattern though it is the wrong time of the day. I have known this procedure to be successful particularly in light winds, but rather more fancy patterns on the whole are better.

What are the reactions of a lake trout when he becomes aware of an artificial fly moving somewhere in his range of vision? He certainly does not say "There is a nice speciment of Phryganea varia which tastes so good or maybe it is only Phryganea absoluta, not quite so juicy." Being rather short-sighted the image of the fly will not be sharp. The most that is likely to register in his brain is – "Something moving and so alive and good to eat. Something large enough to justify the effort of catching it. Something not large enough to be dangerous. Let me at it." The fisherman has won the first trick: he has attracted the trout, and the trout is on his way to take.

What happens then? One of three things. Either the trout carries straight on and takes by first intention; or, as he comes within a foot or two and sees the fly clearly, he becomes alarmed at its strangeness and turns away; or he follows the fly closely, his nose only a couple of inches from it, and after he has followed for several feet, either determines to leave it alone or makes a

sudden spurt and grabs it. All this is a matter of direct observation. In clear water with the light at the right angle, you can see
these things happening before your eyes. But why does a trout,
who would not have left the bottom unless he was minded to
make a capture, suddenly change his mind? How can we induce
him to pursue his first fine careless impulse? The old school,
with their ceaseless playing of the fly, found a partial answer, for
this movement not only attracted the fish from the bottom but,
because the instinct of every creature is to pursue something
which is trying to get away from him, induced the fish to keep
up its rush. He had no time to investigate and question. Unfortunately he was often defeated by the quick changes of
position of the fly and missed it entirely.

What effect at this critical moment has the actual pattern of
the fly? The fish is near enough to see every detail with almost
microscopic clearness, and he cannot really think, if he is capable
of thinking, that the assembly of fur and feather is something
on which he habitually feeds. Not that this need deter him. The
trout is a catholic and adventurous feeder, who does not shy
away from a thing which is new or strange. Trout will take
wasps, and dragon flies have been used successfully as a dap,
though neither wasps nor dragon flies are commonly on the menu.
A grasshopper dapped on a mid-lake shallow a mile or more from
land is taken greedily, though I do not believe the natural
organism could ever find its way so far from the shore without
sinking. We do not know how many fish take a look at these
strange objects and then think better of it. I have certainly seen
trout inspect a grasshopper and turn away. But the main
problem is clear – so to construct your lure as to maintain the
curiosity or ferocity of the trout without going over the edge and
scaring him away.

The answer of England and Scotland, the answer of the
illustrated catalogues, seems to be the bright, not to say gaudy,
fly. I have conscientiously tried these flies on many lakes and in
many conditions. I have tied gaudy experiments myself. Never
have they had more than a fleeting success. Teal and Red, Teal
and Green, Peter Ross, between them they have not accounted
for two dozen trout. The Blagdon lures with attractive names –
Reckless William, Reckless William's Mate, and the Missionary –
did not catch a single fish. They are supposed to represent stickle-
backs and perch fry, but the Irish trout failed to detect the

resemblance. The Irish palette of rich tertiaries, the Irish method of combining these tertiaries harmoniously with perhaps a touch of a more vivid colour, was uniformly more successful.

I am tempted to suggest three rules for the choice of lures for big lakes.

First. They must be large enough for the trout to see in the prevailing conditions and large enough to make it worth while for the trout to come up for them. No. 11 is the smallest size that should be used and if the waves are large No. 7 is not too big. Nos. 10 and 9 are the most generally useful.

Second. The fly should be so constructed as to have the general characteristics of the food on which the trout feed – movement, translucency, colours which blend into each other, and stream-lining for flies intended to fish much below the surface.

Third. Certain colours do better than others according to the light, the nature of the bottom, and the general conditions. I discuss in a later chapter some of the conditions which seem to favour particular colours. Those which I have found it necessary to carry are golden olive, claret (medium and dark) orange and fiery brown dark gentian blue, grey, black and silver. Black and silver are not strictly colours but they are indispensable.

Let me conclude this chapter with a warning against the trap into which all users of lures, and especially those who tie their own experiments, are almost sure to fall sooner or later: the "Single-speech Hamilton", the fly which does wonders on one or two days and never repeats its success. Do not persevere with it. Here are two examples which may emphasize the temptation.

A downpour of rain and a high wind had driven me off the lake. Next day the river would be pouring an ochre stream into Oughterard bay, and the waves would distribute the mud far and wide making the water turbid. Tradition says that in such conditions a fly in the orange-fiery brown range is most successful. I set out to tie something startling along these lines. The body was made from some gorgeous red-copper fur given me by Rogan, the tail of orange Indian Crow, and the shoulder hackle was wound from the orange and black tippet feather of a Golden Pheasant. A fiery brown ribbing hackle completed this outrageous production. Next day the lake was as I had predicted. "What is the name of that fiery devil?" said Long John Power who was boating me, as he saw the new fly. "You have baptized it" I said, "We'll call it the Fire Devil". For two days, till all the turbidity had cleared, the Fire Devil caught every fish. Then it became useless. Long John continued to have faith in it, and for some years I used to receive barely legible postcards begging me to tie him a few of "Fire Devils" but in time even he became disillusioned.

That was a fly designed for special conditions and in those conditions it worked. It would be reasonable to keep a specimen or two in case such conditions recurred. The next example is different.

An Englishman staying with a friend of mine had brought over a collection of flies which had been off-loaded on him as suitable for Lough Corrib. They were without exception the worst flies I ever saw, much too large, with bodies of lustreless mohair in the crudest colours, no wings, and nondescript hackles of poor quality. One in particular excited our derision. The body was a lump of magenta-crimson and the hackle a sickly washed-out green. The Englishman, disgusted by their failure, took to Irish patterns and left his monstrosities behind when he departed. Next year, on an unsuccessful day I saw my friend's boat in the distance and rowed over to see how he had done. He held up three magnificent trout weighing about ten pounds between them. "All on the middle dropper," he said with a grin, and cast his line over my boat. It was the despised fly. I borrowed one and it immediately started to catch fish. Next day we both caught the majority of the fish on the same fly. After that it failed completely and never succeeded again.

What is the explanation? It may have been pure chance. If you spin a roulette wheel often enough the same number will turn up several times in succession. Even patterns tested and approved by generations of anglers have their runs of success and failure. On the other hand there may have been something in the light or water conditions, or an unusual plenty of some kind of food to which the fly bore a resemblance. Unless the conditions for success can be found, and their recurrence recognized, it is useless to persist with a fly which works only in rare and unidentifiable conditions.

10

THE BEETLE AND THE BUMBLE

References to the Royal Horticultural Society's two volume colour chart are given thus – R.H.S. Enamel Blue 48/1.

It is rash to recommend a pattern of one's own, and is necessary to lay down strict standards before doing so. There are so many patterns of proved value that nothing is to be gained by adding another which is no better and no worse than those already in use. The new fly must be able to make out a plausible claim to be superior to most current patterns, either as an all-condition fly, or at least in conditions which are capable of being accurately described and easily recognized, and which recur with reasonable frequency.

The fly which I am about to describe does, I think, pass this test. It has killed more white trout for me than all other patterns of tail fly put together. For brown trout in the big lakes it has not been so outstanding, for among these fish black is not so much a favourite, but it has done better than any other black fly. It has also caught a number of salmon.

How do others rank it? Ernest Phelps K.C., who had fished in three continents and was one of the finest anglers of his generation, wrote, "This is easily the best lake fly I have ever used," and there are others who share this opinion. J. R. Harris on the other hand, thinks it no better than the Connemara Black, a very much easier fly to tie. Endeavouring to take a dispassionate view, I still think it has proved itself sufficiently to warrant a recommendation.

It all began with an order for some assorted lake flies offered in Cummins's Bargain Catalogue. When the consignment was opened, among a collection as brilliant as stained glass, one trim

Quaker of a fly stood out by its very soberness. Body of black ostrich herl, sparsely ribbed with silver, black hackle, black wing with a white tip. Only at the tail was there a little spirt of colour in the form of a bunch of yellow floss. Stood upright on the bend of its hook it was ridiculously like a baby penguin with white belly and small yellow feet. More prosaically it was styled "Heckham-Peckham and Black".

Next March justified the proverb by coming in like a lion but forgot to go out like a lamb, and when I visited Melvin in the last week it was still growling and rampaging. Low dishevelled clouds scudded across the lake not a hundred feet up, the tops were torn from basalt-coloured waves and every reef was surrounded by a patch of foam. The boatman indicated pretty plainly that he thought we should put back, and for all the good we were doing there seemed no reason for disregarding his advice. I opened my fly-box, seeking inspiration, and a small Penguin said quite plainly "This is my weather. Give me a swim."

By the time he was safely attached at tail we were drifting towards a jagged reef which ran, half awash, at right angles to our course. It was just the place for a big gillaroo, for gillaroo haunt the rocks and will take right in the smother of the waves. I suggested to the boatman that he should row the boat cross-wind, parallel to the reef, and butted into a sullen resistance. There were, he said, outlying sentinels of rock which guarded the reef and would puncture the boat as if she were a rotten apple. Nearer than twenty-five yards he would not venture.

Twenty-five yards is not a difficult cast with a snorting wind behind but in trying to drop the fly between two rocks I made the mistake of stretching out my arm so as to allow cast, line and rod momentarily to be in one straight line, I saw no rise in the welter, and the first indication of a fish was a jerk so savage and so sudden that I nearly let go my rod. Somehow the cast stood.

The fish made off without stopping directly down wind, found a gap in what seemed a solid barrier of rock, and slipped through it without fouling the cast. Now he was on one side of the reef and the boat on the other. There could be no question of working him back. He had to be played on a long line while the boat was rowed to the end of the reef and round into the quieter water of its lee. Eventually the penguin returned with a three pound gillaroo in its beak. I fetched in two smaller gillaroo before the rising storm forced us off the lake.

For a couple of seasons I assumed that this was only a special-occasion fly, a thing of wild weather and lowering skies. Then I found out that, dressed much smaller, it was almost as good in sunny weather. I set out to make it even better.

The first improvement was obvious. That bunch of yellow floss was a fly-dressing howler, for floss, once wet, dries out into a hard spike which will never regain its former fluffiness. A thick short topping gave the same colour with more luminosity, and preserved its character indefinitely.

Next to come in for attention was the wing. The white-tipped feather was inclined to split and disintegrate, no disadvantage in a fly designed to transmit light, but spoiling the outline of a fly which was clearly intended to be opaque so as to show against the sky on a dull day. I was doubtful as to the advantage of the white tip. In the Jock Scott the white tipped Turkey has value, for it throws up the darker feathers which partially veil it, but this white tip had no veiling and would be lost to view against the sky. I tried a thin rolled wing made from the secondary of a rook, and found the fly at least as effective and twice as durable.

The body of the original looked as if it could be improved. Ostrich herl is delicate and the teeth of trout are sharp: also it inclines to become flattened. There were plenty of other black materials, silk, wool, seal's fur, quill, chenille. All were tried. One brand of black floss silk was good, but not as good as the black ostrich herl, and the rest were nearly useless. I have suggested an explanation in an earlier chapter.

Next I rang the changes on hackles of different colours but none proved as good as the original black cock. With the alterations made so far the fly was neither better nor worse than the original, it was only more practical and more durable. A very sombre affair it looked, as if a little relief from the dead black would increase its attraction. The black wing would show off nicely a pair of small jungle cock cheeks. So jungle cock was added, and produced a distinct advance in killing power. The jungle cock feathers had to be kept small, and those in which the enamel was tinged with burnt sienna were better than those which suggested a tooth-paste advertisement. But the real transformation came when it occurred to me to try a second topping, tied so as to lie close along the edge of the wing and intersect with the topping in the tail. My black fly stood surrounded by a halo of pale golden light, a halo which was to prove deserved.

That completed the alterations as far as brown trout were concerned. A rather prominent tag of a clear blue silk seemed to improve it for white trout. By now the name had been changed. Friends who tried it and liked it could not remember it as the Penguin, and referred to it as "that black fly of Kingsmill's" which became shortened to "The Kingsmill" a name which has stuck. Here is the developed dressing.

Tail. Golden Pheasant topping.
Tag. (For sea trout) Blue floss (R.H.S. Enamel Blue 48/1), tied rather broad and prominent.
Body. Black ostrich herl, ribbed oval silver.
Hackle. Best quality black cock. If your cock hackles are thin, or chalky, use black hen.
Wing. Rook secondary, closely rolled so as to keep solid, and tied long, low, and rather narrow.
Sides. Jungle cock, small and not too white in the enamel.
Topping. A good Golden Pheasant topping, taken hard up against the top edge of the wing, and long enough to intersect the topping at the tail.

Choose the ostrich herl with a long flue, and be careful that the final topping does not find its way in among the fibres of the wing. If it does so it is useless. It must put a rim of light round an otherwise opaque fly.

I have wondered why this fly is so effective. Is it a lure or does it suggests to the fish some well known article of diet? Most lakes contain one or more varieties of black, or nearly black, beetles and trout certainly feed on them, for they are to be found in their stomachs. Take any black beetle, hold it up to the sky, and see how the light creeps round the shiny wing cases in a kind of halo. Now hold it below eye level and look down at it. On the shoulders of the wing cases you will see two little pools of light. Everything else is black. Can it be that the toppings and the jungle cock suggest in an impressionist way these features, giving to the flat fly an appearance of rotundity? It can hardly be more than a suggestion, but it may last long enough to make a trout say "Hallo. Beetle? Let's investigate" and he who investigates is lost. I don't know. But I do know that for brown trout, white trout, and low-water fishing for salmon, it is a remarkably good fly.

And now the Bumbles. Whereas the Kingsmill was developed on the basis of trial and error, the Bumbles had an element of theory behind them from the beginning. In the last chapter I mentioned how I had been struck by the neglect of Irish fly-dressers to combine their own flair for colour combination and translucency with the English Bumble type of construction. I wanted to see if I could make good this omission and construct a type of fly which would suggest the characteristics of surface life, though without any attempt at imitation. The patterns must be translucent, must have a certain amount of gleam without dazzle, must have gentle and not gaudy contrasts, and must if possible suggest the movement of insects caught in the surface film or blown along by the wind.

My first attempts – those foreshadowed in an old school note-book – were along the lines of a salmon "Grub," a hackle at the shoulder and another of a different colour half-way down the body. They were reasonably, but not conspicuously, successful. Next I extended the area covered by the hackles so that they covered, between them, the whole body. This gave two contrasting bands of colour which pleased neither me nor the trout. Finally I hit on the plan of tying in the two hackles at the same point and winding them along the body together, so that their fibres were commingled. Success followed immediately. The two colours no longer showed as distinct entities. Each was bathed in the reflections from the other, so that a perfect combination resulted. The effect in the hand was of one single colour, and, without a magnifying glass, people shown these flies for the first time often refuse to believe that two hackles of different colours have been used. Held up to the light, while there is still a fusing of colour, the hackle points gleam here and there in sparkles of their individual colour, giving a vivid suggestion of life and movement.

To get the perfect result it was necessary to use bright, stiff cock hackles, and the winding had to be regulated carefully. If the turns were too close the fly lost transparency, if too widely separated most of the life and brilliancy disappeared. Sometimes, if one colour was overpowering the other, half of the too dominant hackle had to be stripped before it was tied on. The ideal fly looked rather bulky in the hand but lost all heaviness when viewed by transmitted light.

Tied in this way with stiff cock hackles the flies had one defect. They lacked mobility. When pulled through the water, even if the pull was made in jerks, there was no perceptible movement of the hackles. This was remedied by tying at the head a long sparse soft hackle, usually taken from a game bird. The main length of this hackle was supported by the stiff hackles wound behind it, but the longer tips were free to wave and struggle as if the creature had a movement of its own. Again there was an improvement.

The method of construction sounds more complicated than it is. There are three hackles. Hackle A is a soft game hackle. Hackles B and C are stiff cock. Take a fair-sized hook, say No. 10 or 9 (O.S.). Choose hackle A so that the fibres are about one-eighth of an inch longer than the distance from the eye to bend of hook. Tie it in at the head and wind one or two turns. Secure, and cut off the surplus. Now fasten in by the stalks hackles B and C, behind but hard up against A. The two hackles B and C must spring from the same point, and they should be no longer in their fibres than the distance from eye to bend of hook. Leave the hackles B and C unwound and pointing forwards, and wind the tying silk over the stumps to the tail. Tie in whatever feather you want for tail, and a length of narrow oval gold or silver tinsel. Spin the seal's fur on the silk and wind the body up to where hackles B and C are tied in. Fasten off body with a half hitch.

Now come the more difficult operations. Hackles B and C are grasped by their tips so that the mid-ribs are closely apposed. Two turns are taken hard up against hackle A, and then they are wound in open spirals to the tail. The hackles must not be allowed to separate even a fraction, which means that a considerable outward strain must be maintained during the winding and this sometimes causes a break and much blasphemy. If you are using a hackle pliers, a little cobbler's wax on the jaws prevents slipping. When you have wound to the tail, the hackles have to be secured, and this is done by winding the thin tinsel through them to the head, each turn of hackle stalk being secured by a turn of tinsel, so as to produce a cross-gartering. The tinsel must be strained very tight and worked through the hackle fibres with a kind of to-and-fro motion, so as not to tie down any of the hackle fibres – a thing not easy to avoid. Finally the tinsel is worked through hackle A and secured at the head.

Tied in this way the fly is everlasting. A less durable method, but one which is rather easier and which produces a neater fly, is as follows. After hackle A has been wound on and secured, take the tying silk three-quarters of the way down the body, and there tie in hackles B and C, this time by their tips. Continue winding to the tail, tie in tail and a length of rather broader oval tinsel. Then spin your fur and make your body, putting one or two turns of the dubbed silk between the tail and the point where the hackle tips are tied in, and the rest in front of this point, being careful not to tie down any fibres of the still un-wound hackles. Fasten off the body at the shoulder. Wind and fasten off tinsel, again taking care not to involve any hackle fibres. Now grasp your two B and C hackles by the stalks, and making sure that they do not separate, wind them spirally close behind and touching the spirals of the tinsel to the shoulder, where they are tied in. Take the silk through hackle A and finish off so as to press hackle A up against the front turns of B and C. Constructed like this it is easier to avoid tying in hackle fibres, and the fly has a rather lighter and more graceful appear-ance than a fly made by the first method, but if in the course of fishing the hackle mid rib breaks at any place the whole fly disintegrates.

Every one can make his own colour combinations. I must have tried several dozen. I give seven. The first three have been tried out in many conditions, and I doubt if they can be improved. The next four could probably be bettered by further experiment.

GOLDEN OLIVE BUMBLE.
Tail. G.P. Topping.
Body. Golden olive seals fur, ribbed oval gold tinsel.
Body hackles. Cock dyed golden olive, and medium red natural
     cock.
Shoulder hackle. Blue jay.

This bumble is based on the colouring of "Invicta", which is itself probably a development of the old Irish "Golden Olive". The correct colour of "golden olive" is difficult to describe. Shop flies are often too harsh a yellow. There should be a hint of green in the yellow, and a touch of "greying". If you can imagine mimosa dipped in green Chartreuse, it will give you the idea. It is half way between R.H.S. Mimosa 602/2 and Chartreuse 663.

There is a variant of this dressing, known as the Green Olive, based on the older fly of that name. The seal's fur and one of the body hackles are green-olive – much the colour of the natural fruit – and the second body hackle is hot orange. These patterns are for brown trout. They are not so successful with white trout.

CLARET BUMBLE.
Tail. Four strands of G.P. tippet.
Body. Medium claret seal's fur (R.H.S. Indian Lake 826/3), ribbed oval gold.
Body hackles. Cock dyed medium claret, and natural black cock.
Shoulder hackle. Blue jay.

This is an outstanding pattern for white trout, and I must have taken over 800 on it. For brown lake trout it is second only to the Golden Olive. The marked preference which white trout can show for this bumble is illustrated by a curious coincidence. A Dublin friend was fishing Glenicmurrin, the big lake of Costelloe, and had a good day, nearly every fish being taken on this fly. He waited at the landing-stage for the other boats to come back. All the other rods had done badly with one exception, a Sligo solicitor whom he knew. He asked what fly had been successful. "Here it is," said the solicitor. "I don't know the name – I was given it to experiment with." It was the claret bumble. At that date I was still working on this fly, and the two specimens which met at Glenicmurrin that day were probably the only two in existence outside my fly box.

There is also a variant of this dressing, the Magenta Bumble, in which the claret seal's fur and hackle are replaced by magenta (R.H.S. Magenta 27) and the ribbing is silver. I owe this variation to Mr. Doherty, the Donegal tackle dealer. I was buying some of his excellent dyed hackles, when he pushed over to me a paper of magenta. "Want any of those?" he said. "No," I replied, "I hate the colour." "Well, the Donegal white trout don't share your views," he said. So I bought some of the hackles and some magenta fur, and tied my first magenta bumbles with very satisfying results. Since then I have found it almost equally good in Connemara. Fairly fresh-run sea-trout prefer it to the claret, but after they have been up for about a month they take the claret better.

THE BRUISER.
Tail. A bunch of flax-blue wool.
Body. Rich gentian blue wool (R.H.S. Gentian Blue 42 or
    Prince's Blue 745/1), ribbed silver.
Body Hackles. Cock dyed gentian blue, and natural black
    cock. These are taken the whole way to the head.
Shoulder hackle. None.

A first class pattern for both brown and white trout, especially
good on a dark day with low clouds and showers. The hackles
are wound rather closer than in the other patterns and the fly
is less transparent, so that its bulk may show against a dark sky.
I owe the name to my friend Cyril Wilson who christened it partly
because of its colour – that of a bruise – and partly because
it had just done good execution for him.

FIERY BROWN BUMBLE.
Tail. Indian Crow.
Tag. (optional) golden brown floss.
Body. Fiery brown seal's fur, ribbed oval gold.
Body hackles. Fiery brown and blood red cock (R.H.S. Blood
    red 820).
Shoulder hackle. Dark grouse.

A fly chiefly for coloured water. I am not quite satisfied with
this dressing, but have not been able to improve it.

GREY GHOST.
Tail. G.P. Topping.
Tag. Black ostrich herl.
Body. Light grey seal's fur (or silver monkey if you can get it)
    ribbed oval silver.
Body hackles. Dyed Irish grey cock (much the colour of a pale
    blue dun) and a natural black cock hackle.
Shoulder hackle. Teal, or grey partridge.

There are days when there is a milky look on the water usually
caused by an east wind haze, and other days of diffused light
when under-water visibility seems much accentuated. Fishing is
rarely good in these conditions, and the best thing to be done is
to change to a finer cast, use a very small black fly at tail and a

larger light coloured fly at dropper. This fly is also worth trying
on very bright sunny days.

SILVER BLUE BUMBLE.
Tail. G.P. Topping.
Body. Closely wound, fine, oval silver tinsel.
Body hackles. Bright medium blue dyed cock (R.H.S. Butterfly
    Blue 645) and natural badger cock. They should be wound
    rather open.
Shoulder hackle. Teal.

MAGENTA AND GOLD BUMBLE.
Tail. Orange Toucan.
Body. Closely wound, fine, oval gold tinsel.
Body hackle. Magenta.
Shoulder hackle. The pink-cinnamon hackle from the wing of
    a landrail.

These two flies are bumble patterns of Teal Blue and Silver
and of Freeman's Fancy respectively. They have a limited use for
fresh run white trout, in low water and bright sun. I do not
recommend them for brown trout. For white trout the silver is
better in July and the gold in August. I include them with hesita-
tion as, although on particular days they will beat all others,
those days are limited and they cannot be regarded as universal
patterns.

The possibilities of colour combinations are endless and they
have all to be tried out in practical fishing, for there is no
guarantee that trout see colours as we do, or that two pieces of
material, identical in colour to our eyes, may not appear different
to trout, if dyed with dyes of different chemical composition. I
would like to see more research carried out into the possibilities
of this kind of dressing.

11

LOUGH CORRIB AND JAMESIE

Corrib, the second largest lake in Ireland, stretches for thirty-five miles in a gentle crescent from Galway on the east to the foot of the Maam Turk mountains on the west. In its hey-day, towards the end of last century, it offered the best lake fishing in the British Isles, not only giving sport to a large number of visiting anglers, but supporting a population of professional fishermen who made a livelihood by selling their catch.

Large lakes are often disappointing, for the shore slopes rapidly into deep water and fishing is confined to a small strip round the edge. Corrib however, has a quite exceptional amount of fishable water in proportion to its area. The long and highly indented shore line shelves gently, and levels out into plateaux sufficiently shallow to be fished with the fly. To the shore of the mainland must be added the shores of the islands which are sprinkled profusely over the lake, 365 of them if local tradition is to be trusted. I never counted them, and I never met anyone who had, nor do I believe that any two people would agree as to their number. It all depends on what you reckon to be an island. There can be no dispute at the top end of the scale, mile long expanses with dwelling houses, farmland, woods and piers; or even about the numerous grassy patches of from five to fifty acres where no one lives but the cattle. But what are we to say about reefs which grip in their bony fingers a couple of thorn trees and half a rood of scrawny grass, or of even smaller out-crops barren of all vegetation. It would be flattery to call them islands, and yet here, picking a careful way among them with an eye to the safety of the boat, some of the best fishing may be got. Lastly there are the offshore and mid-lake shallows, mile after mile of grey limestone pavements, fissured into deep cracks along the joints, pitted and pocked on their faces, scattered over by erratics, a paradise of food and shelter.

The feeding is superb. Gather a handful anywhere from the bottom and you will find it a mass of snail shells, caddis cases, nymphs and leeches. A little higher up swim the fresh water shrimps. The greatest congregation of these I ever saw was in Lough Rea, another Galway lake where, over a long stretch of shore, there were several dozen in each cubic foot of water, but even in Corrib, where they are not so plentiful, there can still be enough to serve a trout with a very good meal in a very short time. Supplement the menu with minnows, perch fry, an odd small trout and an occasional snack of May-fly, daddy and sedge. Small wonder that Corrib trout are fat and have flesh as red as a carrot.

Fishing in Lough Corrib lasts the whole year round. For four months the trout are out of season and the angler must be content with perch and pike, but even the pike would make the reputation of most lakes. A thirty-pounder is always a reasonable possibility. Trout fishing starts in February with the spring trolling, mostly a matter for professional fishermen who put out in one man skiffs, known locally as "punts", so frail looking that it seems impossible for them to weather the rough winds and waves of the season. At the stern are fixed three short rods, home-made affairs of ash or hazel, each trolling a natural minnow. Till a fish takes it is dull work, but then there is plenty to do, for the other lines must be got in, the boat managed, and the fish played at the same time. Englishmen find it hard to believe that big trout can be in condition so early in the year, but most of them are. A friend used to troll Lough Leane, a limestone lake in Westmeath with halcyon spinners in February and March, and each week-end he brought back a splendid basket of fish weighing from two to five pounds, every one of them plump and shapely. His explanation was that the fish did not spawn every year and that it was the non-spawners who took in the early months. Even if this suggestion is true, which I doubt, it says much for the winter feeding in a limestone lake.

March brings the big spring salmon which have escaped the nets and traps at Galway, but the area of Corrib is such that the butter is spread very thin and, although favourite spots are known to the locals, fishing for salmon in the lake is unprofitable work. It is better to concentrate on the trout which by now are taking the fly. In the old days, the professionals did not use rods for fly fishing but relied on the cross line and the otter, both of which are now illegal. A cross line is a line stretched between two boats which are rowed parallel to each other. From this line, on lengths of gut, are hung flies to the number of two or three dozen, and the whole area between the boats is effectively searched. An otter requires only one boat. It works on the same principle as the paravane which was used for severing mine cables during the first world war, and is a kind of water kite. When the boat is rowed, the otter sheers off to a distance of twenty-five to thirty yards carrying its line with it, and then follows a course parallel with the boat. Droppers are hung from the line, as with the cross line, but they are fewer in number. It is a good otter that can carry more than a dozen flies.

Wild stories are told of the execution which used to be worked by these engines. Do not believe them. I once watched an absolutely first class poacher use an otter for three hours and get only one fish. His estimate was that an otter should catch as many fish as three competent rods, while a cross line was equal to four or five.

Wet-fly fishing goes on improving through April and May. Smaller flies may be used than are required later in the year and these months are probably the best for this kind of fishing. In June or late May, comes the Green Drake and everything that can float is put on the water. The lake is covered with boats full of earnest, painstaking, and incompetent dappers. A lot of fish are extracted from the lake in this sad and monotonous way, which is gradually being superseded by the casual dry-fly. Trout in Corrib do not seem to cruise in the same regular beats as they do in Arrow, Derg, or Sheelin and the more expert forms of dry-fly fishing are at a discount.

Towards the end of June, the grilse, locally known as peel, arrive in Oughterard bay and wait for a flood to take them up the river. If there is a more exasperating form of sport than fishing for these peel I have still to find it. They show freely, splashing and porpoising, they swirl under the fly and jump over it, they seem to take it firmly in their mouth and when you strike they are not there. It is told of a pious but keen angler that, when peel fishing, he used to stuff his ears with cotton wool so that he should not hear his own language. Then, just as patience is exhausted, will come a day when everything goes right and three or four fish will silver the floorboards.

July is an abominable month of sun and calm and millions of perch fry, which keep the trout so busy below that they pay no attention to the surface. In the evening you may be fortunate enough to strike a sedge rise, but for some reason such rises are uncommon. If you are unlucky enough to find yourself taking a holiday in July harden your heart, get a good book and go trolling in the deeps for a big ferox. You will not get many and you may get none, but what you do get will be big. I have known them taken up to fourteen pounds and I believe that larger than this have been caught.

August is better, much better. Dapping with the grasshopper and the daddy is now the usual method but the wet-fly does well. September is better still, especially for the wet-fly, and may often be the best month of the season. With September the trout season ends.

The great days of Corrib were over before 1926 when I started to visit it. According to the old boatmen the decline started about the turn of the century and had been going on ever since. I fished the lake for ten years and by the end of that time it had deteriorated so much that I sought other waters. Now, I am told, it is beginning to improve again, but a few days trial in 1960 was disappointing.

Everyone had his own theory to account for the falling off. Too many ducks eating the fry, too many pike, too many anglers, too many outboard motors, too many eels competing for the trout's food, too few eels to consume the bottom feeding and so force the fish to look for food on the surface. All are hypotheses without adequate facts to back them. It is very hard to account for the ups and downs of lakes, and I know of only one case where a definite cause could be assigned. This was the newly-made Poulaphouca reservoir which gave magnificent fishing for several years after it was filled, and then the fish went out of condition and began to die. The trouble was traced to a parasite.

A brother barrister, whose advice on most things is worth following, recommended Corrib to me. Two days afterwards my Belsize sports set out on the road she was to know so well; by tea-time we were pulling in at the "Anglers" in Oughterard, and I was arranging with Pat Naughton to get boatmen for me.

Not long after the sitting-room door opened just sufficiently to allow a little maid to squeeze her head round it. "Jamesie – Donnellan an' – Jimmy McDonagh – is-below-an' is-wishful – to-see-ye," she gabbled in a hand-gallop, and disappeared. Who Jamesie Donnellan and Jimmy McDonagh might be I had no idea, but I guessed that they were my two boatmen and I went down to meet them. They were waiting in the street, a contrasting pair. Jimmy was a pre-Celt of a type not uncommon in the west, lean, broad, of middle stature, inclined to swarthiness, with dark eyes shining between high cheek bones, and strong black eyebrows. In age he looked between thirty and forty. Jamesie was a red Celt. Time had sown sand over his flaming hair and taken some of the colour from the blue of his eyes, but his back was still as flat and as straight as a door, and he walked delicately, like a cat. He admitted to being eighty and Jimmy put him down as more, but he was a man whose age could not be reckoned by the years. He was the leader of the two, which seemed odd, as Jimmy owned the boat. But Jamesie owned the lake, if not indeed the earth. He had struck his bargain with life and it contented him. Old he might be, but he was savouring his old age with as much enjoyment as he had his youth, still vital, interested, and more than a little mischievous. As a Corrib boatman he had begun and as a Corrib boatman he hoped to end. There had however been a period of wandering when his horizon had not been bounded by the hills of Galway and Mayo, when he had sailed the seven seas and gasconaded it in the great ports of the world. Tired of his travels, Ulysses had returned to Ithaca with tales of strange monsters and the blue Symplegades. He was a little feared for his sharp wits and tongue, a great deal respected for his skill and knowledge. Any one of the boatmen could dap and troll, but only Jamesie was expert with wet-fly, and he enjoyed in addition that singular prestige which fishermen who cannot tie their own flies are accustomed to accord to those who can.

Jamesie finished his second pint, refused a third, and collected his hat. Arrangements had been made. "Ye'll have all the flies ye want and more," he said as he turned away. The words were casual, but held just the faintest inflexion of a query, sufficient to give me an opening if I cared to take it. I did care, and produced a couple of fly boxes. The first held a fairly complete selection of Irish standards, and Jamesie, glancing rapidly over the contents, returned it with a curt "Ye have them all." In the second were the prototypes of my Bumbles, and Jamesie's face grew interested. He moved out to the light of the street, pulled from his pocket the spectacles which he rarely used, and set himself to a methodical examination. He tried the hackles with his fingers for spring, turned and twisted them against the sky to catch their brilliance, and with a rusty pin from his lapel probed into their construction. Finally he turned back to me with a puzzled "Where did yet get them flies? I never see'd the like." I told him they were home-made, at which he seemed relieved. "They're a right class of a fly and I'll warrant them. Ye'll kill fish on them to-morrow." With a lift of his hat he was off, talking vigorously to Jimmy, gesticulating as he talked.

Next morning, we met at the little cove near the pier where Jimmy kept his boat. Like all Corrib boats, except the one-man punts, she was beamy as well as long, built to cope with big waves and rough weather, long enough to allow two anglers to cast in comfort while a third, if desired, could dap from amidship. A disadvantage of her size was that against a wind of any strength it needed two men to pull her. On a drift, or when the breeze was light, one was sufficient.

We took up the positions which were to become standard. In the extreme prow my wife contrived for herself a nest with cushions and rug. Jamesie sat in the bow, I at the stern, and Jimmy rowed on one of the two centre seats. Jamesie had his tackle ready, a limber green heart of between thirteen and fourteen feet, with a light untapered line, and I used an eleven foot split cane with a heavier and tapered line. Both outfits, as will appear, were carefully chosen to suit the different fishing methods of their users.

With the wind lackadaisical and the sun bright, I was due for a tedious hour or two, but I had reckoned without Jamesie. He was a talker of genius. Most Irish boatmen have a collection of stories, but their stock is limited, and after a day or two it is a choice between repetition or exhaustion. Jamesie had no set repertoire, and I never knew him to repeat himself. Anecdote, reminiscence, speculation, seemed to seep out of him. What matter that many of his tales were hardly credible? "An admixture of a lie doth ever add pleasure." He was too much of an artist to resist such temptations, but he was also too much of an artist to allow himself to be caught out. However improbable his stories, they were always possible, or at least could not be proved to be impossible.

We rowed quietly out to a point where we could start a drift, passing on the way another boat in which two English visitors were contriving to do most things wrong. Jamesie looked at them in an avuncular way, sighed, and addressed the world in general. "The most of them Englishmen do be terrible bad fishers, but if ye get a right one I tell ye he can be a nailer. There was one of them come to the Corrib when I was a young fella an' I fished with him and it was he could fish. He had a queer name on him, a class of a double name – I don't rightly remember it – there was something French in it."

"Francis Francis," I hazarded. Jamesie turned round with a look of astonishment. "The very name. Bedad that was smart. How did ye guess?" "He was pretty well-known in his day," I said. "So well he might be. He was the best man ever I see. Well, as I was sayin', he come to the Corrib and he had the world of flies. 'What do ye think of them?' he says to me. I told him they were good enough but I had better nor them for the Corrib. I'm thinking he was not too well pleased. 'We'll see,' says he. 'Do ye fish your flies,' he says, 'and I'll fish mine, and if ye win, it will be five shillings in your pocket.' So we fished, and at the end of that day I had the crown, and another the next day, and the next too. On the fourth day, 'There's something in them flies o' yours,' he says. 'Change flies,' he says, 'and we'll try again.' That day he had the better of me. 'Ye know your lake,' he says, and after that he fished mostly what I tied for him and there wasn't a ha'porth of difference atween us. There was one fly of his he shtuck to. It had a body the colour of a red petticoat with a bit of paycock roun' it and a kind of a mishty grey wing."

Was that story true? Or false? Or a bit of both? There is no doubt that Francis Francis visited Corrib at least once, and as an old man he would have overlapped the young Jamesie. The description of the "Francis fly" was minutely accurate. I rather think there was a foundation of truth, but if there was, Jamesie had certainly not forgotten the name. That was only a touch of artistry for which I had fallen. I had still to know Jamesie.

For the first hour I had to be content with Jamesie's conversation and a couple of short rises, but then the wind shifted more to the west, strengthened, and blew a scattering of daddies along the surface. The trout grew more determined, and by the time we had landed for lunch on an island where the rabbit-cropped turf ran down to a beach of white shells, we each had a brace of two-pounders. In the lee of the hawthorn bushes the sun was warm, and it was pleasant to lie and scrutinize at close range the green-veined alabaster cups of the grass of Parnassus, still unseasonably in flower. Not for the first – or the last – time I made the mistake of dallying too long at lunch, and when we re-started the mood of the fish had changed. Only smaller fish were rising. There was then no official limit, but Jamesie never kept anything under a pound, so a couple of twelve ounce fish were put back and our catch was no larger when we landed on another island for tea. After tea a three-pounder followed my fly suspiciously for a couple of yards, then lost his head, grabbed it, and was landed. Jamesie hooked a still larger fish, but the hook came away just as the net was ready.

We had been drifting steadily eastward with a freshening breeze and were now more than three miles from the pier. It was time to row back and two oarsmen were needed to force the boat through the waves. Jamesie put down his rod and took the spare oars, while I cast out from the moving boat. It was my turn to hook and lose a fish. As we drew close to the pier, the last rim of the sun dipped behind the hills and the shadows washed over the lake. I began to dismount my cast, but Jimmy stopped me. "The wind is softening, sir. Tis the right time to try the sand."

A channel deep enough to take a small lake steamer twists down the centre of Oughterard bay. To the east of it stretch rocky shallows, to the west, between the channel and the shore, lies an expanse of sand brought down by the river. Over the sand the water is of an even depth of about six feet, save where a few shreds and snippets of reefs break the surface, and though rarely productive in day time, this was a favourite evening drift of Jamesie's, whose style of fishing it suited. Here he picked up another fish which revived his good humour, always a little in abeyance when the rival rod was ahead of him.

Back at the hotel we weighed the fish, the six just exceeding thirteen pounds. Four of them, to Jamesie's delight, had been taken on Bumbles. "What did I tell ye, Sir? Now don't I know the right class of a fly?" It had been a day typical of Corrib in September when the fish run large but are not very numerous. We never got more than nine on a September day, but the average weight was always at least two pounds. From five to seven fish was normal, anything under this being disappointing, and anything over distinctly good. There was always a good chance of a four or five-pounder. In a few years, however, the fishing had declined, the average fell to four, to three, to two, and at last sadly I said goodbye to Corrib.

Jamesie was willing to be helpful, even forthcoming, in a discussion on flies, but when it came to the business of catching fish, he was a different man. He liked fishing, liked better to catch fish, but best of all he liked to show his superiority over rival boatmen. This was a necessity for his complete happiness. He would rather bring back a mediocre catch which was larger than that of any other boat, than a really good bag which only took second place. So far so good. Anyone fishing with Jamesie could be certain that he would leave nothing undone to get fish. But it did not end there. He craved also the personal triumph of beating the other rod in his own boat, and to make sure of this he was willing to use devious methods. He did draw a line. I have heard him refer with disapproval to leaving his companion's fly-box behind or weakening his gut by the touch of a cigarette. Physical interference was a foul, but when it came to a contest of wits anything was permissible.

It took me a couple of days to smell mischief. Most boatmen are only too glad to set the boat on along straight drift and leave it so. Not Jamesie. From the bow came a continual murmur of directions to Jimmy. "Pull a stroke now" – "Back her a couple" – "Pull easy, easy" – "Back half a stroke" – and so on. This called for no particular comment. I knew that Jamesie had fished the lake for fifty years, and had an eye on him like a travelling rat. All parts of the shallow sliding past under the keel might look equally enticing to me, one part of the bay as good as another, but to his observation, backed by experience and a most remarkable memory, there might be a significant difference. He was always recalling past victories. "Twenty throut did I get to my own rod on the shore of that island in an easht wind and a shining sun, and all of them on a Grey Monkey. It was the September of the year that the ould Queen died and maybe the throut were still in half mournin'." With such a precedent, the wind east and the sun bright, what was I to do but put on a Grey Monkey and let Jamesie control the drift? And sure enough the trout took it, even though no royalty had lately deceased.

I began to work out the effect of his orders. "Pull easy" and

"Back easy" kept the boat working diagonally to left or right across the natural line of drift, and were explicable on the assumption that there was an underwater bank running obliquely to that line. "Pull a stroke" and "Back a stroke" or "Pull two" and "Back two" shifted the boat two or four lengths to right or left of the line she was on and set a new drift parallel to, but some distance from, the old. Each of these manoeuvres gave both rods fresh water, no doubt, in Jamesie's judgment, better water. But what about "Back half a stroke" or "Pull half a stroke"? The result of the first was to allow Jamesie to fish the line I had been fishing, and of the second to put me on Jamesie's line and give him new water. I became suspicious that Jamesie would not take my line, or give me his, unless he thought the change was to his advantage.

On the morning of the third day a trout took a daddy directly down wind of me and about forty yards away. If the boat were left to her natural drift I was bound to fish the spot where the trout had risen; but when we had gone about twenty yards there came the order for which I was waiting. "Back half a stroke." It was time for me to act. "Do no such thing, Jimmy," I said "If anyone is going to fish that trout it will be me and not Jamesie."

The effect of my remark on Jimmy was startling. For two days he had been following directions, comprehending perfectly that Jamesie was trying to get the better of me, amused and yet a little disapproving, for he was naturally loyal to his employer. Still, it was none of his business to interfere. Let me find out for myself if I was able. Now that I had found out he was free to enjoy the biting of the biter. He shipped both oars carefully, put his two hands on his knees, and laughed out to the heavens. "Begob, Jamesie, you're losht. The gentleman has ye discovered." Jamesie looked at us both with dignity, and then delivered a rebuke addressed to Jimmie but aimed at me. "Ye should know by this, Jimmy McDonagh, that that was a thravellin' throut and wherever he is now he is not where he rose lasht."

Jamesie had saved his face but he had been warned. "Pull half a stroke" and "Back her half" ceased to figure in his instructions. He still held the trumps. He knew the lake and I did not. If he said "Pull two strokes," or gave any command which gave both rods a new line, I was helpless. Automatically to halve his order might do us both harm, and anyhow Jamesie would have been quick enough to counter by directing the boat to be moved twice the distance he wanted. I felt sure I was being foxed and could not prove it. I tried bluff. "Look here, Jamesie, either you play fair or there will be only one rod fishing in this boat." Jamesie looked at me. His moustache moved. His eyes creased. Then he in his turn broke into laughter. He had had his fun, and it was time to stop. "Very well Sir. I'll play fair." And play fair – or very nearly fair – he did from that on.

Next morning the produced some of his own flies, and it was easy to see why he had been so interested in the Bumbles. Our methods of tying were dissimilar, and we used rather different materials, but the ideas which we had tried to translate into terms of fur and feather were much the same.

Jamesie had no set pattern – I doubt if he ever made two flies exactly the same. He tied as the spirit moved him, but all his work had a characteristic stamp. He disliked unrelieved blocks of any colour – "soldiers' uniforms" as he called them. If he wanted to tie a golden olive body he did not reach, as most of us do, for a wad of seal's fur ready dyed to that colour. That was much too obvious. First he mixed his golden seal's fur with a very little of the dark fur from a hare's back, just sufficient to soften the brightness of the yellow, then, at one end of the spindle he was going to wind on the silk, he added a fleck of natural wool pulled from a barbed wire fence where a sheep had rubbed, and at the other end a wisp of fur from a fox he had caught killing his hens, or from a neighbour's red setter. When he was as satisfied he spun the mixture on the silk – and there was his golden olive body, not the aggressive unrelieved bar of yellow which so many shop-tied flies display, but a thing of soft shadings and transitions such as any natural insect might be proud of.

It was the same with all his best flies. His clarets varied from blood red to a deep wine-purple, his fiery browns mingled copper and indian red and mahogany. Close inspection was needed to appreciate these mixtures, for the different colours were so combined, and the fur so thoroughly picked out with a needle, that there was no resemblance to a jointed fly or even to a fly such as a salmon "Butcher" where the bands of fur show separately. Such flies came into the "soldiers' uniform" class. He aimed at producing a body which should give the general impression of a single colour, but he gained his effect by the combination of many colours varying but slightly from the central tone that he wanted. His materials consisted of anything that could be teased out and spun on the tying silk. Old bits of patterned carpet, wool manufacturer's sample cards, bits of dress material, and the animal population of the neighbourhood, were all pressed into service – as indeed were the hair-combings of a red-headed tinker.

There was nothing so very new in all this. Irish fly tyers traditionally used this method to combine softness with brilliancy, and as Jamesie at once spotted, I had employed it in the Bumbles. Most of these had hackles of different colours carried down the body, the colours being chosen so as to contrast only moderately with the fur and with each other. It was in the rest of the fly that Jamesie took a line of his own.

Jamesie rarely used hackles, which he considered unnecessary if the body fur was sufficiently picked out, and he disliked wings made of solid feathers because they were too opaque and lacked movement. Instead, he provided his flies with a kind of Elizabethan ruff, which was partly transparent and very mobile. Suppose that he wanted to tie a fly with a wing of the colour known to the old dressers as "bloa" or "blae" and which he referred to as "a mishty wing." This was his procedure.

First he assembled his materials, which consisted of single fibres from the tail or wings of various birds. He stuck to his theory of colour mixing. From coot and moorhen he got an iron grey; from pigeon, tern, and jay the lighter shades; from teal, a pepper and salt and from a parakeet some green fibres to cool down the whole. When he had sufficient to make the mixture he desired, he laid the fibres parallel, with the fine ends pointing in the same direction and all of a length, and gathered them together into a bunch. If there was a tendency for the fibre to interlock, he rolled and combed them till this was overcome – the exact opposite process to that of "marrying" fibres for the under wing of a salmon fly. This bunch he tied on to the hook just behind the eye, with the fine ends projecting over the eye to a length equal to that of the hook shank. The fly now looked rather like a paint brush. He cut off the waste of the blunt ends and spun his body so that it came up to the point where the fibres were tied on. Now came a delicate manoeuvre – the fibres were stroked back till they projected at right angles to the shank, evenly distributed around it and looking like a miniature sweep's brush. When he was satisfied with their set Jamesie worked the tying silk through them and finished off close in front, forming the silk into a little collar which held the base of the feathers firmly pressed against the fur of the body, and ensured that the fibres should retain their position. Held in this way, at right angles to the body, the tips bent and kicked with every movement of the fly through the water, giving a vivid impression of life.

Jamesie's wings, like his bodies, were often the inspiration of the moment; but in addition to the "Mishty", he had two other favourites, the "Foxy" and the "Dark". The former called for the tan feathers of a woodcock and the ruddier shades of grouse, land-rail and red hen; the latter was built on a basis of dark grouse and mallard.

Flies such as these could never be a commercial success. They needed too much time, trouble, and skill to tie. Jamesie made them for himself and as a gift to a few of his more favoured employers. Now that he is dead no one is likely to tie them, and indeed, even before his death, he was giving them up in favour of the bumbles. He acknowledged at once that the cock hackles down the body gave greater brilliancy than, and as much transparency as, his own picked-out seal's fur; and that by choosing carefully the colours of hackle and body it was possible to get the effect he desired, a fly in which the predominant tone was produced by a combination of varying shades and colours. He criticised, however, the stiffness of cock hackles in the water when compared with his own soft feathers. This difficulty we eventually got over by adding a few turns of a soft hackle at the shoulder, thus securing the necessary movement.

We experimented over a number of seasons, trying out different methods of construction and every colour and combination of colour that we could think of. "Experimented" is perhaps too grandiloquent a word, for we were a little haphazard in our efforts. Jamesie, in particular, was too individual to be tied to a set plan. The appearance of a few dead wasps on the water would be followed by a fly gorgeous in black and yellow chenille with a rusty dun hackle, which was really rather like a wasp, but never collected a fish. I expostulated with him for producing such aberrations when we were supposed to be investigating the fishes' preference for one or other shade of blue. He answered me, as usual, with a story.

"There was a lad once that lived along by the Cornamona shore but he didn't fish any, an' when they axed him why he wouldn't fish, he said as how it was too easy an' he had more things to do. That saying' of his riled the boys an' they kep' afther him till at the latther end he allowed he would show them. He got a salmon hook, an' he lashed any feathers he could find to it till it was more like a bird than a fly – like one of them yalla-headed wrans it was. He got an old dappin' rod, an' when there was a wind big enough to shweep out the conthraption, he started off on a drift with all the boys watchin' him. He hadn't gone more nor ten or twelve perches when a fish took him, an' he landed it, God knows how. Do you know what that fish weighed, Sir? Eight pounds four and a half ounces on the scales. 'Easy!' says he 'Easy!' when they were weighing it, and from that day he never held a rod again. He was a lad that had a head on him, I'm thinking. You never know what some fish'll take."

Jamesie knew every lake in the west of Ireland from Sligo to Limerick. In the last century it was common for anglers to go on a round tour, changing from brown trout to white trout and from lake to lake. Jamesie was so good a boatman that he had been taken as a personal henchman by a number of these peripatetic sportsmen. His observation was exact, and his memory the most remarkable I ever have encountered. If I received an invitation to unknown waters he could always describe every feature of the lake, the best drifts for trout, and, with a detail which was often accurate to a yard, the places where salmon stood year after year. I never knew him to be wrong. Often he could go further and describe the dressing of a particular fly which he had found of service, and here again he was uncannily right.

Jamesie divided flies into four classes, light, dark, medium and fiery. The light comprised flies whose bodies and general tone were silver, grey and yellow. Among the standard dressings this class would be represented by Golden Olive, Invicta, Grey Monkey and a simplified Silver Doctor or Silver Grey. The dark included the deeper shades of claret – the colour of the lees of the wine – black, and sombre blue. Black Claret, Teal and Black, Zulu, Kingsmill and the Bruiser are examples. "Fiery" covered copper, orange, and fiery brown. The typical fly of this category was Fiery Brown itself, but it would also have embraced Orange Grouse and Dunkeld. "Medium" included such flies as Claret and Mallard, and a considerable range of brown bodies. The indications for the choice of one type or another were as follows.

Light flies were best when the bottom itself was light, of sand or grey limestone. A silver-bodied fly was especially suitable to lakes like Carra where the water is unusually clear and the bottom whitish marl. Jamesie's prescription for this lake was a silver body, a thin wisp of teal for the wing, and a pea-green hackle. A large silver fly was also suitable for a strong east wind at the end of the season, and a smaller size silver body had general utility as a fry-suggesting pattern. Golden-olive was the most useful colour of all the light flies, especially with a west wind and high clouds, and in the evening on the sand of the bay. Grey – I never quite sorted out the indications for this colour. Jamesie would look up at the sky and into the water and announce, "T'is time to put up a grey fly," and he was usually right, but he found it difficult to assign reasons. In general it could be said that light flies were for light bottoms and light days.

Dark flies, as might be expected, were for the opposite conditions, a black, peaty bottom, an overcast and lowering sky; but a rather small black fly was good at tail on a sunny day.

Fiery flies were for peat-stained or slightly muddy water.

Medium flies were maids-of-all work, a loose category. Jamesie's typical medium fly was in general colouring a warm golden-brown olive, with a ruff in which brown mallard predominated; but he used his characteristic pointillism freely in the body which had flecks of crimson, purple, and orange as well as brown. No two bodies were exactly alike, but it was a most effective fly.

Jamesie believed in making up the cast with one fly which was particularly suited to the conditions, one medium, and one which was suited to opposing conditions. He thought it wise to give fish a choice, and pointed out that the character of the bottom was continually changing. If the fly of the type which he thought most suitable was proving a success he put on another fly of the same general type, but not identical. If a fly which, according to his notions, ought not to be suitable, was doing well, he did not always double up on this type. He had also a fancy for using a freak fly on one of the casts. "You never know what some fish'll take," was a phrase which recurred frequently in his conversation. The only freak flies which I can remember to have justified the experiment were the "Single-speech Hamiltons" mentioned in the earlier chapter. I agree with Jamesie's classification and his general rules as to when each type should be used. There is such a bewildering variety of patterns from which to choose that I will say no more than that any collection should include the following colours – golden olive, green olive, grey, silver, black, fiery brown, medium claret, dark claret and gentian blue.

12

THE WISDOM OF JAMESIE

In the daytime I was too busy fishing to keep notes of Jamesie's talk, and at night too tired. As usual I trusted to my memory, and as usual it has failed me. On the water hardly a day passes without some of his hints coming vividly to mind, but here in the study it is hard to gather these gleanings into a sheaf. The bulk of his knowledge was instinctive, unrationalized and uncommunicable. Season after season, in calm and storm, sunshine and shadow, he had watched and brooded over his lake and all that went on above and below its ever-changing surface, retaining in his memory much of what he had noted, but letting more glide imperceptibly away into his subconscious. There it had undergone a slow process of assimilation and digestion, losing its original form, becoming an inarticulate part of him. Only now and then would the product emerge in a sudden spurt of decision, a compelling "hunch", as to the thing to be done. Jamesie's hunches were not infallible, but they worked sufficiently often to exclude any theory of blind chance.

Apart from these intermittent hunches, which he could not himself explain, I was able to extract at last some general theories. Trout, thought Jamesie, were everywhere, deep and shallow, in bay and on point, by reeds and among rocks. "There is no spot in the Corrib where ye may not find a fish". But the density of the fish population varied from place to place; and even where the density was approximately the same, fish took better in some places than others. Winter and early spring found most fish in the sheltered bays, but as the year mellowed there came a movement to the broad shallows which were to be found far out in the lake. September brought a backward migration towards the mouths of the spawning streams. It was not a steady purposeful run like the ascent of a salmon, but a slow and casual drift, the fish feeding and dawdling as they went, like cattle on a mountain. In they came, working their way from island to island, point to point, not so much following the indentations of the shore as cutting across the mouths of the bays to the next promontory. At the end of the season Jamesie favoured places where the land stretched out a long finger under water across the route of the travellers.

All the Corrib boatmen were good. They knew the lake as a landowner knows his own demesne. But Jamesie knew it as a blind man knows the house he lives in, with an absolute certainty. Though he could not see the bottom he could sense it, and in a shallow a mile long could smell his way to the few square yards which constituted a pet spot. Jamesie believed in pet spots, where, year in year out, trout took better than in other places, and he had his ideas as to the reasons which brought this about. First there was food. Snails were more abundant in certain patches and perch fry in others. Next came shelter. Fish have no eyelids and so shun a bright light by seeking the shadows of rocks and clefts in the bottom, to emerge only at evening on to the open sands. Shelter was also important to enable them to avoid the attentions of their enemies the pike. According to Jamesie pike fed only in the daytime and this was another reason why trout could roam further afield when the light failed. Lastly there was the question of currents, which were important, because trout always lay facing a current, and because of the food which was current-borne.

Jamesie opened my eyes to the amount of currents which exist in a lake. I had taken into account only the water from the main feeding rivers, and assumed that it mingled rapidly with the lake water and lost its identity. One calm day when there was a small dirty flood in the river, he showed me how the river water made its way more than half a mile out from the shore in a narrow, gradually widening, course, leaving clear water on each side. When there was no flood this tendency of the river water to keep itself to itself was not apparent, but it existed all the same. Then there were the wind currents. A strong wind drove the waves in front of it. In unobstructed reaches the movement of water so caused was negligible, but where a chain of islands lay at right angles to the wind, the water was forced through the openings in a slow steady current. This also he demonstrated by anchoring the boat in such a gap, and showing me the nymph shucks and other small pieces of debris which was being carried along a foot or two below the surface.

A very favourite spot with him was the shelving of a bank, where the shore sloped into the water, or where a small hog's back had formed itself further out. At some level on the slope the trout would be found resting, but the level varied according to the height of the lake and the temperature. The level of Corrib may rise or fall several feet, and Jamesie knew within narrow limits at what part of a bank the trout would congregate for each level. But other factors than height of water came into play, and there had to be a good deal of trial and error before the correct depth for any day could be ascertained. Jamesie would quest and twist along a bank, like a dog after a running grouse, till he found what he reckoned to be the correct depth for the existing conditions.

One day there was a fair hatch of lake olives in the lee of an island. I could count about twenty in sight, but not a trout rose to them. I asked Jamesie why this was. For answer he picked out from the bow a three-pounder which he had just caught and laid its plumpness on a seat. He prodded it with his fingers. "Look at that, Sir. It's rale mate that fellow wants to fatten him." He removed one of the olives from the gunwale and perched it on the neb of the big trout where it looked like a butterfly on an elephant. Then he brushed it lightly and all that was left was a thin smear. "What'd be the use of one of them wisheens to him – or a dozen of them? Wouldn't he have more loss chasing them than he got by ating them?"

That sentence of Jamesie contains one of the keys to success in fishing big lakes. A trout is not going to expend more energy in chasing his food than he will gain by assimilating it. The question is one of calories. In a river trout feed regularly on small flies because they use up very little effort in getting them. The hatch is more concentrated and a trout with an eye for a good place can hover close to the surface, waiting for his food to be brought to him on the conveyor-belt. He need only move a few inches to right or left, give an upward roll and the morsel is his. A lot of these morsels acquired with a few flicks of his tail make up a meal. The lake trout is less fortunate. He lies anything up to ten feet below the surface, and to raise his weight through ten feet of water takes real effort. If he comes up near the surface his window gets smaller and smaller the higher he rises, and the chance of a fly coming into its diminished circle is slight. He can cruise if he wants to, but here again he has to cruise deep if he is to see a wide area of the surface, and has to come up for each fly. If he cruises shallowly the little moving port-hole of his vision will only pick up a fly at rare intervals, unless the hatch is one of quite exceptional density. Rises to smaller insects, such as ants, caenis and the duck flies do occur, but usually in sheltered places, and I have only rarely encountered these rises.

I have spoken of the trout's window. Only in this circular aperture can he see anything on the surface, or see through the surface. Outside his window the surface appears to him like a mirror, reflecting the bottom but impossible to see through. Anything floating motionless on that surface is invisible. Suppose however it is not motionless, but fluttering like a daddy, or scuttering like a sedge. Then the surface film is bent, and the mirror distorted in a way which causes any trout in the neighbourhood to take note and and shoot upwards, with the knowledge that when the disturbance comes into his window there will be something to reward him. He need not cruise. The fly heliographs its position from afar, and the trout wastes no time in fruitless circling.

The practical lesson is to use a fly sufficiently large to make a trout consider it worth while to chase it, and to keep your top dropper working in the skin of the water so as to distort the surface and signal its whereabouts. Where there is a strong wind and big waves the surface mirror is already so distorted that a little extra distortion may not be noticed by the fish. Then it pays to fish all three flies under water, or to put an outsize bumble on the top dropper and fish it so as to cause a regular wake which can be seen despite the waves.

Jamesie and I fished in rival and contrasting styles and though each could, and when circumstances required, did adopt each other's methods, yet the difference in our tackle was such that the change over was something of a makeshift. Jamesie was a master of the mid-Victorian style which had evolved to make the best use of the tackle then available. Before the oil-dressed line was invented lines were of silk, or silk and hair, closely plaited but undressed; and the flies were as often as not dressed on hair instead of gut. To cast such a light tackle required a long and rather whippy rod, and even with the wind behind, the distance which could be covered was not great. There were advantages to compensate. The long rod and light line enabled the flies to be played on the surface at a sufficient distance from the boat in a variety of attractive ways, and even when the modern dressed line and shorter stiffer rod were introduced a number of good fishermen preferred to stick to the old methods in a modified form. Of such was Jamesie. He liked a rod of not less than thirteen feet and a thin level line, only lightly dressed. So equipped he gave new meaning to the familiar phrase "playing the fly". I had fished with more than one person who favoured what a friend called "The Great Exhibition style", but it was not till I met Jamesie that I saw it used by a real master. It was an exhausting business. Despite the leverage of the long rod his hand and arm were never still. The wrist kept up a continuous quiver, and the arm swept left and right, up and down, like the arm of a violinist. At the end of his line the flies responded, sliding and circling, bobbing about like egg-laying spinners, making short spurts along the surface like sedges, or long swoops like a wind swept daddy.

Whether Jamesie cajoled, deceived, or exasperated the trout into rising I never decided, but rise they did. I never knew any-one provoke more rises than Jamesie but the proportion of fish landed to fish risen was disappointing. This was the greatest drawback of his method. Some fish, who were really trying, missed the fly because of its erratic movements; and others, following up, took fright when they saw the boat and sheered off at the last moment.

With his light equipment Jamesie could not shoot any length of line, and the end of his draw found his flies so close to him that it was difficult to strike accurately. His method was most successful in the evening when the sun was down and the boat cast no shadow on the bottom, or when a strong wind allowed him to play the flies at a greater distance from the boat, and helped to conceal the boat itself. A minor disadvantage was that his tackle could not be cast across the wind and so, if a trout was seen to move outside the line of drift, he could not cover it unless the boat was moved. Jamesie's skill managed to conceal some of the defects of the method which were patent with less expert fishermen, such as the old squire of Lough Melvin. After watch-ing him I had abandoned the Victorian style and partly adopted, partly evolved, another, which avoided most of its disadvantages, but at the same time sacrificed some of its virtues. I may call it "the long draw". It is on the whole the best method of fishing for big brown trout in a lake, especially when conditions are difficult, and, though rises are fewer than with the older method, the proportion of fish hooked is much higher. Any equipment which will comfortably cast a distance of twenty yards and will make a fair job of casting cross-wind is adequate. Extra strong rods are tiring and quite unnecessary; the ordinary ten-foot dry-fly rod of medium strength, with a tapered line of suitable thickness to match the rod, will suit most people. Rods shorter than ten feet are a mistake and a longer rod will facilitate a change over to the older method when desired. Perhaps the most suitable rod I ever owned was a light two-piece of eleven foot six inches, which I foolishly sold because its length made it awkward for transport.

The main virtues of the method are three. It covers a larger area of water and so shows the fly to more fish; it gives the fish plenty of time to follow the fly and make up their minds to take it; and it enables the rod to be held continuously at the best angle for striking. Its demerit is that the shorter rod and greater distance of the fly loses that degree of control over the working of the fly which is given by the older method. To call it a new method is hardly correct, for the basic principles remain, only the length of cast, the manner of draw, and the way of striking being altered.

To prepare for a long draw you must first cast a long line, the length depending on the wind and weather conditions. On difficult days with little or no breeze, twenty yards – and as much more as you can manage – are desirable, but ordinarily fifteen yards will be sufficient. Imagine, then, that you have laid your flies upon the water some eighteen or twenty yards away, and you want to draw them seven or eight yards before casting again. To do this by the older method of raising the rod top is impossible, as before you had recovered the requisite amount the top would be in the water behind you. Instead of raising your rod top keep it low, at an angle of not more than thirty degrees to the water surface, and make your draw by the use of the left hand alone. There are several ways of doing this. The easiest is to catch the line just below the bottom ring with the left hand, pull it down to where the right hand can catch it, and go on repeating the process till enough line has been drawn in. This pulls the flies in a series of jerks, which is often effective. As the line is recovered it is allowed to fall into the floor boards, where it lies, ready to be shot at the next cast.

Another way, which I prefer, gives a continuous as opposed to an intermittent draw, but one which can be varied in pace within wide limits. The hand movement which produces this result is at first rather difficult to learn, but soon becomes quite automatic. With the rod balanced comfortably in the right hand at the correct angle take hold of the line between the reel and the bottom ring with the left forefinger and thumb, palm upwards, and fingers in line with the forearm. Pull the line a little downwards and to the left, till your hand and arm are comfortable and your whole position is balanced. You may find it convenient to rest your left elbow on your left thigh as you sit. Now you are ready to begin the draw. Bend your left wrist outwards as far as possible, retaining the finger and thumb grip, and keeping the palm upwards. This draws in about four inches of line. Now hook the remaining fingers over the line above your original grip, which relaxes as soon as the fingers have got a hold, and bend your wrist, palm still upwards, as far inwards as you can. This draws in another four inches, and you will find that you will have now about seven or eight inches in a loop in your palm, while your thumb and forefinger are in the correct position to take a fresh hold. As you take your new hold, your other fingers relax and the loop of line drops down. Continue the movements till you have recovered enough line (which is allowed to fall on the floorboards as before) and shoot all the loose line with your next cast. I have described the movements separately, but in practise they merge fluently into each other, and the flies are drawn in steadily without any pause. At the beginning of the draw, the flies are too far away, and the angle made by the line with the water is too narrow to permit of working the flies on the surface. The only variation you can make in their movement is to draw at different speeds and to alter the angle of draw by moving your rod to right or to left. When the draw is nearly finished you can lift the rod point a little and try your skill at making the flies dance and dib on the surface.

What is to be done if, as so often happens in this method of fishing, you see a trout following the fly, eyes fixed on it, nose about six inches away, almost as if he was being towed? I wish I knew. I have tried quickening the draw, slowing up, main-

taining the pace, stopping altogether. There is no standard recipe
to success. If you are lucky he will make a sudden spurt and be
hooked, but as often as not he loses interest and goes home to
read a book.

Correct striking with this method is instinctive. You are
perfectly balanced, the rod at the correct angle, the line taut.
When the fish takes you cannot avoid raising the rod gently and
firmly, while at the same time you emphasise the strike by pulling
in line with the left hand. It is a two-handed procedure which
comes perfectly naturally. The hook goes in above the barb, and
there is no danger of a break. I have never been broken on the
strike except on the evening already described, when it was almost
dark.

Cast radially, first to the left, then straight in front, then to the
right, so as to cover the greatest area of water, and keep a good
look out for any movement of a fish outside the line of drift
which can be covered by a cross-wind cast. For some reason fish
seem more ready to take when the cast is made cross-wind.

There are various other ways of producing the long draw. If
there is a good wind you can try quartering, or "ottering" as
Jamesie called it, which is done by rowing the boat, slowly, partly
down and partly across wind, holding the rod top high, and
letting the line float out in a big belly like a spinnaker. The flies
take a course parallel to that of the boat and the draw can be
prolonged indefinitely, but striking is rather uncertain because
of the high rod and the slack line. Where there is a reef running
diagonally to the wind this is the best way of searching its side.

Another way, perhaps the most effective of all, is to row the
boat up, or up and across, wind and to cast at right angles to the
course of the boat, allowing the flies to work round in a quarter
circle. Bow rod casts a comparatively short line, just sufficient to
keep well clear of the oars, and fishes the lane of water near the
boat; while stern casts far out and fishes a lane outside that
searched by the bow rod. The flies move slowly at first, quickening as the boat gains on them. There is a particular point, about
half way along their travel, when the arc of the curve sharpens
(this sharpening can be accentuated by proper rod control) and
it is at this point that the trout nearly always take. Watch this
point, and sooner or later you will see a trout come charging
through the wave crests to pounce on the fly like a golden tiger,
one of the most exciting sights that fishing provides.

I have had many good days on Corrib but I shall describe only two short spells. For the first luck and luck alone was responsible. The second happened to coincide with a new experiment, and at the time I was inclined to take credit to myself, but as I have never been able to repeat the experiment with equal results I must, though with some reluctance, attribute everything – well, nearly everything – to good fortune.

The day had been wearisome calm for the most part with an occasional hot sigh of wind coming from an overcast and moody sky. Sulky mutters of thunder grumbled over the mountains to the west, but came no nearer. No fish, no rise, no fly, no life anywhere. Less than two hours of the day were left, and we started to row dispiritedly towards the jetty which was our centre of operations in August. The sky grew still darker and heavier. Then, without warning, there was a flare overhead, a shatter of thunder, and the rain struck down on us with such vehemence and viciousness that we began to search for the baler. In twenty minutes the tumult had passed, a cool breeze stole over the levels of the lake, and the water – I can use no other word – smiled.

In the boat were four exceedingly wet people who should have hurried home to change, but our spirits responded to the uplift and we decided on a final attempt among the pockets and knife-edged reefs which characterize this part of the lake. There was still no fly, nothing but the change in the day's aspect to account for what happened, and what did happen can be best conveyed by the simple statement that in a few minutes over the hour we caught eighteen fish out of which thirteen fell to my share. Nothing but pure chance could account for this disproportion. Jamesie and I were fishing the same flies and identical methods, since, with the trout rising so frenziedly, I did not waste time on long casting or fancy draws. Even with firm handling it takes about three minutes to net a trout of over a pound, so it will be seen that I was almost continuously in fish. Nearly every trout that rose was hooked and only one fish escaped after being hooked. The average size was on the small side, the total weight being twenty-three pounds.

The day's adventures were not at an end. Near the jetty stood a cottage in whose yard I used to leave my car, and as it was a Friday I slipped in to leave some fish for supper. The woman of the house exclaiming at our soaked condition, bid us to the fire, and turning to me said, "It's cold and thirsty you must be.

Will ye have a sup?" In an Irish cottage if the teapot is not on the hob, hospitality prescribes a glass of milk, and I accepted gladly. To my surprise she took a jug from the dresser and poured out nearly a cupful of clear water, warmish water too, as I noted with mild disapproval when I took the cup. Still, thirsty as I was, I set out to drain it. Not till I felt the ardour of the liquid on my throat did I realize that I was gulping poteen, raw and warm from the still. (Next day I was to come across the still, hidden in a thicket of scrub on a nearby island.) No doubt I should have coughed and choked, my eyes should have streamed, and my head reeled. None of these alarming things happened. My throat was warm but rather pleasantly warm, my eyes no more than a little prickly and my gasp of moderate dimensions. I finished the cup but retained sufficient sense to ask my wife to drive the car. I may add that neither that night nor next morning did I feel any ill effects, and also that the fish were counted before I went into the cottage, not after.

The second incident calls for a short technical explanation for the method which I then used for the first time is one which, while not the open sesame I thought it to be, has had success on other occasions, both with brown trout and salmon, though for some reason it is useless with white trout. I had done my share of teaching novices and had marvelled at the proverbial beginner's luck. Then I noticed a peculiar thing. It was always the very worst cast that produced the unexpected fish. The line would drop in coils on the water and lie there like a dissolute boa-constrictor, the novice would begin to retrieve the mess, and then a fool of a fish would shoot up from the bottom, pick a fly out of the entanglement, and get caught; and always the fly selected was moving on a curved path. Then there was the fact already noted, that when casting from a moving boat the point where fish most often rose was just when the fly was beginning to circle. Jamesie too, I had observed, was given to starting his flies in one direction and reversing the movement of his rod so as to coax them into a semi-circular course, with good results. Perhaps a curved path seemed more natural to the fish. I set out to find how this curved path could be combined with the long draw and, after experiment, found the answer in the "S" cast.

This is the way it is done. (A good wind and a long rod are advantages). Cast your line at right angles to the wind, outside the line of the drift, and cast rather slackly. The result will be that the wind catches the flies and gut more than the line, and when cast and line fall on the water they will lie in a semi-circular curve with the convex side facing up-wind. Now mend the nearer portion of your line down-wind, without disturbing the further portion which is in the water. This will put another semi-circular curve in the upper part of your line but the convex of this semi-circle will point down-wind. The whole outfit, line and cast, should now be lying on the surface in the shape of an "S". If you keep the point of your rod low, not more than two or three feet from the surface, and pull in by hand in the way already described, the pressure of water on the line will force the fly to move in two curves in the shape of a flattened "S", which certainly does seem on occasions to attract fish when other methods have failed. Jamesie was not with me that remarkable afternoon, for I was fishing with Cyril Wilson, the best amateur fisherman on the lake. His bungalow was on the shore of Porta-carron bay, and we set out at 3 p.m. for a few hours fishing in the water of medium depth which lies in the centre of the bay. The wind was north west, full and steady, and the waves big but unbroken. The month was September. We came back shortly before six, and in the meantime I had landed five trout weighing fifteen pounds – five, four, three, one and three-quarters, one and a quarter, in nicely graduated succession. All had been taken on the "S" cast, the successful flies being the Kingsmill and the Claret Bumble. The remarkable thing was that my host had not a fish and, if my memory is correct, did not even get a rise. Ordinarily he would have taken at least four fish to my three and I was inclined to attribute my success to the new method. Cyril, with his greater experience, said nothing and only grinned. He knew that these things happen and that it would not be long before he had his revenge. Nor was it.

Year after year Jamesie had seemed the same, old indeed, but growing no older and no feebler. Then came an August when only Jimmy was at the Angler's to greet me. "Where's Jamesie?" I asked. "He'll be along presently but he's given up boating," said Jimmy. "He says he's too stiff to pull. He does still fish a bit with his son of a Sunday". As he spoke Jamesie appeared at the end of the street, perhaps a little less elastic in walk, perhaps a little more consciously erect, but certainly not failing. Neverthe-less he stuck to his decision, and thenceforward Jimmy and I went out alone, and Jimmy did the work of two men. While Jamesie was there Jimmy had allowed himself to be over-shadowed, but now he was in control and a more tireless, willing boatman never rowed in Corrib. No matter how hopeless seemed the day Jimmy would not give in. "Thry one more drift, Sir, atween the islands," and if that failed there was another drift to try, and yet another which must not be left unfished. Corrib was his idol against whom he would hear no word. He and I were there to show forth its wonders. He did not fish himself, except occasionally a little dapping, but he saw to it that I did, and if he worked hard, made certain that I did likewise.

There came a spell of hot calm weather when fishing was a weariness, and an Englishman, who owned a powerful outboard engine, suggested a trip round the lake if we could find a pilot. I promised to ask Jamesie and he was delighted to come. Never had the old villain been in better form. He took the tiller, exulting in the speed of the boat and in the broad arrowheads which she carved on the surface. His flow of legend and reminiscence never ceased. Presently we came to a shallow which was a nightmare of boulders, some just showing above the surface, some more dangerously hidden. Jamesie did not slacken pace, but wove his way through the obstacles as if he was in a bending race. I moved up to the bow, not exactly distrustful of his knowledge, but still a little anxious. Ahead and only about a foot under water I could see a rock as big as a billiard table. Jamesie put the tiller over and we missed it, but only just. I made a mistake. "Easy on, Jamesie," I said. Jamesie stiffened. His judgment had been impeached, and that before a boatload of Englishmen. He throttled down the engine to a safer speed, took his bearings carefully, and spoke. "Sure I know every rock there is in the lake" – here there was a ferocious bump and the keel scraped across a whale-back – "and that's one of them". The shock had been sufficient to upset several people off their seats and I was nearly pitched over the bow, but anger gave way to laughter. Only I was not satisfied. Jamesie's feet had been firmly planted when the bump came, so that he had not moved, and I had noticed his slight lean on the tiller after he had taken his bearings. Moreover the joke was not original. It was known all over the west of Ireland and had even appeared in print, attributed to the captain of the Dun Aengus which plied between Galway and the Aran Islands.* I took an opportunity to move down to the stern sheets and sat beside Jamesie so that I could talk to him without being heard. "Jamesie," I said, "I am ashamed of you." "How's that Sir?" "To run the boat on a rock for the sake of getting off a joke that everyone but an Englishman would know wasn't your own." Jamesie affected to be affronted and turned away without answering, but presently I saw a line deepen on his cheek and I knew his moustache was throttling a smile. "What are you thinking of, Jamesie?" I said. "I'm thinking," he answered, "that some Dublin counsellors are a damn side too smart for us poor counthry boys."

"How is Jamesie?" I asked Jimmy when I came down next season. "Dead, Sir," he said. "Dead these three months." I should have expected it, of course. But it was a bitter little pang when it came. "Why did you not let me know," I said, "so that I could have come down for the funeral?" "Ye couldn't have come, Sir," he said, "for I saw on the paper as how ye were defendin' a man for murther. I wasn't goin' to throuble ye."

I have no doubt that Jamesie got safely through the golden gates; but there might have been a little delay while two old fishermen exchanged a tale or two.

---

* Dr. A. A. Luce, in his book *Fishing and Thinking* which appeared when the first edition of this book was in the press, tells an identical story of a boatman on Lough Conn. The remark has become "folk".

PART III

———◆———

WHITE TROUT IN RIVER AND LAKE

13

WHITE TROUT WAYS

Anglers usually come to sea-trout fishing after previous experience with brown trout or salmon, and their ideas and muscular reactions are already conditioned by that experience. They naturally tend to persist in the ways they have already learned, with but minor modifications. It is difficult to persuade a salmon fisherman to strike properly or a brown trout fisherman to forget about natural insects and imitation of the natural. In this chapter I give a short account of the life history of the sea trout of Connemara, their migrations and habits, which will, I hope, be a guide to those who are new to this kind of fishing.

The sea trout has as many names as royalty. Outside Ireland every district, almost every river, seems to give it a different title. In Ireland, wherever you go, it is called simply and descriptively the "White Trout". In weight and preferences it varies widely. A Swedish angler looks for fish running up to twenty pounds; in the Hebrides and some rivers in England and Wales fish of from five to ten pounds are regularly caught; but in the west of Ireland a four-pounder is rare, a five-pounder almost a specimen fish. It ascends at different times in different rivers. In Connemara it is usual to stop fishing when the sun sets, which is the time when an angler on the Slaney would start to put up his rod. In Kerry and West Cork – to say nothing of the Dovey in Wales – the worm is the most successful bait but I have never seen a worm used in Connemara except once when I tried it as an experiment, without success. About so temperamental a fish generalization is dangerous. My own experience of white trout has been confined almost exclusively to Donegal, Mayo and Galway, and most of it has been in Connemara where I know all the fisheries except Inver and Kylemore, though my particular study was Fermoyle. Any opinions expressed in the following pages should not be assumed to be correct for districts other than those mentioned.

The white trout, like the salmon, is a migratory fish, spawned in fresh water, living the life of a small brown trout for the first two, three, or four years of its growth, then changing into a silver coat and descending to the sea to grow fat. Unlike the salmon, it never goes far out into the Atlantic, but feeds around the coast and on sea banks where, as in the North Sea, there is no great depth of water. The rapidity of its growth and its ultimate size depend on the richness and extent of the feeding. The west coast of Ireland has no banks to compare with those in the North Sea, the English Channel, or the Baltic, and so our fish run smaller than those who feed in these more favoured areas. A salmon never returns to the river until he has spent a year in the sea, and he may stay in the sea up to five years before coming back. A white trout usually returns as a grilse in the same year as he has gone down. The lowest lake of a system will have a number of these grilse, weighing only about six ounces, as early as July, but the main grilse run, the so-called "harvesters", is not till the end of August or beginning of September, when the fish average a little over half a pound. These grilse spend the winter in fresh water, but only about a third of them spawn, the genital organs of the rest not yet being fully functioning. Some white trout do not spawn even in the second year of their return, but once a white trout has spawned, with few exceptions he goes on spawning every year till he dies.

In Connemara the upward run of white trout begins about the middle of June, and local tradition, corroborated by the watchers who in favourable conditions can see the fish passing under the bridge at Costello, says that the pioneers are nearly all big fish. They push up rapidly as far as the state of the water allows, but they are so few, and the extent of the lakes so large, that no one fishes seriously for them till July is under way, and by this time the early fish are already growing stale and difficult to catch. In August and September, when the day was calm, I have often seen in the upper lakes small groups of five or six fish playing round just under the surface, with their back fins showing. All were about four or five pounds in weight, very coloured, and impossible to catch. These, I imagine, were the pioneers. In July the run thickens and reaches peak about the third week, though weather conditions may advance the peak or retard it. The late

August or early September run is chiefly of "harvesters", though a few fresh adult fish continue to dribble in. 1955 was a year of exceptional drought, and when rain came at last, in September, there was an immediate run of fresh fish, all in poor condition. They had been hanging round the estuary of the Cashla in thousands, waiting for a flood, and their numbers had been too great for the food supply in this small area to keep them fat.

Fishing used to continue – and in some places still continues – for the first half of October, and both the larger trout and the salmon are said to take well in this month. The season should end with September. Even in the last week of September an experienced fisherman will put back many a fish as being already out of condition, though some anglers bring back, and even exhibit with pride, trout and salmon that are nearly black, with nothing to give them weight except their skin, their bones, and their spawn.

November is the spawning month for white trout. These fish choose small gravel to make their redds and will spawn in the tiniest of streams. As the hillside streams rise and fall very rapidly, the trout may deposit their ova in a place which next day is a dry gravel bed. Sometimes the larger fish spawn at the shallow edge of a lake where a stream comes in. Attention to the spawning beds is the most important part of the management of a white trout fishery. Bog mould is brought down by floods and silts into the gravel, forming a pan which the fish cannot break up. Spawning beds must be well raked every year, and in boggy rivers it may be necessary to throw in gravel to make new spawning beds. When Lord Dudley was tenant of Screeb, he greatly improved the fishery by putting lorry-loads of gravel into the river, and Pat Spellman doubled the annual take on the Fermoyle fishery by continual attention to the spawning beds. The river breeds, the sea feeds, and proper care of the beds gives a generous return.

A certain amount of white trout redds are disturbed by the activities of the salmon who spawn later, but, as salmon prefer much larger gravel for their operations, so long as big gravel is available the loss is not serious. Walking along a stream it is easy to distinguish the redds of the two species.

It takes from ten to twelve weeks for the ova to hatch out as alevins and it is a further four to seven weeks before the yolk sac is absorbed, the mouth developed, and fry life begun. Meanwhile the exhausted parents do not, as might be expected, make for the rich feeding of the sea as soon as spawning is over. Local watchers in Connemara maintain that the parent trout do not descend till April or May, and certainly there are kelts in the lower lakes in April, but I suspect that a certain number return from February onwards. Experimental netting in Donegal has shown white trout descending in February, and the full water of the early months would prevent the fish from being observed on their downward run. It is difficult to believe that the perfect condition of July fish could be produced by a mere two and a half months feeding. Some fish certainly over-winter in the sea, and in Kerry big sea trout may be caught in March with sea lice still on them. I have not heard of fresh fish being caught in Connemara earlier than June.

Nearly every river in Ireland contains white trout, but they seem to prefer acid water to alkaline and, when they do enter a limestone stream, they take the first opportunity of escaping up a more acid tributary. Galway bay gives an interesting example of their preferences. Its northern shore is a succession of one famous white trout fishery after another. At its eastern end flows in the Corrib river, which drains a lake larger than all the white trout lakes put together. A few white trout – and those often large – enter the Corrib river but I never caught a white trout in the lake, nor do I know of anyone who did. Although many of the streams which feed Corrib rise within a mile of the head waters of the streams which feed the white trout fisheries, Corrib lies chiefly on limestone, and so has alkaline water, and the white trout lakes lie on the peat and granite, which makes them acid.

When a white trout has made its way into the river, or the lowest lake of a system, its journey is far from ended. The best spawning streams are usually high in the hills, discharging into the upper lakes, and the trout know this instinctively. A number of barriers lie across their path. There are the rapids, where the stream tumbles down over little falls no more than a foot high and which can be negotiated in any normal water; cascades consisting of successive falls not more than three feet or so high, which can be run or leapt in a small flood; and real falls of six or seven feet, which require a flood somewhat out of the ordinary. These obstacles regulate the rate of the ascent of the fish and much of success in white trout fishing depends on knowing the river bed intimately, so as to be able to judge the extent and rapidity of run permitted by any given flood, and the reaches which it will allow the fish to traverse. Major obstacles may occur anywhere along the system – at the very mouth as in the Gowla, or half way up as in the Cashla.

As the season progresses, more and more fish come streaming up from the sea into the lower waters, and it is these waters which fish best in July. Every flood is a summons to the fish to press on and to leave the lake or deep pool in which they have been resting, so as to cover as much as possible of their journey to the spawning beds. Some will stop as soon as they reach the next lake, others, if the flood holds, will push on to the second or third. If the flood drops suddenly, they tail back to the lake they have last traversed. With each flood the process is repeated, so that towards the end of the season the upper lakes are better stocked than the lower. Even the lowest lakes are never quite depleted, for new fish are always arriving and as nearly every lake has at least one small spawning stream flowing into it, some fish remain to spawn in these tributary streams.

White trout who have been long in a lake without being able to progress become harder and harder to catch, but a flood and a change of lake will make them eager once more. When first I started to fish in Connemara, the usual practice after a flood was to search with special care that part of the lake where the river flowed out, on the assumption that newly arrived trout would scatter round the exit before finding more permanent quarters. This, at any rate in small lakes, I think to be a mistake. I have had many opportunities to fish a lake which had just received a fresh supply of trout, and twice I was on the spot when a lake received its first run for the season. The day after the flood fishing was best where the river flowed *into* the lake, and in subsequent days the fish seemed to distribute themselves round the shores, drifting backwards from the river entrance towards the river exit. I believe that trout newly arrived in a lake swim against the course of the current (which in a flood is perceptible throughout the lake unless it is a large one) until they reach the river entrance. Here a proportion rest, tired with exertions and unwilling to face more rough water. Others press on to reach the next lake but even these may drop back if the flood falls suddenly. The area round the river entrance is the first to be populated. A certain number of fish who arrive at the tail of the flood may stay in the exit bay, especially if the lake is large. While the flood is still high enough for trout to run through, a person who knows his lake and the course which the current takes (discernible in calm water by the scraps of floating debris) can do well by holding the boat away from the course of the current, and fishing across it. Running trout are often willing to take.

When the dispersal has finally taken place the trout will be found unevenly distributed. The areas around the river entrance and exit, shores of islands, rocky bays of suitable depth, mid-lake shallows, and shelving banks are the favourite places. The fish may go into deep water, but in Connemara they do not take there. (It is, I am told, different in the north of Scotland). Your boatman will know the best drifts, but there is a simple way of finding out whether you are on likely ground. Take the oar by the loom and thrust it vertically down into the water. If you cannot touch bottom when the whole length of your arm is immersed, you are fishing too deep. If you cannot wet half your oar, you are fishing too shallow. Anything between these limits will hold fish.

Salmon, when they come into a lake, usually take up a fixed position and stay there till they move on to another lake. That big white trout, of three pounds or more, do the same is the opinion of one of the most observant boatmen I know. The bulk of the fish have ambulatory habits, and at certain times of the day take a swim round. On calm days I have been able to trace their movements by slight disturbances of the water, and know people who, from cliffs, have been able to see groups come into a bay, swim round it for a while, and then leave. This habit accounts for some of the accepted traditions of white trout fishing. After a long spell of idleness you may drift into an area of sudden activity. Both rods are in fish, perhaps one rod has two on together. When you have landed or lost the fish there is a temptation to try again over the same place, but this is hardly ever successful. The boatman will tell you that this is because the fish are boat shy, and the passage of your boat has put them down; yet, fishing from the shore with no boat to alarm the trout, you will still find little profit in re-fishing a patch which has just given several rises. I think it more likely that the initial drift encountered one of these travelling groups. There are how-ever certain places where drifts may be repeated – channels between shoals and passages between islands or between island and shore. Those are the constricted routes along which trout moving from one part of the lake to another are forced to travel and, though the group which was first met will have moved on, another may be taking the same road.

Salmon do not feed in fresh water. This statement is not pedantically correct, for I have seen peel taking an odd May-fly and probably they absorb some worms other than those which the fisherman offers them, but for practical purposes it may be accepted as accurate. White trout certainly do feed in fresh water. Looking out over a calm lake, where the rises slowly spread and intersect like the Olympic rings, one is tempted to suppose that the white trout are making a meal of it, but four out of every five rises are made by small trout or parr. Even if the extra size or turbulence of the ring marks out a white trout, there is no guarantee that it is a feeding rise, for white trout like salmon will break surface for sport. White trout, moreover, seem very inept at taking a floating and motionless fly. Their sea feeding on sand eels and sprat has turned them into chasers rather than suckers-down, and from a becalmed boat I have often seen a white trout make two or three futile efforts to absorb a sedge or daddy and suffer the ignominy of having it snapped from under its nose by a small brownie.

The feeding of white trout in fresh water is spasmodic and limited. This can be deduced from the rapid decline in their condition after they leave the sea, and is confirmed by examination of their stomachs. I ought to be able to present a table showing the stomach contents of several thousand fish, and I have wickedly neglected my opportunities for preparing such a monograph. From time to time I took out with me a magnifying glass, a white saucer, and a razor blade, and at lunch time eviscerated the fish, tipped anything found in their stomachs into the saucer of water, and examined it. In all I must have investigated about one hundred interiors. Rather over half had no food, except an odd water flea or Daphnia. About thirty per cent. had the remnants of three or four insects, and about fifteeen per cent. had double that amount. No fish had as much as I would expect to find in a Slaney trout of six ounces after the morning rise. There were never any worms or traces of small fish. I found only small sedges, crane flies, assorted diptera, heather moths, and a very odd beetle. The herling – that is to say the sea trout grilse – seemed more disposed to feed than the adult fish.

Admittedly the food supply in these moorland lakes is scanty, and a trout might be hard put to it to collect a dozen insects in a morning, but there are occasions when a moderate sprinkling of olives and small sedges are to be seen, and more often than not the white trout ignore them. White trout have their time of "taking", and if a rise of fly coincides with this time they will not overlook the natural, but a rise of natural will not necessarily bring them on the "take". The "take" seems to be the result of a sudden burst of activity quite unrelated to food.

Anglers accustomed to brown trout fishing, and aware that white trout do feed, are led astray by the idea that they must imitate the natural and by a tendency to concentrate too much on the neighbourhood of reed beds and other places where they expect the most fly to be found. I have known a Test angler, who acquired a white trout fishery, to allow the best portions of a lake to become choked with rushes in the belief that the hatch of fly, and as a consequence the catch of fish, would be improved. Rushes are of little use in promoting fly life, and the only result was to damage, luckily not irretrievably, one of the finest lakes in Connemara.

The "take" is usually from 11 a.m. to about 1.30 p.m. After lunch there is a slack period, and from 4.30 to 7.30 p.m. may come a revival of activity. In July when the fish are fresh-run the afternoon lull is less pronounced. The "take" is, I believe, associated with the desire of the fish for a gentle constitutional. Certainly in calm weather the fish can be seen moving near the surface while the take is on.

The white trout seems to dislike excess of any kind. Too hot a day or too cold, bright sun or low clouds, calm or black squalls, too high a lake or too low, all these are bad for fishing. A spell of settled weather after a big flood, a moderate temperature with gentle winds and high dappled clouds, those are the conditions the fisherman prays for.

Three conditions are fatal. The first is a rapidly rising lake. For the initial two inches of a rise salmon will take well and trout moderately, but, when the water really starts to climb up the banks fishing is over till the fall begins. The second is when the lake is low and the water over seventy degrees. One of the two blank days which I have had in Connemara was on Lough Inagh during the hot weather of 1955. Despite a favourable wind, not a fish rose to me or my companion in a whole day's fishing. The third condition which I have found disastrous is when there is a kind of electric tension, often associated with the Northern Lights in the night sky. A very odd fish may rise, but the wise man forsakes the lake and goes after grouse. Minor electric tensions with local thunder are also adverse, but they last usually only for a few hours and when they pass the trout rise readily.

The white trout of Connemara are not large. In this district I have taken only one fish of four pounds, and not more than a couple of dozen of three pounds or over. Two-pounders are fairly plentiful. Herling run from half a pound to three-quarters. The size of fish which are on the move varies from day to day. Some days only herling are awake, and on others – usually when the wave is big and steady – nearly every fish seems to be large. An average weight of one and a quarter pounds is reckoned to be satisfactory. Only twice have I averaged over two pounds, and in neither case was the catch large. With a large basket – indeed with any basket of over a dozen – it is almost impossible to exceed an average of two pounds. It is customary to keep any fish over half a pound, and if you have a couple of half-pounders in a basket of a dozen, it means that the remainder must average over two and a quarter pounds to make your total average up to the two pounds.

How many fish can be expected in a day, given ideal conditions? A great deal depends on the month. July, when the fish are running, is the best; August, after the first week, is indifferent; September shows an improvement. Most of the good Connemara lakes have records of over fifty fish to a boat in a day, and I know of one boat which took eighty-six in a day on Glenicmurrin – mostly rather small fish. All these catches were made in July, a month when a barrister is still busy at work and of July fishing I cannot speak from personal experience. My best period was fifteen successive fishing days in September which produced 245 white trout, an average of over sixteen a day, and four salmon.

If the lakes are not over-fished even adverse conditions will not prevent reasonable sport, the more interesting because of the difficulties to overcome. In September 1939 I arrived at Fermoyle to find that there had been no rain for weeks; the lakes were at their lowest and for the fortnight of my stay no flood came. What wind there was – and usually there was none – came in faint puffs from the east, the least favourable quarter, and the sky was cloudless, though occasionally there was an east wind haze, another adverse factor. Using a "tail" of 3x gut to my cast, a single fly, and the greased line technique described in a subsequent chapter I got 114 fish, an average of eight fish a day, the worst day being a singleton and the best a dozen. There was an undue proportion of herling and the average weight was only thirteen ounces. This certainly is not good fishing, yet there was some satisfaction in being able to get the better of adversity even to this limited extent. I should add that the lakes had been very lightly fished owing to the adverse weather.

Local knowledge may turn a bad day into a good. One morning I looked out of my window to see a big flood coming down from the hills. Derreen was too high and the butt of Fermoyle already turbulent; still, if I hurried over my breakfast, I might beat the flood to Rusheen, the next lake below Fermoyle. A hasty row across Fermoyle, and a scamper down the river, brought me to Rusheen just as the water was beginning to push a spearhead into the lake. The wind was adverse but I had brought my two-handed trout rod and, fishing from the shore, I was at once into a nine and a half pound salmon which, aided by the stream, tried to return to the sea. By the time it was landed the river was a torrent, and fishing useless in the lower waters. The rain however ceased by lunch, and it struck me that if I went up to the Clogher pool – a four mile drive and a two mile walk over the flank of Clogher hill – the upper water might have fallen sufficiently to give a chance with a salmon. As we walked over the bog another cloud burst began, but once more I just managed to reach the pool in time to get one salmon and lose another before the second spate swept down. Next day with a falling flood, Clogher pool gave me two more salmon, and might have given double the number if I had stuck to it and not made a mistake by going off to a stretch which was not yet in order.

Success in this mixed salmon and white trout fishing means thinking in terms of the barometer and thermometer, height and colour of water, strength and direction of wind, rather than in terms of natural insects and rises.

Anglers new to white trout are often disappointed when their first fish are laid on the boards and think them to be out of condition. White trout are torpedo shaped, something like a mackerel, and, weight for weight, have not the shoulder or depth of a brown trout. It is like the difference between a greyhound and a foxhound. They swim much faster than a brown trout and, when first hooked, are almost as much in the air as in the water, eight successive jumps with practically no interval between them being not unusual. At each jump, down must go the rod top to avoid the chance of broken gut or a hold wrenched free, and when the fish touches the water, up it must go again to retain contact. A friend has compared this interchange between angler and fish to two mandarins exchanging compliments, but this suggests too leisured a performance. Rather is it like the quick successive engagement and disengagement between expert fencers. Now and then the timing goes wrong, and angler or fencer is caught out. Disaster does not necessarily follow. The gut may stand the strain and the hook retain its hold, though the mouth of a fresh run white trout is very tender and the hook can rip through it much more easily than with salmon or brown trout. Salmon fishermen find it difficult to appreciate this softness of mouth in a white trout. When they have accustomed themselves to strike, they strike too hard. I have seen at least two men who could lay claim to being in the master class with salmon, but who lost trout after trout by tearing the hook away.

14

THE PRIEST'S OMNIBUS

Whenever anything in our house has to be turned, squeezed, bent or extracted, a cry goes up for "The Priest's Omnibus", and some part of that paragon of tools will do the trick. This chapter tells how I came to possess it.

It had been planned not as a fishing holiday, but as one which would give my wife a rest and the children a trouble-free beach. However, the map showed a river adjacent and so a rod found its way into the car. The hotel proprietor, a German, was not encouraging. Yes, he had the fishing rights on the river, and he had heard that there were white trout and even salmon, but his guests never brought anything back but "Things so", and he indicated a three-ounce fish with dramatic finger and thumb.

The map showed that the river divided just above a bridge some two miles from the sea. Reaches below a junction are generally good, and the contours indicated a flat stretch where I might find deep pools. Next day I set out for the bridge. There was a pool sure enough, fairly deep and wide, but with banks encumbered by bushes and too much sheltered from the wind. It produced three fish, all of them under the pound. Half a mile further down, the river plunged into a close tunnel of trees, but in the interval there had been two short pools, rather too rapid, and another ending in a narrow slow-flowing tail constricted by a shingle spit. The short pools each gave a fish. The shingle tail was very calm, very exposed and very slow. I attacked it with a single fly, kneeling and fishing up as carefully as if I was nymphing on the Itchen. It yielded eight fish. With thirteen in all, from half a pound to two pounds, I returned to be greeted by a perfectly hysterical proprietor and that night all the hotel ate white trout for dinner. Clouds of incense floated around me, but I was not at ease. The proprietor evidently expected a repeat performance – any amount of repeat performances – unaware that I had been fortunate enough to catch the river at the right point of a falling flood. Next day I tried the same stretch again, and got only eight white trout, but a small salmon on top of them helped to preserve my reputation.

In Ireland whenever a salmon is hooked the countryside seems to sprout population, and while I was playing the fish the parapet of the bridge was a row of watching faces. When it was landed all of them disappeared except one, who waited while I carried up my prize. From past experience I suspected that he would be the local poacher, the very man I wanted. Poachers, whatever their methods (and in Ireland we have a nice variety), must know the places where fish lie and, being on the whole an easy-going and broad-minded lot, are not averse to giving some help to a reasonable angler. A reasonable angler is one who is wiling to pay for his information.

The conversation opened along well-known lines, congratulatory comments on his part, deprecation on mine. Then I made a monstrous error. I asked a direct question as to where were the best pools. He shrank into himself like an alarmed sea anemone and disclaimed all acquaintance with fish. Only after prolonged fencing did we find a way out. His grandfather, he said, had been a famous fisherman and apparently a very garrulous old gentleman. The grandson had a retentive memory. In the form of stories heard from his grandfather he gave me all the information I wanted, and a suitable recognition of his ancestor's prowess was not refused.

In case any reader may find himself near this river (it is the Eany in South Donegal) I may mention the two best pools to which my acquaintance introduced me. The first, on the main river, is easy of access, being directly below the next bridge above the junction. In favourable conditions it is good for two or three decent sea trout. The second, on the smaller river about half a mile above the junction, is approached deviously along a cart track, through a farm yard, and between two pig sties. For its size it is about the best sea trout pool I have met. About fifty yards long, hour-glass in shape, it has all the ugliness which characterizes the first class pool. Sea trout, when they leave the sea, prefer a lake to a river and if they cannot get to a lake, they choose a pool which is the nearest thing to a canal. Feeding little in fresh water, they have no need for a brisk stream to bring food past their noses, but they do require to conserve their energy for spawning. A fringe of water lilies along the edge is a sure sign of a good pool, for water lilies do not like a strong current any more than sea trout.

Conditions were now worsening. The river was low, the weather bright, and the wind fitful. Trout could still be caught, but they were smaller and fewer. Delicate casting, fine tackle and small bright flies were needed. Freeman's Fancy and the Gold and Magenta Bumble were the best. The proprietor eyed me with disfavour. He felt I was not really trying. When my conscience, which had slumbered while the fishing was good, woke up to remind me that this was meant to be a family holiday, and I deserted the river for a couple of days, he looked as if he would like to put me out of the hotel.

There came a night when the rain crashed against the window with a noise sufficient to waken even as heavy a sleeper as myself, and in the morning pools were everywhere. The places which had served me well up to this would have their banks under water, but I had walked a large part of the smaller river with this contingency in mind, and had picked out some spots which were likely to hold fish in a flood. White trout do not make runs as lengthy as salmon and will take a breather in the quieter parts of streams before moving on to the deep pools where they are going to settle down.

The hour-glass pool had become a lake, but, a little further down, the river ran between high clay banks in a steady flow which slackened at a turn and bore towards my side. Under the slacker water there was, I knew, a big rock which in normal times stood up well above the surface but was now invisible. A wall of gorse ran along the bank, and only at one place was there a loophole from which I could fish. As my fly swept behind the rock, there came a boil but no tightening. My next cast had the same result. Evidently the fly was coming across too quickly. He might take at the third cast, but if he did not, my chance was gone. A white trout hardly ever rises more than three times. Something had to be done to slow up the traverse of the fly.

Under the far bank the water moved noticeably slower. If the fly could be drifted down in that quieter patch till it was opposite the fish, there was a chance of bringing it more gently across. The far bank was a clay cliff bare of vegetation, and this gave me an idea. Off came the dropper. I cast my tail fly hard at the vertical clay, shooting three or four yards as I did so. Gut and six feet of line smacked against the bank and slithered down into the water, bunched, but not tangled. Now it was a question of "mending" to prevent the centre current getting a hold, and "feeding up" to allow the fly to drift down. The height of my own bank made both tactics easy and all went well. The cast straightened out, the fly took the proper course till it was level with the fish, and a final exaggerated mend allowed it to come slowly over his nose. This time there was more than a boil, and it was unmistakably a heavy fish. He made straight off downstream and round the bend, the line bearing on a clump of willow-bay half submerged by the flood. Islanded in the gorse, I had no chance to follow, and he seemed set for a return to the sea.

At last the reel drum moved more slowly, and I was able to brake. Something queer had happened. The pull was still strong, but there was a deadness about it, a lack of direct contact. In a moment the mystery was solved, for the fish exploded into the air almost at my feet. He had turned in his tracks, leaving forty-five yards of drowned line in a big loop down-stream, and could do pretty well what he liked. This was no salmon. He was everywhere – a swirl under the far bank, a gleam up-stream, and then crash, crash, crash, as he leaped into the air over and over again so rapidly that it looked as if he were bouncing off the water. There was no possibility of control till those loose yards had been recovered on to the reel, and even then I could not stop his fury. His own efforts and not any pressure from me at last exhausted him, and the rest was routine, save for the final difficulty, known to every fisherman, of landing a big fish with a short net from a high bank. It was done at last, and he lay before me a white trout of just over five pounds.

"The best trout ever I saw caught. Man, but he could lep! " My friend had emerged from the gorse, his caution temporarily abandoned in his enthusiasm. I got a couple more while the flood was high, and the next three days restored the proprietor to enthusiasm. By this my fishing was organized. The compass gave me the orientation of all the pools, and while still at the hotel, I could tell which of them the wind would be striking in a favourable way, and how the sun would be shining on the water, always an important consideration. As the best pools are widely separated, a car was necessary to get from one to the other, and a certain amount of time was taken up in jointing and disjointing the rod – (for I will never carry a rod sticking out of a window), but soon I became expert in doing this in the minimum of time. It is not necessary to detach line or cast, only to pull out enough line to allow the separated joints to be laid side by side, the cast wrapped round the bundle, and the whole put on the back seat.

The river ran down again, and with fishing at a discount we went for a drive, crossing the bridge below the junction. The water whispered over the ford only an inch or two deep; the smaller branch looked as if it were stagnant. A moorhen crept out of the sedges to enjoy the sun, flirted her white petticoats salaciously and departed with a sharp "Eeyek". Distant shots reminded me that yesterday had been the twelfth.

Our drive took us in a half circle, crossing the larger branch by a bridge some miles up-stream. I stopped to make a small adjustment to the car, while my wife looked over the parapet. She began to gesticulate, and I ran over. The river was a muddy torrent. There had been no rain on our route, but I knew what had happened. Those distant shots had been thunder, and in the steep valley of the Blue Stacks, where the river begins, the clouds had burst. With haste we might get to the junction pool before the flood.

We made it easily. Everything was as before. The moorhen repeated her turn. Silence and heat enveloped us. Then in the distance, we heard a mutter which swelled to a grumble and then to a roar as the flood burst round the bend. It came in a steep-fronted wave, thick with debris, carrying with it the pitiful carcass of a late-born lamb. The bushes bent beneath its attack, the smaller river, invaded by the water from the main branch, flowed backwards in a rapid stream, and over the ford there was now more than three feet of water. Still the river rose. There could be no fishing today, but tomorrow! Alas, by tomorrow the flood had gone. The downpour had been short and local. The river dropped as rapidly as it had risen.

The last day of our holiday came. The afternoon would be taken up with packing and preparations, but there had been rain in the night and so I was out early to get a few trout before lunch. Wind and water were perfect. Three came from the shingle tail, two from the bridge, and five from the hour-glass pool, so with about a stone of fish on my back I left the river for the last time. On the way back to the car I met a young priest, rod in hand, who asked me how I had done. I showed him. "Well," he said, "I fished this river as a lad, and now I'm back on holiday from America, and I've had three days on it, but I never saw a bag of fish like that. How did you get them?" The cast was still on my rod, the magenta and claret bumbles as droppers. Examining them, he asked whether they were not too small, and what had become of their wings. "Try them yourself," I said and gave him three or four.

Next day as I was pulling away from a Donegal garage where I had refuelled for my drive to Dublin my wife said, "Stop, there's a man running after the car and waving." I stopped and my acquaintance of yesterday came up panting. "Wait," he said, "I must get you a bottle of whisky." "But why?" I said. "Those flies of yours – I never had such a day!" I declined the whisky but he insisted I must take something as a memento. "Listen, I have a gadget – it does everything – it's American – you can't get it in this country. It's in my car." He ran back to where his car was parked, and returned with the tool. And that is the story of the Priest's omnibus.

Except for the priest, I did not meet another angler, which struck me as peculiar, so I determined to ask my friend the reason. By now we were on the best of terms. Ever since the capture of the big trout he had begun to expand, often turning up to watch me fish. I suspected at first that he wanted to head me off from places where scales and trampling betrayed the use of a net, and this may have been so, but he certainly showed a keen interest in up-stream fishing and the use of small flies, both of which were new to him. He explained the absence of other fishermen as occasioned by the belief that the river fished well only during a few hours of falling flood. Anglers from a distance found it difficult to hit off the right time, and local anglers, not having motor cars, fished only the pool nearest to them while the flood was still high and big flies were effective. When the flood ran down these flies were useless (he did not add that other methods of capture, difficult to employ in a flood, in low water became easier and more profitable than angling). As for guests at the hotel, they were accustomed to brown trout, and fished rapid water where no self-respecting white trout would lie. I had been lucky enough to tap his local knowledge. I had a car, and methods which extended the period in which trout could be caught. To his explanations I should add that the weather had on the whole been favourable, and that the run of fish was later and rather better than usual.

15

TACKLE*

Walking along the banks of a salmon river in spring, you may see half a dozen techniques at work, each with its own specially adapted equipment. A good salmon fisherman must know how to fish sunk fly or greased line, must be able to spin with Silex, multiplying, or fixed-spool reel, and must have some acquaintance with rolling a worm or drifting a shrimp on a single hook. On his choice of the method which is right for the day and the water, success may depend. Nor can the equipment for any of the methods be said to be stereotyped. Within a general framework of uniformity, there is room for experiment, discussion and dispute. Styles of casting, of working the fly or bait, of fishing a pool, vary so much that a fisherman can be recognized from the manner of his fishing long before he is near enough to be identified by his face or his clothes.

No such diversity of methods or equipment is required for white trout fishing in Connemara. Wet-fly is so much more successful than any other form of fishing that it has become almost universal. There may be a few days when the dap or the dry-fly is of service, an hour or two in high flood when a small shrimp on a single hook will interest a salmon, but the tackle used for wet-fly can easily be adapted to these occasions. As for spinning it is an abomination pardonable only when the flood

---

* During nearly the whole of my fishing life rods were made of greenheart or split cane, casts of silkworm gut, and lines of oil-dressed silk. Nowadays glass fibre and carbon fibre are taking the place of split cane, nylon has completely ousted gut, and plastic lines with various interiors are preferred to oil dressed silk. I have left most of this chapter as originally written in 1958 for it correctly represents the practice in that year but have added at the end some observations on the new materials.

is really dirty. In twenty-five years fishing of Connemara waters I have spun twice, and then for half an hour.

The equipment is very nearly standardized, so much so, indeed, that I would hesitate to describe it, were it not that inspection of rod racks and tackle cases shows that there are still many who handicap themselves by the use of unsuitable gear. Usually the mistake is to choose rods, lines and gut which are too heavy and too strong and flies which are too large and too gaudy; but I have seen the opposite mistake of using a seven-foot brook-rod and a 4x cast. Minor faults resulting in lack of balance are common.

The tackle makers have a good deal to answer for. In their effort to give popular and descriptive names to the various thicknesses of gut (the original classification was in Spanish) they invented the hierarchy of "Heavy Salmon, Light Salmon, Sea trout, Lake trout, etc." The Sea trout gut was about 7/5 or 8/5, heavier than a modern angler would use for salmon, once the rivers have fallen to summer level. Sea trout rods were proportionally over-powerful. Such tackle may be justified where the sea trout average over five pounds, but even in such Rolls-Royce waters it is unnecessary, and in ordinary waters it reduces the chance of hooking fish and destroys any excitement in playing them.

The secret of suitable tackle is balance and proportion, and the correct way of establishing the right proportion is to work from the fly back to the rod, and not, as is so often done, from the rod down to the fly. Once the sizes of fly likely to be taken by the trout are known, it is easy to find the thickness of gut necessary to make such flies swim attractively, and to pull the hook home; the gut decides the thickness of line; and the thickness of line determines the spring and strength of the rod. There is a permissible margin in every case, and room for individual preferences, but anyone who builds up his tackle in the way suggested will not fall into a major error. In Connemara, however light the wind, I never found it necessary to fish smaller than a number 12 (O.S.) lightly dressed, and the largest fly required in high water and big waves is No. 7 (O.S.). Nine-tenths of the fishing will be done with 11, 10 and 9 (O.S.). For these sizes 2x gut is correct. It makes the fly swim well and fish well, and is strong enough to sink the hook over the barb. A level cast of 2x is the most usual. I like to make two modifications. I carry a

LOUGH MELVIN, CO. LEITRIM

The lake on whose shores stood the Big House. It holds a greater variety of game fish than any other lake in Ireland—salmon, pike and four distinct species of trout. Notice the foam streaks. For some reason fishing is rarely good when these streaks are about.

(*W. N. Stokes*)

LOUGH CORRIB, CO. GALWAY

(*W. N. Stokes*)

SUNSET ON LOUGH MASK, MAYO-GALWAY

On a calm evening such as this the dryfly expert, fishing sheltered creeks and inlets, comes into his own. Fish up to eight pounds have been taken in this way.

"AT LAST"

With the first flood after a long drought, the imprisoned salmon surge up the falls. The river is the Conway, the drought that of 1959, but it illustrates exactly what the author saw on the Feugh when the drought of 1911 came to an end.

THE HEAD WATERS OF THE LIFFEY
A typical mountain stream where the trout are numberous and free rising, but small.

THE RYE WATER IN SPRING
Small limestone streams such as this hold big trout, which may be taken in Spring with rather large stream-lined flies, fished down-stream and well sunk. Notice that the point of the rod is kept low to allow the flies to sink and imitate fry.

(*J. R. Harris*)

THE KELLS BLACKWATER IN SUMMER
Another limestone stream which in summer is best fished with a dry fly.

THE MELANCHOLY PURSUIT OF DAPPING
The rods in this picture are being held too low for such a light wind.

(*J.R. Harris*)

(*W. N. Stokes*)

VANISHED EDENS

The top photograph shows the Erne, most perfect of salmon rivers, before it was submerged by a hydro-electric dam. The lower picture shows Henry Stokes, F.R.C.S., doyen of Irish fishermen fishing Costnawanny, the pool below the wood in the upper picture.

(*W. N. Stokes*)

(*T. C. Kingsmill Moore*)

A CONTRAST ON THE SLANEY

The rough stream when it is almost too low for fishing, and when it is definitely too high.

(*T. C. Kingsmill Moore*)

(*T. C. Kingsmill Moore*)

FISH WATCHING

From the rock on the left of the upper picture, sheltered behind the dwarf pine, a considerable area of the bottom of the pool can be kept under observation in low water. There are usually a couple of salmon, two or three eels and half-a-dozen trout to be watched. The lower photograph, taken from Galway Bridge, shows a collection of salmon waiting to ascend.

(*T. C. Kingsmill Moore*)

TYPES OF WATER

Rapid swirling water among boulders. Good fish lie in sheltered spots behind and in front of rocks, waiting to pounce on food as it shoots by. An easily visible fly is an advantage, and it need not be too exact an imitation. The lower picture shows a quietly rippling stream below a weir. Here the fish have more time to examine the fly, North Country patterns, with their close resemblance to flies drowned by the weir, are the most successful.

(*T. C. Kingsmill Moore*)

CONTRASTING POOLS

The upper pool, having a bottom of large rocks and irregular rock ledges, is in continuous and varied motion. It has given me dozens of trout and salmon, including a 30-pounder. Wet fly is best. The lower pool is generally so still as to require a dryfly, but when ruffled by a wind, as in the picture, wet fly can be fished. The fly has to be pulled through the water, as in lake fishing, and the stream-lined form of the Traditional tie has an advantage.

(*T. C. Kingsmill Moore*)

(*J. R. Harris*)

BARRIER FALLS

On many white trout fisheries there are falls so steep and so high that fish cannot surmount them till the slope of the water and height of ascent are reduced by a really big flood. The upper picture shows such a fall above Luggeen on the Inver system; the lower is the fall below Derreen on the Cashla system.

(*T. C. Kingsmill Moore*)

(*T. C. Kingsmill Moore*)

WHERE WHITE TROUT WILL LIE AND WHERE THEY WILL NOT

The upper picture is Clogher pool, and it shows all the characteristic dullness and featurelessness of a first-class white trout pool. The dark spots on the water in the foreground are water lily pads turned up by the wind. The lower picture shows a series of cascades and rapids a little lower down the river. White trout can run these in moderate water, but never stay in such a vigorous flow.

(*T. C. Kingsmill Moore*)

THE BUNDORRAGH
A lovely little sea-trout and salmon river flowing out of the wild glen of Delphi in Mayo.

THE PATH TO CLOGHER
It traverses part of one of the block-moraines which cover much of the hillsides. Sometimes these great masses of rocks are jumbled together so chaotically and the rocks are so superimposed, three or four deep, that only a goat or a fox can get through them.

UPPER AND LOWER PORTIONS OF THE BUTT OF FERMOYLE

The "butt" of a lake is where the river enters it, and is always one of the pick places for sea-trout and salmon. The butt is best fished from the piers shown on the left of the lower picture, and the ability to cast a really long line is a great advantage.

(T. C. Kingsmill Moore)

THE ERRIFF, CO. MAYO

A salmon and sea-trout river famous for a century and a half. The angler is fishing the throat of a pool,
generally the best place for salmon, but too rapid for white trout.

AN EVENING'S WORK WITH THE DRYFLY ON THE LAKE

The photograph was taken by the light of the headlamps of a car. The trout are from $5\frac{1}{2}$ lbs. downwards.

"tail" of 3x to attach to the end when the conditions are such as to require the use of a No. 3 hook. This is a four yard cast, which makes it necessary to reel some feet of gut through the top ring when netting the fish. If a loop is whipped at the end of the line, and the cast attached by interlocking the loops it is perfectly safe to do this as there will never be a jam; but there will be a little extra strain put on the gut by the friction of the rings; and therefore it is wise to make the top yard of the cast of 1x, followed by two yards of 2x, with a "tail" of 3x kept in reserve for a calm day.

Two objections, mutually inconsistent, have been urged against a cast constructed in this way – first that it is too weak, and second that it is too strong.

Those who fault it for being too weak point out that when fishing for white trout you may at any time hook a salmon, and that 2x gut will not be strong enough to stop a salmon from careering into weeds and sedges. This is perfectly true. No gut finer than 6/5 would stop the first rush of even a small salmon, and gut of that thickness would result in empty baskets. If a salmon is hooked near reeds and determines to go into them, let him go, and take your time. Unless he fetches a compass so as to collect a mass of resistance in the belly of the line, or yanks a dropper firmly into a tough stalk, guile and cajolery will work him into open water. Usually however, a salmon, when hooked, stays quiet for a few seconds, sufficient to allow a good boatman to place the boat between the fish and danger, so that when the rush comes it will be directed out into the lake where 2x or even 3x gut will kill any salmon likely to be met. Salmon in these fisheries are not large, averaging about seven pounds. Anything over ten pounds is unusual. I have been broken three times by fish who made for weeds or rushes the moment they were hooked, but never by a fish once he was in open water.

There is this much to be said for those who favour a stronger cast – it is just as inexpert to use tackle which is needlessly fine as to use tackle which is needlessly coarse. If the circumstances are such as to call for Nos. 8 or 7 (O.S.), these large flies will swim and fish better on 1x, and half drawn or quarter drawn are not out of place. When wind is blowing half a gale fish are not scared by thicker gut, and the extra strain which can be exerted will save the labour of the boatman when a salmon makes away up-wind.

Now for the second criticism, that 2x is unnecessarily strong, and that 3x or even 4x is adequate and more sporting. There is a great deal of snobbery in over-emphasis on fine tackle. Its advocates are anxious to impress their audience with their superior skill and delicacy of handling. Anyone who does not lose his head can land a large trout or even a salmon on 3x gut in open water, but it takes more time and causes the fish more distress. It is not necessary to use such fine tackle, for sea trout are not abnormally gut-shy, and probably fewer fish will be hooked, since the flies will not fish as well as on gut of more substance. The tail fly will swim with the hook slanted downwards, sagging at the neck, while the droppers will not protrude but will cling to the main cast and wind round it and generally make a nuisance of themselves.

For the range of flies and gut mentioned what kind of line is necessary? Of course it must be the best quality of oil-dressed waterproof silk. Nylon lines are too light and too bulky for their weight. If all the fishing is to be done from a boat the line can be level, but probably there will be pools and butts to be fished from the shore, where longer and more accurate casting is required, and this calls for a taper. The thickness usually known as "light dry-fly" is best. I have just put a micrometer on mine, and it is .040 of an inch in the centre and .023 at the point, corresponding to 19 and 23½B. wire gauge.

Any first class reel of aluminium alloy weighing about seven ounces, and with a contracted drum of about 3½ inches in diameter to allow a quick recovery, will do. But get the very best quality. The various fly reels which I have now in use are from twenty-five to fifty years old, some of them having been picked up secondhand. They are all the best products of their respective manufacturers, and have never caused a moment's trouble. Cheaper reels have had to be discarded after a few seasons. The rod should be able to cast up to twenty-five yards at a pinch, should have backbone to deal with heavy fish, and above all must be gentle in strike. Any light dry-fly rod of about ten feet long answers this description, but have nothing to do with the heavier dry-fly rods, butt-actioned with a powerful top joint, which were popular about the turn of the century. Such rods will wrench the hook out of fish as soft-mouthed as a freshly-run white trout, and in a large fish may break the gut on the strike. I have seen a fisherman of great experience break cast after cast in good fish. The rod was of the wrong type, and from a long course of salmon fishing he had lost his touch with trout.

My own favourite rod is of a pattern no longer made. While strong in the bottom joint, it has a top joint no thicker than that of a light nine foot wet-fly rod. At my request the manufacturers made the last eight inches of the top joint even softer than was usual, to mollify the strike. It will cast over twenty-five yards, kills a big fish quickly, is delicate with a half-pounder, and is the best rod for hooking that I have ever handled. Ten feet long, it weighs only seven and three-quarter ounces, and, as most of the weight is in the butt and the action in the middle joint, it is very light to fish with.

The simple and easily procured equipment which I have described will serve every purpose for salmon and sea trout in Connemara and the West generally. Having said this let me confess that I always take with me, and occasionally use, a double-handed trout rod twelve and a half feet long. The makers call it a trout rod, but to my mind it is a light salmon rod, ideal for greased line fishing on big rivers in May. In Connemara, when the flood is still high, salmon fishing is at its best and sea trout fishing at a discount. Now is the time to fish the pools, and to try the butts and other selected parts of the lakes from the shore, in the hope of a salmon. Long casting may be necessary – the wind is often violent and adverse and a salmon when hooked may take it into his head to go far out into the lake with the force of the river current behind him. The ten-foot rod is adequate, but the light salmon rod with its greater reserve of strength and casting power, makes for luxury. The rest of the equipment is stepped up proportionately – a heavy tapered dry-fly line, half-drawn casts, and Nos. 8 or 7 (O.S.) flies.

Leaving aside for the moment some more controversial points, such as whether to use gut or nylon and the best patterns of flies, I turn to minor but essential equipment, and here I think is the place to voice a protest against the ways of the manufacturers. I have spent my life looking for the ideal fly box, the ideal net, and the ideal boat cushion. I found them all. They were perfect. But when I came to look for replacements – even the ideal wears out in time – I was told that the articles were no longer manufactured. In the hope that these despairing cries may reach the hearts of the former makers I shall describe them.

The fly-box was the Wheatley-Kilroy which used to be stocked by Messrs. Farlow. The flies were held in coiled springs, held firmly, held without crushing, always on view, easy to select, easy to remove or replace. They did not rust or fall out. A large stock could be carried, and the size of the coiled springs could be varied to suit hooks of different ranges. No other box, book, clip, or contraption combined all these virtues, and now "we regret that this box is no longer procurable".

Connemara gillies do not like using a gaff, preferring a net, even for salmon. This means that the net must be strong and fairly capacious. At the same time, as there is much walking to do between lakes, it must be easily portable and collapsible. For use in a boat it should have a four-foot handle, and for use on a river, when there is no gillie and it has to be slung, there should be another handle not more than two feet long. The V-shaped collapsible type is the most suitable, but it must be strong, light, rigid, and certain in action. All these requisites were to be found in one pattern. It never failed to open or close when it was called on, and never did either when it was not. It was big yet light, strutted so as to be rigid when open, and provided with a fool-proof locking ring that prevented it from turning in the handle. When I wanted a second of these nets, the manufacturers replied, "we have long since ceased to produce this pattern". Two months later I received a note that in stocktaking a single specimen of this incomparable net had been discovered, but it was the last. Did I still want it? My reply was a telegram threatening an international incident if anyone else got it.

Rain in Connemara is frequent and heavy, so the bow and stern seats are often not only wet but swilling with water. The weight of the body drives the water up through the thickest mackintosh, unless you are raised a little above the wet, and any ordinary cushion is useless for it becomes no better than a sponge. Someone thought of the idea of making a cushion of rubber strips about an eighth of an inch thick and a little over an inch wide, set on edge, and fastened together into six-sided cells like a honeycomb. The rain ran down the mackintosh and fell through the honeycomb on to the seat, while the fisherman, perched on top of the honeycomb, remained dry and comfortable. For fifteen years I have not been able to renew the cushion which I originally purchased. No one seems to have heard of the invention.

If there is no great distance to walk, the best anti-rain combination is a short mackintosh coat and a heavy full mackintosh skirt, with some form of souwester. This, worn with gum boots and with the aid of the honeycomb cushion, will avoid the fisherman's trade mark, a wet behind. If there is much rough walking to be done – and there generally is – such an outfit is too heavy and too hot. The light anti-gas clothing issued to A.R.P. wardens during the war was excellent, but supplies are now exhausted. Some of the medium quality plastic materials could be made up in the form of a short jacket and trousers, just long enough to cover the tops of gum-boots, with the seat reinforced against wear. This could be rolled up and carried in the fishing bag, would be cheap, and should last for two or three seasons. Button holes and button attachments would need to be very heavily reinforced, as plastic rips easily, and here again the manufacturers have never paid sufficient attention to the needs of the customer.

Gum-boots are universally worn. They should be chosen with thick ribs to the soles, so as to save the fatigue involved in slipping about where the going is slushy and greasy.

Some form of anti-midge cream or liquid is an absolute necessity, for somewhere about the Miocene period Connemara midges got crossed with jungle hornets, and now combine the size of one with the sting of the other. Mylol is the best preparation I have discovered.

What are the main changes in tackle which have come about in the last 20 years? Nylon has finally and conclusively ousted gut. Thickness for thickness it is stronger and less visible. The early specimens of nylon were only obtainable in short lengths and were liable to weak spots and sudden failures. All this has now gone. Nylon can be obtained in lengths up to 100 yards and is so reliable that testing is more a routine than a necessity.

Gut thickness was measured in "mils", or thousandths of an inch. 2x, 1x, 0x, on the *Fishing Gazette* scale were respectively 9, 10, and 11 mils. Nylon is measured in thousandths of a millimetre and the corresponding numbers are 22, 24, 26. Because of the absence of knots and its lesser visibility 24 may be used where 2x was recommended and in turbulent conditions or when larger flies are needed for any reason 26 or 28 are not amiss. Sea trout may be moody, captious, unpredictable but I do not think they are gut shy, certainly less gut shy than brown trout.

The fashion has grown up of selling nylon not by number but in terms of alleged breaking strain. A standard based on diameter is more satisfactory. The important thing is to select the diameter which will make the size of fly swim correctly. The fly must not droop at the neck but there should be a certain degree of flexibility.

The only disadvantage of nylon is that we have had to learn new knots. Those old favourites, the figure of eight and the Cairnton, were completely satisfactory with gut but with nylon, owing to its increased elasticity, they are liable to slip. What are we to use instead for tying on our flies? For sizes 11 (O.S.) and smaller the single Turle is satisfactory; for really large spring salmon flies Stanley Barnes's Two Circle Turle is secure. The Two Circle is, however, not an easy knot to tie well and is clumsy looking when finished. For intermediate sizes I recommend the One-and-a-half Circle Turle which is neat, swims the fly well and which I have never known to slip. This knot is not illustrated in Stanley Barnes's *Anglers Knots* and should be better known. Here is a short description. Take a down eyed hook of suitable size, pass the nylon through the eye, make the usual Turle loop and pass the loop up over the fly. If you were to pull on the standing part now you would have the ordinary Turle. Do not pull on the standing part. Instead, holding the eye of the fly and the over-hand knot which made the Turle loop close together between right thumb and forefinger, take the far side of the Turle loop in your left hand and wind it towards you, over, down under and up again, passing the loop a second time over the fly. Now pull on the standing part to close the loop taking care that the projecting end of the original over-hand knot lies back along the shank of the hook and is trapped under the loops. The circles should lie immediately behind and touching the eye of the hook.

Another knot for attaching nylon to a fly, which is gaining increased favour, is the half-blood jam, tied with four coils. This is safe but not so elegant as the Turles. It has, however, a certain advantage for tying on dropper flies. The one-and-a-half circle Turle needs a fair length of nylon to tie comfortably, it takes up a good deal of nylon in the knot itself, and it is difficult to undo. Probably you will only manage one change of a dropper fly before the dropper has got too short to use. The half-blood jam needs less nylon to tie, uses less nylon in the knot and a snip of the scissors through the coils gets rid of it.

Both the blood knot for joining lengths of nylon and the half-blood jam for attaching nylon to the eye of hook or swivel have recently come under criticism on the ground that they slip. All I can say is that I have never known either of these kots to slip when I tied them myself. It is necessary to see that the coils are properly bedded and for this a liberal supply of saliva is a great help. One of the more severe critics, Mr. Richard Walker, has devised a new knot which he calls the Grinner and which he claims to be stronger than the blood knots and never to slip. It is illustrated in the 1978 Autumn number of the *Flyfishers' Journal*. The half Grinner is made like this. Start as you would for the half-blood. When you have completed three coils round the standing part bring the end in a big loop up to where your coils began and make three more coils away from the eye and inside this big loop. Tighten by pulling first on the free end and then on the standing part. This knot should do all that is claimed for it, but is more clumsy than the half-blood.

With gut, dropper lengths were usually attached to the main cast by a larkshead loop, either tied above a knot or so that the sides of the loop fell on different sides of the knot. With nylon there is no need for knots and so this method has been abandoned. Most people now cut the cast and then retie it using a double over-hand water knot and leaving one end long enough to use as a dropper. This gives a poor strutting to the dropper, very slightly weakens the main cast and produces a dropper which after a change or two of the fly, becomes too short and necessitates recutting and reknotting the main cast.

I much prefer the following method. Make a harness loop in the main cast. The loop can be adjusted so as to be very small, just large enough to admit a match. Attach the dropper length to this by a four turn half-blood jam. The dropper is well strutted out from the main cast and I have never known it to slip. When it gets too short a snip through the coils removes it and a new length is tied on to the harness loop.

The loop at the end of a cast was usually made by a single or double over-hand loop. This has now been superseded by the Blood bight, which is stronger.

All these knots except the one-and-a-half circle Turle and the Grinner are illustrated in Stanley Barnes's *Anglers Knots*.

Lines have undergone a complete change and, I submit, a change for the worse. Gone are the lines of oil dressed silk and instead we are offered lines made of various types of plastic and plastic coated. They come in four types, floating, sink tip, sinking and rapid sinking and they faithfully perform in the way indicated by their description. All these types can be necessary. For dry fly the whole line must float. Though in a fair breeze it may be an advantage to have your top dropper furrowing the surface, in a very light breeze it is a mistake to allow your flies to skate and the sink tip must be called on. Finally there are some days when, for one reason or another, probably a rapid change in temperature between adjacent layers of water, white trout take better with the fly well sunk and we must use a sinking line. With modern lines this means carrying three or four reels, or at least three or four drums, an intolerable burden. With the old oil dressed silk all you needed was a minute tin of a suitable grease and a half ounce bottle holding water to which a few drops of detergent had been added. Properly greased, which means an economy of lubricant and an excess of elbow grease to polish it home, such a line will float all day. If you want a sinking tip rub down the last two yards with a rag moistened from your detergent bottle. For a sinking line you have only to extend your rub for about twelve yards up the line. Add to this that the silk line casts more easily and accurately than plastic lines and that it lasts much longer. Oil dressed silk lines used to last me for ten years if properly looked after while modern lines are often cracked after two or three seasons.

Rod materials are in a stage of transition. The materials of my fishing years were greenheart and split cane. Greenheart could make a very delightful trout rod and older salmon fishermen were faithful to their Grant Vibrations and Castle Connells. But greenheart of the first quality has become increasingly difficult to obtain and greenheart rods wear out sooner than split cane. Split cane will, literally, last a life time. (In the sixties I was still fishing a 16 foot Hi Regan which had left the manufacturer in the 19th century and a 14 foot Gold Medal which had been a wedding present to the father of a friend in 1905.) My trout rod, bought in 1928, is still in mint condition though it has had one new top. Split cane had no serious rival.

Now split cane is giving way to rods made of glass fibre, carbon fibre, or a mixture of both. I have no experience of them but angling friends, on whose skill and judgment I am prepared to rely, tell me that they are as good or better than the best split cane. They are certainly lighter, but lightness can be a somewhat over-rated advantage. Anyone purchasing a new rod should insist on being allowed to try it out on water so as to make sure that it suits his personal style and physique. Purchasers do not realise the great differences there are in rods. They may have their main action in the butt, the middle or the tip. The action may be stiff and very rapid, moderate and slower, or noticeably gentle. What suits one man may be all wrong for another. A friend of mine who cast chiefly from his wrist, swore by a butt-actioned Pope, which was anathema to me who use chiefly the elbow and shoulder. The enormous increase in anglers fishing from the shores of reservoirs and lakes led to a demand for rods which can cast a very long line and the consequent cult of the stiff rapid-actioned rod. There is no dispute that in the hands of a skillful caster of powerful physique such rods will cast the greatest distance but they need very accurate timing and strong muscles to produce the necessary rapid acceleration over a relatively short arc of travel. The ordinary mortal will find casting easier and more pleasant with a rod of moderate action and he will probably cast further than he could with a stiff rod. In a boat the stiff rod is quite out of place.

To emphasise the desirability of trying out a rod on water may I mention a personal experience. When, in 1928, I wanted to try a rod, chiefly for use from a boat for brown and white trout, I made my requirements known to Messrs. Hardy and they sent over to their Dublin agent six rods for me to try out. I spent a very pleasant afternoon on the shore of a small lake doing so. All were first class rods and I could make a fair fist of casting with any of them but one was, for me, outstanding. In use it seemed not so much an extension of my body as part of my body itself. Yet, of the 32 trout rods listed, with descriptions, in the catalogue it would have been about the last I would have chosen from the description. Nor would I have chosen it from trial in a shop. It needed a line attached to bring out its virtues. So do not buy the fashionable rod or the one which the shopman, probably quite honestly, recommends. Insist on a trial and choose the one that suits you and your requirements.

16

FLIES AND TACTICS

Flies? There are innumerable patterns from which to choose and plenty of scope for personal preferences. Provided that the size is correct and certain general principles kept in mind the exact pattern is not of such very great importance.

White trout flies should be dressed on a hook with a wide gape, so as to take as big a grip as possible. A wide gape means that there is increased leverage at the bend, and therefore the wire of the hook should be extra strong. White trout prefer a compact, chunky, thick-set body, the antithesis of the slinky type of fly used for greased-line salmon fishing. Fish winged flies at tail, and hackle or bumble patterns on the droppers. Choose dark colours rather than light, rich colours rather than gaudy, rough bodies in preference to smooth.

The fish do seem to single out particular colours on certain days and in certain places, and the factors which govern their choice appear to be the nature of the bottom, the light, the kind of sky, the colour of the water and the length of time that has elapsed since the fish left the sea. Flies therefore can best be discussed in broad categories of colour.

Black. Though black is not strickly a colour but the absence of all colours, it is convenient to treat it as a colour, for from beginning to end of the season black flies are probably the most successful. Everyone has heard of the Connemara Black, of which there are several dressings, the simplest being a black seal-fur body, ribbed silver, jay hackle, and mallard wing. I do not rank it high among the black flies and after lengthy trial have discarded it. For a tail fly my choice is the Kingsmill, Watson's Fancy, or Black and Silver. Doing my best to discount personal predilections I still think that the Kingsmill is the best fly for

Connemara fish, and is is particularly good where the bottom of the lake is dark and peaty. If the bottom is sandy, or sand and rock intermixed (parts of Lough Inagh on the Ballinahinch system and Lough Curreel on the Inver fishery come to mind) Black and Silver may be better. This fly has the tail-half silver, the front-half black, a black hackle, and a very light mixed under-wing with mallard over it, and is a fly with more sparkle than the Kingsmill. Butcher, with an all silver body, black hackle, and blue-black duck wing, fishes well in the same surroundings as Black and Silver, and is rightly popular. Watson's Fancy with its splash of scarlet in the tail half – all the rest of the dressing is black as night – is always good, and particularly good towards the end of the season.

These flies have corresponding hackle patterns which can be used as droppers. Thus the Black Zulu reproduces the character of Watson's Fancy; Silver Zulu (with a blue tail instead of a red, or no tail at all) echoes Black and Silver; and Black Pennell consorts happily with Kingsmill. There are other worthy black flies – Teal and Black can stake a claim – but anyone who selects from the varieties mentioned will not go wrong.

Claret. Next in general utility to black comes claret, and for fishermen claret embraces three colours, a raucous and offensive magenta, a true rich claret (the colour of a good burgundy) and a blackish claret which is a traditional Irish colour. As the season progresses and the fish are longer in fresh water, their preference shifts from magenta to claret, and then on to black-claret. For a tail fly nothing beats that Peninsular veteran, Claret and Mallard. If the body fur is magenta, the hackle should be magenta and the ribbing should be silver tinsel; but for the other colours a black hackle and gold tinsel ribbing are best. For droppers, Claret Bumble and Magenta Bumble. Of the other claret patterns the only one worth mentioning is Claret and Jay.

Blue. Here again there are two colours to be considered, a light Cambridge blue and a rather dark gentian blue. The light blue is valuable only on bright days in the early part of the season, when sometimes, though by no means always, it can be very good indeed. Teal, Blue and Silver is the best combination, and there is the corresponding bumble, dressed with a silver body and teal, badger cock, and blue hackles. There is also a dressing erron-eously called Blue Zulu, with the body of pale blue silk ribbed with broad silver, and a black hackle tied only at the shoulder. Pale blue is more a special-occasion than a general-utility colour, but the darker blue for general-utility ranks next after black and claret. The only winged fly which uses this colour for the body is the Glenicmurrin Blue. Among hackled patterns, a friend has done well with a fly which has a thick body of blue chenille and a black hackle, and "The Bruiser" is a most effective bumble.

These three colours form the working palette of the white trout angler, continually in use and responsible for four-fifths of the fish. Green may be ignored. Golden olive and all shades of yellow, so invaluable for brown trout, will take fish, especially in high water, but need not be carried. There are, however, certain colours which are so valuable on special occasions that they cannot be left out, and a few flies which do not fall conveniently under any colour classification.

Orange and fiery brown may be needed when the water is deeply coloured, and the two best patterns are Orange Grouse, which needs no description, and Keating Killer, a fiery brown with prominent jungle cock in the wings. Grey, sometimes indispensable, is represented by Grey Monkey and the Grey Ghost bumble. The conditions which call for grey have already been described in earlier chapters. Silver and gold tinsel bodies are for blue skies and sun. As the season progresses the silver tinsel of such flies as Butcher, or Teal Blue and Silver, give place to gold, and the only gold tinsel winged fly which earns its place in the fly-box is the vulgar but successful Freeman's Fancy. I tied a bumble echo of Freeman's Fancy once, a thing with a gold body, orange tail and hackles of red landrail and magenta, and Captain Wheeler, who then owned Inver, reported that on a bright August day it succeeded when no other flies were taken.

Of the flies which do not yield to any particular classification, two must receive mention because of their success. The first is a wet Daddy-long-legs, mousy-coloured body, rusty dun hackle, and long legs of knotted fibres from a cock pheasant's tail. The other dog-of-no-particular-breed-but-nevertheless-an-excellent-ratter   is the worm fly, (so called), which consists of two Bracken Clocks tied on No. 3 or No. 4 hooks, and mounted tandem-fashion on a piece of gut so that there is a space of about a quarter of an inch between the hooks. It used to be a very successful tail fly in September, especially off rocky shores. Does this queer combination represent anything? It may be a coincidence but in

September the bogs are crawling with woolly-bear caterpillars, and the peacock herl bodies of the worm fly with their long sepia hackles are, when in the water, an excellent imitation of these hairy creatures. One sunny day, when looking idly at the reflection of a rock in the water, I was surprised to see two cater-pillars crawling about on the underside of an overhanging surface from which they could easily have dropped into the mouths of waiting trout. But would trout tackle such a choking mass? I attached some caterpillars to dapping hooks and tried them on the surface and sunk below it, but without any success, and another intriguing theory disappeared.

It is probable that every experienced angler for white trout will miss from this list of flies some pattern in which he has particular faith, and it would be easy to extend it. But it is, if anything, too long. As the seasons pass, the temptation to crowd the fly-box with patterns that have proved useful on odd occasions, becomes easier to resist, and we tend to concentrate on the varieties which have proved their worth in foul and fair weather. Nowadays I rely almost entirely on the Kingsmill, and the Claret and Blue Bumbles, and some others do the same. Only if these patterns fail, or if the prevailing conditions point clearly to the need of another pattern, do I change.

I have not dealt with specific imitations, the use of which is narrowly limited. If there should be a rise of olives or sedges in sufficient numbers to warrant the use of an imitation, any of the standard attempts at reproduction will serve. White trout have not the habit of scrutiny which a chalk stream trout develops. They are D'Artagnans, and act in a brave fury of impulse. Nor is there any need to trouble about special patterns for salmon, as salmon take the ordinary white trout patterns as well as any. A fancy for more elaborate dressings can be satisfied by carrying a few small Silver Doctors, Claret Jays, and Orange Grouses, in the salmon patterns of those flies.

Tactics! Most of what has been said about the technique of lake fishing for brown trout is applicable to the white trout lake, but there are certain modifications. White trout seem to be more sensitive than brown to the presence of a boat and to the disturb-ance caused by oars. In the sea they are the prey of fish-eating sharks which abound in these waters, of the herring hog, the tope and the big conger. The loom of a boat must be very like a shark overhead, and the swirl of an oar suggests the disturbance of a conger's tail. The explanations may be imaginative, but it is certain that any unnecessary movement of boat or oar should be avoided. Casting from a boat which is being rowed up wind is rarely successful except on rough days, though there is no harm in trying it as the boat has to be worked back to the head of a drift, and while this is being done the time may as well be used in a way which might produce a fish. But all the methods of drifting which put a run on the boat are to be avoided. In a white trout lake there will be much less water to fish than is covered in a day in Corrib, though it will be more heavily stocked with potentially rising fish. Every part of the lake which is suitable for fishing must be covered in close parallel drifts, arranged, according to the prevailing wind, so as to leave no unfished lanes between them and yet not to overlap. This calls for some planning between angler and boatman. The smaller the lake the more important is it to keep the drifts tightly together. Derreen used at one time to be fished without oars. The angler fished over the stern while the boat was allowed to drift very slowly down wind restrained by a mackerel line which was fastened to the prow and paid out as required by the gillie standing on the bank. To start another drift, the boat was hauled back quietly by the line, and the gillie moved down the bank for a yard or two, and another drift was begun. In this way the lake would be fished closely with the smallest possible disturbance of water. The method worked only with an unvarying wind. If the wind was inclined to veer a few points in either direction, the drifts could not be kept parallel, and some water was missed while other places were fished twice.

I always prefer to fish alone in a boat. A plank is placed from gunwale to gunwale just in front of the stern boards, and I sit on this facing the stern. The boatman can work the boat into every nook among reeds and rocks, and I can cast all around me. If it is a stormy day the boat can be kept head to wind and allowed to drop back slowly. Lastly, there is no need of the awkward turn of the body which, when you are drifting sideways, is necessary to bring the fish up wind of the boat.

With white trout the strike must be quick, controlled, delicate, and must be varied according to the way in which the fish takes – coming in, going away, sideways, or straight up and down. If the fish takes as he is going away from you, it is necessary only to hold against him, and a hard strike can cause a break; but if he

takes while coming in towards you, the strike must be very firm
or the hook will not go home above the barb. When the fish takes
sideways to the boat, following a dragging fly, there should be a
fractional delay or you may pull the fly away from him; and if he
jumps clear of the water and comes down on the fly the temptation to strike must be resisted till he has disappeared under the
water. Striking is akin to shooting. There must be an instant
assessment of motion, and a corresponding allowance, and as in
shooting, even the most skilful have their off days.

In no other form of fishing is it so necessary to keep perfectly
balanced, never to raise the rod above an angle of forty-five
degrees, and to recover the line by drawing in with the unengaged
hand rather than by raising the rod. Striking must be done
partially by the rod and partly by a pull with the left hand. You
will hear it said that it is unnecessary to strike white trout. It is
true that a big white trout will often hook himself, but smaller
fish must be struck. I once took over the instruction of a complete novice. He learned to cast and work his flies rapidly enough,
but nothing would persuade him to strike and in consequence he
did not hook one fish in a dozen rises.

A slow and steady draw is usually most successful with white
trout, while salmon prefer a more jerky motion. There are, however, occasions when it pays to strip the flies through the water
as rapidly as you can, as this seems to stimulate a dormant chasing
instinct. When the wind is light the flies are best drawn across
the waves; when it is heavy, draw the flies sideways parallel to the
troughs. Whether to draw from right to left, or from left to right,
must be discovered by experiment; for the correct direction varies
with the light and the day.

Many of the lakes have beds of tall rushes and trout will lie
in clear patches among the stalks. The flies must be dropped
accurately, and if a fish takes, he can usually be bustled the yard
or two into more open water and then allowed to play himself
out. It pays always to use a switch cast which makes the flies last
longer, inspires confidence in your boatman, who has no fear of
being hooked, and, because the flies are longer in the water, tends
to catch more trout.

Dry-fly is hardly ever necessary but may be tried on calm days
and slow river pools. White trout take a dry-fly much better if it
is dragging, and in a lake it is a good plan to twitch it along the

surface in short jerks. Pattern I have found to be unimportant –
a small bumble is as good as anything.

Never go in to lunch if the trout are rising well. White trout
will go off the rise suddenly and completely and you must make
the most of the time when they are inclined to move. In the
record day for Clogher lunch was taken while the trout were still
active. After lunch not a trout stirred.

Short rising! This is a topic which I have been shelving, for
I cannot supply the answer. There are two types of short rising.
The first occurs in July and early August with fresh run fish,
normally of the smaller type. On a day which seems almost
perfect you will rise fish nearly every cast, but only about one
in three or four will be hooked, and that one will generally go
free after a couple of jumps. I have tried innumerable remedies.
A long-shanked hook, with the dressing confined to the front or
even quarter of the hook and kept small, is a help, but only a
help. Some people attach a diminutive triangle to a length of gut
which keeps it an inch or so behind the fly. This will foul-hook
a percentage of short rises, but it is not fair fishing and I have
always refused to try it. I can only suggest that you use very
small flies and experiment, first with allowing them to sink well
and drawing them very slowly, and then with the opposite tactic
of raking them fast along the surface. Sometimes one method
gives results, sometimes the other. There is no hard and fast rule,
nor are the results anything to boast about.

In the first kind of short rising I think the trout do not want
the fly and are only playing. There is a second kind of short
rising, usually confined to larger fish and the month of September,
when the fish is eager for the fly but owing to some peculiarity of
the light finds difficulty in taking it. He may often be seen swimming round looking for the fly he has missed. The remedy is to
cast again at once. You will get another rise, frequently another
miss. Cast a third time, and even a fourth. You will have to pull
in a yard or two of line between each cast, but you are likely to
get your fish in the end. I remember a morning on Clogher when
five successive fish, none of them less than one and a half pounds,
were all caught on the third or fourth cast. When making the
second and subsequent casts pull your flies sideways, parallel to
the boat and at right angles to the drift. The trout will see them,
whip round, and charge after them apparently with furious

anxiety to take. They seem indeed almost over-eager, which may account for their bad marksmanship.

In western rivers the white trout are to be found almost exclusively in still, deep pools which require a wind, preferably an up-stream wind, to ruffle the surface. Whenever possible these pools should be fished across and up-stream. Keep well back from the bank and cast so that the tail-fly nearly hits the opposite bank, rather up-stream from where you are standing. Then raise the rod and bring the cast across stream with the droppers in the skin of the water. Do not worry about drag: it attracts the attention of white trout and they do not object to it, especially if there is a good wind. When you have brought the cast into your bank, move up a couple of yards and repeat the procedure till you have covered the taking portions of the pool.

If there is no wind you may still get a fish or two in the glassy glide of the tail. Here it is better to use only one fly, fished more up-stream and without drag.

When the flood is still high and the water moving more rapidly, it may be easier to fish down-stream, and either of two methods may be successful. In the first, the flies are brought across, rather rapidly, on the surface with pronounced drag; in the second, they are fished as deeply as possible and with the minimum of drag. Some days one method works best, some days the other.

Only once, in dead low water and hot sun, did I find white trout ready to take in a rapid stream. Lack of oxygen had enticed them away from their more usual haunts.

17

THE COUNTRY OF THE CASHLA

Down the west coast of Ireland, from the top of Donegal to the town of Galway, a succession of small rivers tumble down the mountain sides and make their way through bogland to the sea. All of them have a run of sea trout and most of them a fair number of salmon. Where there is no lake at the head, or in the course, fishing is confined to a few days, sometimes only a few hours, of falling flood! but if there is a lake or, as is not unusual, a string of lakes, the run-off is delayed and the lakes provide fishing of varying quality throughout the season. The main problems are identical – correct estimation of the upward progress of the fish and of the nature and effect of each flood, correct choice of water to fish according to the prevailing wind and weather – but the answers vary somewhat with the topography of each river. Not till you have walked a river from source to mouth, examined the watershed, and done a certain amount of sounding in the lakes, can you hope to make the most of your opportunities.

Though I have fished well over a dozen of these river-lake complexes I can claim complete intimacy with only one, the upper Cashla or Fermoyle fishery. I visited it nearly every year for twenty years, as guest or paying guest of four successive owners, and with friends rented the lodge and fishery for short periods on numerous occasions. Nearly all the rest of this book is devoted to this fishery and the lessons it tried to teach me, lessons which, with minor modifications apply to all these western fisheries. Fermoyle is now let out in daily rods for a moderate sum, and an account of its characteristics may be helpful to those who come after me.

The north shore of Galway bay is bordered by a belt of

158

granite eight to ten miles wide, sheeted over by bog, intersected by rivers, and sprinkled with lakes of every size. Most of it is low lying, but between the Screeb and Spiddal rivers it rolls up in wave on wave to form a moorland plateau which at its greatest height crosses the thousand foot contour. Through the heart of this plateau the river Cashla carves a ten mile course to reach the sea at Costello.

It is a desolate country, the haunt of peregrine and raven, of wild goat and blue mountain hare. For fifty square miles when I first knew it there was no dwelling, no cultivation, not even a tree.* On the surrounding lowland a few houses huddled into tiny villages and a finger of habitation probed upwards towards the fishing lodge of Fermoyle, but on the upland proper, man had never been able to establish himself. He had tried. There were the ruins of two lodges, and a cottage which had sought shelter from the elements and the evil spirits behind a square rampart of fuchsia, but the elements, or as some said, the hostile presences of the land, had burnt or battered them down in a few years. Only the sod shelters where the night watchers rested in the spawning season bore witness to man's existence.

Save for the growth of bog the country is as the ice left it, and marks of the ice are everywhere. A glacier taking its source from the Twelve Pins swept south eastward over the end of Galway bay to the estuary of the Shannon. In its advance it scooped out hollows which are now lakes and scraped the countryside as bare as a bald head. Down by the coast where the bog has been cut away you may see acres of smooth planed granite with here and there deep grooves where some boulder, held in the sole of the glacier as a diamond in a glass cutter's tool, rent its way across the foundation rock. Retreating, the ice left moraine dams which formed further lakes, and covered its earlier work with a piled up chaos of erratic boulders of every size from a child's head to a cottage. Then after an interval of drier climate, the bog took over. In the valleys it grew deep, lapping slowly up the sides of the megaliths and eventually covering them, but on the flanks of the hills you may still see the great masses of rocks strewn haphazard on each other, formless, truculent, and in places almost untraversable. The bog did more than merely cover the desolation

---

* In the last few years a considerable amount of afforestation has been attempted and the character of the landscape has in places been greatly changed by this.

which the ice had left. It built up into a spongy blanket from six to twelve feet thick, which allows a watershed of not more than forty square miles to maintain a river and fourteen white trout lakes.

The properties of peat are peculiar and should be understood by every western fisherman who wants to forecast the probable conditions of a lake or stream which may be hidden miles away in the mountains. Peat will go on absorbing moisture till it reaches saturation, at a point when water constitutes nearly niney-five per cent., of the whole, forming a vast sodden reservoir. If no more rain falls the bog starts to lose water by evaporation, drainage, and gravity, till half its moisture has disappeared, at which stage water still makes up eighty per cent. of the whole. This statement usually provokes flat contradiction but can easily be shown to be correct. Imagine a bag into which have been put five black marbles to represent the solid matter of the bog and ninety-five white marbles to represent the water. Now take out half the white marbles to represent the loss of half the water. What is left? Forty-seven and a half white marbles and five black. In other words the water still makes up rather over eighty per cent. of the whole.

This somewhat abstract piece of physics has practical applications for the fisherman. After a long wet spell the bog reaches saturation point, and is then as impermeable as concrete. Even on gentle slopes a heavy shower will find its way into the river at once, causing a rapid flood. On the other hand if the weather has been dry and the bog can suck up the rain before it reaches the river, there will be no appreciable rise. These statements require some qualification. The upper slopes of the watershed may be so steep that even when the bog is dry, a certain amount of the rain runs off before it has time to soak in; and if there has been a very hot arid spell the surface may form into a scurfy skin which is for a short time resistant to moisture, and from which the rain shoots off to form a small and dirty flood. As soon as the crust softens the bog regains its natural power of absorption. Most western rivers have steep short floods only sufficient to enable fish to run from lake to lake, but even when the flood subsides, the oozings from the bog are sufficient to keep the lakes at fishing level throughout any normal season.

The upland plateau which I have been describing reaches its full height of 1,140 feet at the north-west corner, in a hump so formless and undistinguished that alone among the neighbouring heights it has no name on the map or in the speech of the countryside. Some grateful fisherman should remedy this, for its ungainly shoulders intercept the rain clouds sweeping in from the Atlantic and enable it to provide the head waters of four white trout fisheries as well as sending a tributary scampering back to Corrib. The precipitation of moisture must be quite exceptional, for the flat summit is intersected in every direction by steep-sided gullies in which the green branched candles of the club moss gleam, looking strangely exotic on a Connemara mountain. It is, too, something of a Pisgah from which a fisherman may survey the promised land. Close by are its daughter fisheries, Fermoyle, Costello, Furace, Screeb; beyond Screeb is Inver, and beyond Inver Gowla, and in the furthest distance you can catch a line of silver where the lakes of Ballinahinch lie in a half circle round the foot of the Twelve Pins.

A short mile to the east of the summit lies Shanawona, the top lake of Fermoyle, and already in that short mile a brisk stream has come into being. There is no bright spring with sand grains dancing in its up-surge, no spout of water from a limestone rock. No one can say exactly where the stream begins. There is only an amorphous percolation made up of small oozings and seepings, wet films glistening on granite, drippings from grass and heather, underground trickles nosing a way through spongy peat. Somehow, imperceptibly, all these insignificant down-droppings become confluent, and in half a mile there is a brook flowing briskly over a gravel bed where hundreds of sea trout and an odd salmon spawn every year. All over the watershed the same kind of thing is happening, thanks to the peat.

The top lake of a fishery high up in the hills is rarely as good as those a step or two lower down, but it has the advantage that it comes into order when the lower lakes are still choked up with excess of water. An hour's heavy rain will put Shanawona on the rise, and, no matter how long or heavy the rain, the level will begin to fall about an hour after the rain has ceased. A four mile drive and rather over two miles of rough mountain and bog walking are necessary to reach Shanawona from Fermoyle Lodge, so if you start out as soon as the sky has cleared the lake will be fishable by the time you reach it.

From Shanawona the river battles and burrows its way through the obstructing boulders for a mile and a half to reach Clogher, dropping two hundred feet in its course. As there are no major falls or cascades a small flood allows the trout to make the ascent, and as there are no pools or resting places they take the journey in one spurt, without delaying on the way. The result is that this part of the river is not worth fishing. Other high mountain streams, less consistently rapid in their course, such as the Tarsaghaun in Mayo, do fish well in a flood, and have their place in a fisherman's time-table, for they give sport for a couple of hours before any other part of a fishery is in order. It is necessary to be on the spot when the rain ceases and to start fishing as soon as the flood begins to drop. Concentrate on those places where a running fish would be tempted to pause for a rest, the tail and throat of small pools, the slacker water on the inside of a bend, and easy flowing streams. Once I arrived on an upland Donegal river to find it in a flood so high that fishing seemed useless, but walking down the bank I discovered a small area of slack water no larger than a billiard table, where a projecting horn of bank diverted the current and caused a back eddy. Out of this I took five white trout in twenty minutes, the whole, I imagine, of its temporary resting population. I ought then to have sat down and waited for it to fill up with newcomers, but instead I wandered on looking for another such place and failed to find it.

Clogher, the next lake, is the most attractive in this fishery. Nearly all the lakes are described in greater detail subsequently. Here I am dealing only with general problems of choice and timing, of water supply and the ascent of fish. It is sufficient to say that Clogher is not in order for about twelve hours after a heavy flood has begun to subside. It takes not only the overflow from Shanawona but also from two side lakes which discharge their waters into the river above it, and another river from an adjoining valley comes in further up the lake. In addition there is the seepage from a couple of square miles of bog and the direct shoot-off from encircling hills.

If Clogher is too full the river below it will almost certainly be at its best, for it is a universal rule that a river comes into order before the adjoining lake. Between Clogher and Carrick (another one and a half miles and a fall of 130 feet) the character of the river changes completely. It consists now of long deep pools, with two cataracts, one below the Clogher and the other below the Carrick pool. These cataracts can only be run in a flood much heavier than will suffice to take fish from Clogher to Shanawona.

After making their way up the cataracts, fish are ready to rest a while in the next piece of quiet water. The Carrick and Clogher pools are the two best in the Fermoyle fishery. Even if the water is low you should get a few trout from them, provided there is an up-stream wind, and in a flood a wind is not necessary. Should you be lucky enough to find the right wind combined with the right water, Clogher pool is almost a certainty for a salmon or two. When the flood is at its highest, it pays to concentrate on salmon and leave the trout alone, remembering that salmon will lie in much stronger water than trout and favour the neck of a pool, while trout usually favour the centre and tail.

Carrick is a sulky lake, slow to regain its proper level. Still another side lake and many hundred acres of bog and mountain have contributed their water to the river, and the outflow from Carrick is restricted. It may take a couple of days for Carrick to settle down, even for salmon.

Another mile with indifferent pools leads to a cascade which is in view from the windows of the Lodge, and which is the key to the amount of water which has fallen in the hills. Ordinarily it is hardly visible. After heavy rain it shows in two broad white streaks, and if these streaks coalesce into one sheet a big flood is on its way down. A white trout fisherman is so dependent on correct timing that he must always be on the look out for such natural tell-tales to guide him in his choice of water.

Tiny Derreen is hardly more than a river pool which has got notions above itself. It fills rapidly – you can see the water climbing up the banks and spreading several feet deep over the surrounding levels – but it empties nearly as rapidly, and true to its river-pool character, will fish well for salmon even when it is high.

In the half mile of river between Derreen and the lake of Fermoyle is the dominating feature of the fishery, a steep fall some eight feet high, passable by fish only in a really big flood. It may be weeks after the run of fish starts before such a flood occurs, and many more weeks before there is another. Until there is a big flood the lakes of the upland are empty. Meanwhile the lower lakes of the plain, to which the white trout have access in almost any state of water, get more and more populated. Large numbers may be taken but they soon grow stale and disinclined to rise. Many fisheries have such falls somewhere along the course of the river, controlling the ascent of the fish, and it is as well to find out before you start your holiday whether the fish have yet made their way above the fall.

When the flood comes, the pent-back salmon and sea trout stream up to the river and attack the falls in their hundreds. At the height of the run, air and water are full of jumping, swimming, struggling fish. For the first day or two after they arrive at each successive lake they take eagerly. If conditions are good, a fisherman may beat the half century, and should anyhow be assured of quite exceptional sport.

An attempt was once made to let fish over the fall by damming up a side lake and fitting sluices which, when opened, should cause an artificial flood; but the flood was not large enough and the attempt failed.

Below the fall lie the lakes of the plain, Fermoyle, Rusheen, Muckinagh, Clonadoon and Glenicmurrin. There is little difference in level, Fermoyle, the highest, being only twenty-four feet higher than Glenicmurrin, the lowest, while Clonadoon and Muckinagh are side lakes joined to the main river by short spurs of water a couple of hundred yards long and are only a foot higher than Glenicmurrin. As fish do not need a flood to travel between any of these lakes, it might be thought that the trouble of calculating the effect of floods was over. There is, however, one unexpected feature, neglect of which robbed me of what might have been the best day's fishing of my life. When the flood comes pouring down from Fermoyle it does not go in full volume to Glenicmurrin. A large portion backs up the spur rivers into Clonadoon and Muckinagh, both big lakes, and they act as delaying basins. As the flow is no longer out of, but into, these lakes the trout start to swim against the current and come to Fermoyle: but Glenicmurrin, if it is low, does not fill up for two or three days sufficiently to induce the fish (especially the salmon) to leave it in any quantity. As the river drops, Clonadoon and Muckinagh begin to drain again and a proportion of the fish coming up from Glenicmurrin enter and re-stock them.

Glenicmurrin is the largest of all the lakes and will hold three boats. Together with the two miles of river joining it to the sea it forms the separate fishery of Costello, probably the best known of all the Connemara waters. As far back as 1833, when an English fisherman visited our waters and recorded his experience in *An Angler in Ireland,* he referred to the river as "the fabulous Hydaspes" and was told that one rod had killed over two hundred trout in a day. He himself caught thirty-five trout running up to five pounds on his first day, and twenty-seven trout and two salmon the next. Even then however, white trout fishing could be unaccountable, for in his third day he caught only three. In those times fishing was concentrated on the river, gratings being fixed at the mouth of the lake to prevent the ascent of the fish. Behind the gratings were sluices, and when these were opened the size of the lake ensured a really effective artificial flood. It is easy to understand the slaughter that took place among the packed masses of fish when such a flood was released. I believe Costello was the first place to experiment with the artificial spate.

Not every fishery has such a variety as Fermoyle, nor has the modern angler such a choice as was afforded to guests at Fermoyle, when the number of rods was limited to five or six, and each day a certain amount of water was left unfished. But wherever he is fishing, the white trout angler must learn to think in terms of water supply, flood, wind, and run of fish, and nowhere could he learn to do this better than in the watershed of the Cashla.

18

SHANAWONA AND THE GREASED LINE

Imprisoned under the peak a daddy-long-legs made dry scraping noises in its efforts to escape; on one of the boat knees, where the paint had been laid too thick, a blister was swelling in a way which was vaguely repulsive. Nothing else in the boat moved. The rod was idle across my thighs and Jimmy, oars shipped, sat in a despondent huddle, staring into the water.

For six weeks, so Jimmy said, there had been no rain. Corrib was feet below its normal level, and shallows over which the boat had drifted profitably in June, now showed their teeth above the surface. Day after day a white sun dragged its course through a sky of dusty blue, and the heat was intolerable to man and fish.

Yesterday evening, after my arrival, I had managed to hook a couple of pounders in the moth-light, but yesterday there had been some attempt at a breeze. Today the surface was polished, each island doubled, standing on its own image. Only a merganser could catch trout on such a day and even the merganser did not seem to be having much success. My eyes followed him as he worked his way in a circle round the boat, and far away to the north-west they caught a darkening of the surface. Wind!

It was not likely to be more than a flaw, and a gentle flaw at that, which an island could absorb and nullify for half a mile to its lee. What was the nearest place where the breeze when it did arrive would have had its course unobstructed over open water for nearly the full breadth of the lake? Portacarron point! If we were lucky the wind would sweep down in the gap between Jones's island and the mainland, undiminished in volume.

There was time to take up our station and watch the slow advent of the breeze. The pace of its approach showed that it was hardly more than a breath, and in the distance the water was again paling. Five or ten minutes of a mildly ruffled surface was the most we could expect. It was Jimmy's business to see that we drifted over the choicest part of the point when the breeze was at its best.

In that small ruffle it was a case for long casting and a long slow draw, with the boat eased imperceptibly across wind, so as to prolong the time the fly was in the water. We both knew our parts and presently, deep in the water, there showed something like a wisp of smoke, which darkened and took shape into a three-pounder following the fly. For a couple of yards he kept pace with it, his nose not more than two inches from its tail, but his mouth never opened, the expected spurt never came and he sank back to become a smoke again, and vanished. The wind passed, and the lake was dead.

"It's no use fishing Corrib in this weather," I said in irritation. "Now if I were fishing Fermoyle, I might do some good." "You would not then," replied Jimmy, to whom any reflection on Corrib was treason, "for them that has it took are going off not able to catch a fish. We'll try a turn by the shlates in Bog bay." The shlates produced no sign of life, but as I fished, an idea prompted by Jimmy's remark grew in my mind. If the tenants were leaving, if even they were getting half-hearted about their fishing, some of the lakes would be unoccupied and I could hope for a day or two.

"Row back to the pier, Jimmy," I said. "I'm going to send a letter to Pat Spellman asking for leave to fish."

"The post'll be gone." Jimmy was cross. "Mick does be leaving early these days, and letters don't be left at the lodge above twice in the week."

I risked it however, and caught the post. Next day when I returned from the lake, there was a most friendly note from the tenant, enclosing the key of the Shanawona boat with leave to fish this lake "as often as I liked."

Shanawona? It was a lake I did not know, but the map showed it, perched almost on the crest of the upland plateau, the top lake of the fishery. What the map did not show was how to get to it. It appeared to be some three miles south of the Oughterard-Maam Cross road, and by striking S.S.W. from the gap between compass. The walk was going to be tough, over one range of Lough Bofin and Lough Agraffard, I should be able to find it by compass. The walk was going to be tough, over one range of hills, down to a valley, and then again up seven or eight hundred feet on to the plateau.

As we left the road next day and toiled up the bare granite ribs of the first range, the sun shone hotter than ever. All the colour had been bleached out of the countryside. The slippery grass had faded to an ash-grey, and over the rich blacks and browns of the peat a dry grey scurf had spread. The heather was prematurely over, while large patches showed withered and dead. We dared not traverse the slope, for we were following a compass line and had to go straight over everything. Up we went, and down we went, to the valley where the Yellow river, a noisome, oily snake of stagnancy, gave us some trouble in crossing, and then at last up on to the final plateau, beyond the crest of which we hoped to find our goal. It had looked easy on the map, but the upland was full of hollows, with bog pools varying in size from a tennis court to a football ground. None seemed to have any exit, or indeed any inflow, yet the air was loud with the music of water; water running, water splashing, water tinkling. My companion reminded me that we were now in the core of the haunted country, and probably on the fairy highroad from Carraroe to Rosses. What we were hearing might be fairy music, a theory which at first seemed strengthened when we realised that the sound really was coming out of the earth under our feet. Eventually we traced it prosaically to underground streams flowing over the granite core many feet below the bog.

Meanwhile, where was Shanawona? We had topped the crest, and could see what we took to be Clogher in the distance, but no Shanawona. In another hundred yards it appeared suddenly almost at our feet, cupped in high banks which had hidden it from our view. It shone blue as agate, absolutely calm save for a couple of deeper bands, where a sigh of wind crept down a hollow of the hills and spread over the water. The small brown trout, however, seemed busy over something and an occasional larger ring showed where a few white trout were stirring.

The boat was – of course – on the far side of the lake, but it was a small lake, easy to walk round. We were soon afloat, fishing wet-fly in the orthodox methods of the day. Not even a short rise rewarded us, so I changed to dry-fly, casting wherever I saw a white trout rise. They did respond to the dry fly to the extent of rising, sometimes two or three times, but always missing, till finally a more expert brownie would annex it. I had not learned at that time that a white trout generally misses a stationary fly and that even a dry-fly is taken best when moved a little.

We went into lunch without a fish, and Jimmy was the only one in a good temper. Corrib was not being put into the shade by the white trout lakes. During lunch I went through my fly-box, selecting a small and very sparsely-dressed wet Orange Grouse, with a hardly visible wing and only a few soft fibres of hackle. Then I greased a long length of my line – I had forgotten the Cerolene but there was plenty of fat in the ham sandwiches – and attached the fly to the dry-fly cast. It would not float – indeed with that sparse soft dressing it would sink rapidly. The line had been greased only to facilitate long casting and keeping in touch with the fly.

By the time we were ready to re-start a breath was blowing from the east, enough to raise a pin-ripple, and to move the boat in a barely appreciable drift. The slowness of the drift was no disadvantage, for the greased line made it easy to cast a score of yards and fish a wide arc. Once the fly had alighted it was drawn in slowly, fishing at least six inches under the surface, till half the line lay on the bottom of the boat, when it was time to cast again, making an intervening false cast to help in gaining the distance. The fish responded to the new method at once, taking fiercely with an explosive up-and-down rise. Hardly one was missed, as, owing to the greased line, fly and rod point were in direct contact and the strike instantaneous. By tea time I had fourteen fish and my companion, a thoroughly competent angler fishing in the orthodox way, had not one. A freak distribution between the two ends of a boat is common enough but this difference was at least suggestive. Further experiment would have to await another day. We wanted to explore the country a little more and then get home.

A short climb on to a mound of moraine debris blocking the eastern end of the lake showed me a distant sheet of water which could only be Lettercraphroe. Lettercraphroe, largest of the Fermoyle lakes, has not yet been mentioned for a very good reason. It is an angler's tragedy, the finest white trout lake that never holds a white trout. Of an even fishing depth, a maze of islands and promontories, with boulders nuzzling up to and through its surface, it is a lake of dreams. All round, for three-quarters of a circle, some higher, some lower, lie white trout lakes and it also, if my geology is correct, was once a white trout lake, for there are indications that it once stood at a higher level and drained down a long valley into the Spiddal system. But the advancing ice scooped it deeper and the retreating ice threw a saddle of moraine across the head of the valley. The impounded waters burst their way out of the northern end into another valley which leads down to Corrib. Now it holds only innumerable brown trout of about four ounces.

For the moment Lettercraphroe did not spell tragedy, but relief. I knew that a bog road, unmarked on the ordnance map, ran close to its southern end and if, next day, we started our route from there we would be travelling over more familiar country. I very much disliked the idea of being caught in a hill fog anywhere along our route of the morning.

One of the disadvantages of fishing lakes far distant from the road is the possibility of a sudden fog. I have known a countryman to be hopelessly lost for twenty-four hours till the fog cleared. In theory it is easy to escape. You walk downhill till you find a little stream, follow it till you hit a larger stream, taking you to the river, and then follow the river down, circumnavigating the lakes till at last you arrive at a bridge and a road. In practice this is exhausting, for the sides of the streams and lakes are the worst going in the countryside, and it is not so easy as it sounds. It is always wise to choose and follow an exact route, noting the compass bearings and noting also any peculiar features at distances of about a hundred yards apart. Such a route I intended to plan next day. It turned out that I was wise to do so.

The approach from the south-east, leaving the little road at the southern corner of Lettercraphroe, was half a mile shorter, and, though it still involved a climb, much easier. For most of the way marks in the form of peculiarly shaped boulders were available, and those were given names to impress their characteristics – the "knife edge", the "rifle sight", the "Greek helmet" and so on. A narrow stream-gully formed part of the route and could be followed in any fog; so could a hog's back ridge. There were, however, two stretches, one of wet bog and another of grassy upland, which were relatively featureless and on which a compass would be necessary. We noted the bearings carefully for future use.

The weather remained the same, brilliant sun and no wind, so we determined to try out the new method thoroughly, in competition with the old. First we used a dry-fly and had the usual experience of a number of ineffectual rises and no connection, though one small white trout managed to get himself hooked at the third attempt. Then I substituted the small wet-fly on my line, while my companion cleaned the grease off his and fished wet in the normal way. We changed rods occasionally. At the end of the day the score was twelve to the greased line, and none to the wet line. The importance of long casting in these conditions also became clear, for my young companion, who was not able to throw quite as long a line as I could, got fewer rises.

Next morning he had to return to school and for two more days of the same weather I fished alone getting eight fish the first day and six on the second. The experience of future years was to show that Shanawona, a small lake and most of it too deep to fish, always needed a rest after two successive days of raking.

Then came a note from Pat Spellman. The tenants had given up in despair. The entries in the fishing register for the four days I had fished Shanawona were eloquent.

> Sep. 20 – "Dead calm and bright."
> Sep. 21 – "Ditto ditto."
> Sep. 22 – "Not a breath of air, bright sun, very hot."
> Sep. 23 – "Ditto. Party left as weather unpropitious. Indian summer."

Hardly a fish had been caught in the lower lakes.

As the tenants had gone, Pat suggested that I try Clogher for the next day, and the day after he would boat me on the home lakes. Clogher, normally a much better lake than Shanawona, gave only eight white trout, but, still in the flat calm, a salmon swallowed a diminutive Kingsmill on 3x gut, and was successfully netted. The day after I found Pat bouncing with excitement for all his seventy-four years. News travels fast in Connemara, and he had heard that something strange and successful had been going on in the fishing line. Now he wanted to see for himself. The stage was set for a demonstration. Derreen was a mirror flawed here and there by the rises of white trout. Pat could slip a boat through the water with less disturbance than any man alive, and even in that shallow pool could put me within casting distance of anything that moved.

It came off. Fish after fish was spotted, and the wet-fly put a little beyond and to one side of him. Then the recovery began and within a couple of yards would come a bang and an explosion of water. In all we got eighteen white trout, some of them really good, and lost a salmon which came unhooked. Next day the weather broke.

From that season I have used a greased line as a matter of routine, except in a strong wind when a heavier line, ungreased, helps to keep flies steadier in the water. The great advantage of the floating line is in a calm or in faint airs, for it enables the long casting which such conditions demand, and even at the end of the longest cast it is easy to keep in complete touch with the fly. In moderate breezes it is unnecessary, but useful, because it eases the strain on a rod with a light point especially when the switch cast is used. No doubt this device must have been discovered independently by dozens of people, but I had never seen or heard of it before and I think that day on Shanawona marked its introduction to Connemara. Pat talked, and in a few years it had become general on Fermoyle and has spread to the rest of the fisheries.

19

SHANAWONA AND THE MIST

Last year it had been all sun and no rain. Now it was all rain and no sun. For two days it had been coming down, solid, persistent, turning Oughterard bay into yellow soup and blanketing the hills. Resignedly I commandeered a small table and tied flies, but my companion chafed to see the days of his holiday running to waste. On the third day he burst into my bedroom. "It's stopped raining – can we go to Shanawona?" I looked out. Mist swirled in the village street and, behind the hotel, hung in a dense curtain. It is bad enough to be forced to return from a hill-top lake in a fog: it is madness to start out in one. I said so – and while I protested, looked at the boy's face and capitulated.

That was why, after an agonising crawl along the mountain road, we stood at the quarry, looking out into the blankness, ready to make our venture. We took counsel. There was a small wind which caused the mist to swirl, so that sometimes the loom of a figure could be seen at fifty yards and at other times would be lost at twenty. The wind, if it remained steady, would give us the most important of aids in a fog, a point of orientation. It would raise little waves on Lettercraphroe, and their lapping would be a further guide over the most featureless part of our route. We had a compass, and we had last year's notes of the marking stones, with the distance in paces from one to the next, and the compass bearings of each stage. Lastly, our course had been planned at some cost in shortness, to touch natural features such as streams, gullies, and tarns, which were recognisable by some peculiarity even in a fog. We determined to make the attempt.

There were delays. We found that our note of paces had to be corrected, for steps tend to get shorter in a fog. Sometimes we had to cast round to find a mark, one of us staying still while the other two went exploring within hailing range. We were puzzled by what looked like an unfamiliar range of hills, and in fifty yards it had resolved itself into two moraine mounds no larger than houses. We got a fright when five herons in close formation swirled out of the mist into our faces and fled, squawking, back into the mist again. But, in only half on hour longer than the usual time for the walk, we hit Shanawona within ten yards of the boat. "Smallest 'rumpeted."

On the mountain road there was consternation. Sherry Shepherd, the owner of the fishery, nosing his way into Galway with his wife Molly and John Spellman in the car, recognized my white Belsize gleaming ghostly beside the road. He was a man of impulse. No one, he declared, could find his way to Shanawona in that mist. A search party must be organised at once. John recalled how he himself had been lost in a mist for two days. Molly, as usual, with her unemotional commonsense restored perspective. If I could not find a lake, whose position I knew, how could a search party find three people who might be anywhere within twenty-five square miles? She was prepared to back my mountain sense to find a way back even if I did lose myself. It would be time to start worrying if the car was still there when night fell. So it was decided.

Meanwhile we had started our fishing, and eerie fishing it was. The mist had thickened, and in three oar strokes the bank vanished. Only a small circle of water was visible and the mist walled us round and domed us over so that we seemed to be fishing in a kind of inverted bowl. Luckily the lake was narrow and the wind blowing straight across. Once out of sight of the shore we surrendered ourselves to the wind till the opposite shore loomed up, when we pulled back against the ripples to pick up the mark where we had started the drift and began another further down. No properly adjusted trout should have dreamed of rising in these conditions, but the lake had not been fished for six weeks and a few fish responded. By three o'clock we had fifteen and, mindful of the mist, I suggested packing up. The boy pleaded for one more drift so one more drift it was. My last cast in among the boulders of the far shore fouled a rock, or so I thought, but the rock began to move and turned into a salmon to complete the basket.

The way back gave little trouble, for the wind strengthened

and the mist thinned. On the road we met the car returning from Galway. Sherry jumped out, full of relief and congratulations. From the back seat came Molly's flat and yet somehow delightful voice. "And please remember that I was the only one who said you were not as big a fool as you looked. You can take that as a compliment."

For two successive years, a fortnight in each year, I took Shanawona at the nominal rent of £5, for it was difficult of access and rarely fished. Having the lake to myself I was able to do what I had long wanted, namely to make a detailed study of one piece of water and everything connected with it. The first task was to make a working chart. A lump of lead, a ball of string with knots every two feet, and a compass was my primitive equipment. I prepared a number of postcards, each with an outline of the lake enlarged from the six inch ordnance which served to record field notes of the soundings. At night these were transferred to a larger map, a copy of which hangs, or used to hang, in Fermoyle lodge.

The results were surprising. Everyone knew Shanawona was a deep lake, but no one had realised that some of it was over fifty feet in depth. It was rather under half a mile long, and two hundred yards across at its maximum. Most of the northern shore plunged down so steeply that the fishable water could be covered with a short cast from the bank. A shallower shelf filled the south-east corner and extended along the south-west shore to the other end, where the river ran in, but in most places the shelf was only twenty to thirty yards wide. All the rest of the lake was too deep to be of any use, and the available fishing water could be fully covered by one rod twice in a day.

Fishing owners, especially if they are hotel proprietors, will tell you that a lake cannot be overfished by fair fishing. Shanawona disposed of that statement. Given comparable conditions, the numbers of the take went steadily down with each day. After three days it had to be rested for at least a couple of days, when it regained its form. It was not a question of a diminished supply of fish, for the amount I took out was negligible when compared with the stock; nor was it a question of the fish becoming boat-shy, for the falling off was as great in those parts of the lake which were fished from the shore. The only explanation of which I can think is that the fish became so accustomed to the sight of the flies that they lost interest and curiosity. After two days rest they had forgotten, and were ready to be interested again. In lakes lower down in a chain, where fish are continually passing through, and in larger lakes where variations of wind dictate different drifts and portions may go unfished for days, this falling-off is not so noticeable; but in Shanawona the water was so limited that, whatever the wind, I saw to it that no part escaped, and this fishing law of diminishing returns was always in evidence.

I have said that the deep portions were not worth fishing. To this there was an exception. After a long hot spell with the lake at its lowest, as on the day when I first fished it, some of the fish seemed to desert the shallows for the deeper water, perhaps for coolness, and could be taken there; and even at other times I suspect there were fish in the deep water, though I failed to rise them. Local tradition said that the pioneer trout of June ran up to Shanawona on the first flood, and in calm weather I have seen fish of four or five pounds playing round just under the surface of the deepest portions, but as my fishing was in September they were already too stale to take.

Perched up on the shoulder of the highest mountain in the neighbourhood, Shanawona was particularly affected by weather conditions and electrical tensions. Black squalls swooped down on it with a more adverse effect than in lower lakes, and it was often in mist or cloud. Wet mists are bad for fishing but dry ones are worse, and the only tolerable day I had in a mist was the one I have described. Of electrical tensions I will give one typical example.

All day the clouds had been building themselves round the lake with that upward twisting which presages thunder. I was touchy and depressed and the trout were no better. By four o'clock there were only two half-pounders in the boat, and I left the lake to its sulks and went off to explore the upland. Half an hour later when, ear to the turf, I was trying to trace the course of an underground trickle, I found myself singing and looked up. In every direction the cloud battalions were in confused retreat and blue sky was showing. I hurried back to the lake to find it a flat calm, but the trout also had felt the departure of the depression and faint lines on the satiny surface showed that they were swimming around. There was no wind for drifting. There was no need to drift. We rowed to the mouth of a small bay on the south west shore, shipped the oars, and waited. Soon the exhilarated fish were moving within casting distance, and if a small wet-fly on a greased line was cast in front of a fish and pulled across his route, it was taken more often than not. In the short hour before I had to leave nine fish were netted and the boat had not drifted a dozen yards. The trout were not rising – there were no insects for them to rise at – but merely obeying some impulse to go for a swim. If there had been even the faintest ripple their activity would have gone unobserved. The "time of the rise" with sea trout is almost independent of the presence of insect life. It is the time when for reasons of their own they choose to come near the surface and move about.

Shanawona, because of its depth, introduced me to a new tactic in hooked fish. A big trout, risen at the edge of the deep, would sometimes sound straight down. One such fish went down and down, the rod point already nearly in the water, till my backing showed and I began to wonder what had happened to the bottom of the lake. The mystery was solved by a splash only a few yards behind the boat. The fish had gone to the bottom and turned straight up, but the cushion of water between his downward and upward courses was sufficient to keep the line running straight down from the rod even when the fish was coming up. It took some furious reeling to regain direct touch.

It was a mistake to rent so small a lake for a continuous period. Such lakes should be kept as reserves, and fished when the larger lakes have gone stale. Then, just because they have been let alone, you may get a couple of days of good fishing.

It always pays to try any piece of water, however unpromising, which has the smallest outlet to the river. Shandullaghaun, a miniature lake not far from Shanawona, is drained by a cut not more than a foot wide which runs underground for much of its course, and the lake itself looks to be completely overgrown with reeds. It was never fished till one day when I discovered a patch of clear water about the size of a tennis court, fishable from the shore. Out of this tiny area I have taken dozens of fish including one of three pounds.

20

CLOGHER AND THE CLOUDBURST

Clogher was always a favourite with the knowledgeable, which puzzled those new to the fishery. The approach is arduous whichever route is chosen. One involves a long two miles over a dreary bog, the other, almost as long, is a switchback down to Lettercraphroe, up over a spur of Clogher mountain, and down again through a rockfall where the wild goats with immense horns and topaz eyes stare you out of countenance. The lake can be as dour as a Calvinist minister, and its record day – with two of the finest white trout fishermen in Ireland at work – is only thirty-six, while the other regularly fished lakes have records about the half hundred. Two things stand to it. On a good day the trout average a much greater weight than in any other lake. It is not customary to enter the total weights of the baskets in the register, but it is a certainty that the thirty-six from Clogher would have turned the scale against the fifty from other lakes. I never quite averaged the two pounds on Clogher, but several times came within an ounce or two of it. The second element in its favour is the variety of water, which gives scope for intelligent choice and different methods.

Clogher is about twice the area of Shanawona and has four times as much fishable water, for it is all shallow save for two holes each of about half an acre. An island divides it into two nearly equal halves, a north-eastern and a south-western. The island is prolonged to the south by a jumble of rocks reaching to the shore which are impassable except in high water, but at its northern end there is a channel opposite the Black River by which one can always get from one half to another. Nevertheless, this island governs the fishing, for the passage involves a delay sufficient to discourage dodging about in search of more activity

178

at the other end. Once you have chosen the half where you want to begin, that half has to be given a thorough trial, however much you suspect (as you always do) that you are missing something good at the far end. The choice is made more difficult by the very different characteristics of the two halves. The western half holds no salmon, but the greatest number of trout running from one and a half to two pounds. It is noticeably the sulkier of the two, but if the trout do happen to be on the rise the sport is the finest in Connemara. In the eastern end you may chance on a salmon almost anywhere, and I have seen two trout of four pounds taken from it. In general however, the trout run smaller and rise more readily. Into it flows the river from Shanawona, carrying a load of silt which has spread out on either side of the butt, giving ideal conditions for the growth of reeds and rushes. As this butt and its surround is the best part of the lake for salmon, and also excellent for trout, Sherry Shepherd used to cut back the reeds twice a year, but this has been neglected in recent years and now the butt is almost unfishable. The last two salmon which I saw hooked in the narrow channel still remaining were free in a few seconds. I understand that the present owner intends to take steps to clear the butt again.

Clogher has given me superb sport. To my own rod on four successive fishing days I took twenty-two, twenty-four, fourteen and seventeen. Another day gave me three salmon and a dozen big trout. On still another (with the help of my wife who hooked a three and a half-pounder by the tail in a squall and in the middle of a nest of rocks) a salmon and twenty-two trout. Yet somehow I feel that I have never seen its full possibilities, a day when in the western end the rise should last through morning and afternoon, instead of petering out after an hour or so. For some reason which no one has discovered the rise at this end is always short, usually between eleven and twelve, with a little further activity between five and six. Even on the day of the record, not a fish was caught after lunch. A quarter of a mile downstream from the lake, lies the Clogher pool, long, deep, and hardly moving, which requires high water and a S.S.E. wind. If this combination turns up, it used to be a certainty for one or more salmon. In low water if there is the right wind you will get trout.

The most memorable day on Clogher could not, from the fishing angle, have been worse. When I arrived with the friend who had introduced me to the west, we looked without much hope at the even grey sky and the milky light on the water, conditions which produce the maximum of sub-surface visibility. Such days are always bad, though by using a very small black fly and a slightly larger grey bumble, a few fish can be induced to take. This morning it was very few. Only two were in the boat by lunch. There was something brewing. Both of us felt it. Up above that grey pall the clouds were trooping. The pall itself grew lower and darker. The air seemed to press in on us, to be a tangible thing. Then came a single flash of lightning followed by a blast of thunder, and the rain was on us with a hiss and a snarl. The landscape disappeared. The surface of the lake leapt up in white spray two feet or more, and before we reached the island our feet were awash. The rain lasted in full fury for perhaps half an hour, then dwindled to a drizzle through which Clogher hill began to show. It looked as if the miracle of the Gadarene swine was being re-enacted, this time with sheep as the performers. Down every grassy steep were rushing masses of white. We actually did think they were flocks of frightened sheep till a further thinning of the drizzle showed them as sheets of water, falling in no regular channels but spread over the whole face of the hill. The sheets came lower and lower towards the level ground at the hill foot. Most of this water would escape the lake, flowing away into the river below it. Not so the deluge which had fallen on the cluster of hills to the north and west, and by now was racing down to us. Once the lake began to rise rapidly the chances of fishing would be over, but there would be ten minutes or a quarter of an hour, while the surface crept up its first couple of inches and in that interval salmon would be likely to move. We considered. Clogher is served by two rivers. The Black River drains an area of about two square miles on the western slopes of the ridge which strikes north from Clogher towards Shanawona, and has no lake on its course. The main river comes from Shanawona with a tributary from Lough Anierin. Reckoning that the two lakes would act as delaying basins which would intercept the flood, and that the Black River would come down first, we took station opposite its infall and waited.

By now the sun had come out brilliantly on an absolutely calm lake. Not a trout was moving. They had recovered from the bombardment. The Black river still picked its way delicately through the boulders of its bed, and in the windless silence we could hear only the spinet-like notes of water dropping from the bank into the lake, and the faint swish from the white curtains sliding down Clogher hill.

A squawk drew our eyes to the sky, to see once again the classic, oft-repeated, never, as far as I have observed, conclusive, combat between a peregrine and a heron. The heron lumbered along with its slow clumsy wing flaps, neck drawn in, long legs trailing behind. High above, the falcon circled till she reached a point favourable for her stoop, then fell like a meteorite, aiming at the vulnerable junction of neck and back. Till the peregrine had come within about thirty feet the heron appeared to take no notice, and then things happened in a flash and a flurry, so quick that, though I have seen the performance a dozen times, I can never be quite sure of the sequence of movement. I think the heron does a half roll, and at the same time twists its neck so that the yellow dagger of its beak points straight upwards along the path of its descending enemy. The legs are at the same time drawn in. If the peregrine met that venomous beak she would be spitted through and through by the force of her own impetus, and she knows it, so by some aerial acrobatics she side-slips out of danger, and is carried by her rush far below the heron which resumes its course, while the peregrine spirals upwards to gain height for a new attack. Normally the performance is repeated three times, and then the peregrine gives up. The heron flops along to its destination and the peregrine streaks off like a jet plane.

As we watched, wishing that we had a pair of field glasses, a roar burst on the air. I looked at the Black River. It was still placid, without an inch of rise. Our calculations had gone wrong. Out of sight the main river had come down. We rowed as fast as we could to the butt and found it a cauldron. A broad gush of muddy water was already thrusting far out into the lake, sweeping the reeds flat, obliterating the reefs. Looking up the valley we saw what had happened. To the west of the river outlet runs a line of low cliffs a couple of hundred yards long, where the peregrines nest. In ordinary conditions no stream intersects them. Now the whole line was an unbroken curtain of water, curving far out from the edge. At a dozen places further up the valley the same thing was happening, and, long before the top lakes had filled, the river had come down in spate.

Fishing was over. We watched the lake rise visibly, saw more reefs submerged, and made our dripping way home, to hear of roads washed away, bridges damaged, and crops destroyed. That is the way it can rain in the west.

If a friendly millionaire were to offer me any white trout lake in Connemara I would choose Clogher. Always I pushed out from its shores with a feeling of anticipation and excitement. It has given a basket in half a gale and in complete calm. There was no telling where fish would rise best, or whether they were going to be large or small. Often disappointed, I never ceased to hope for the day which I felt was due to me, when morning and afternoon, all over the lake, along shores and shallows, butt and islands, the big fish would be moving and I should "bring *such* fishes back." It never came. Perhaps I shall fish it again and perhaps –

21

CARRICK-KILL-AWALLIA AND DERREEN

"Carrick", it was generally called, for the longer name was rather a mouthful, but Jamesie was faithful to Carrick-Kill-Awallia, rolling out the rich syllables with enjoyment. It gave him an opening for one of his characteristic stories. He told it one day sitting on the shore of Inisthawee, whittling a thole pin to his satisfaction. "Ther's another lake by the name of Carrick or so they call it now, but the rale name is Carrick-Kill-Awallia. Have ye fished it? Ye have not? Well maybe ye will, an' when ye do, fish careful round the big lump of a rock by the reeds for there is always a salmon there. An' take notice of another big lump of a rock that's flat on the hillside. There's more than salmon under that I'm telling ye. 'Tis that rock gave the name to the place."

He looked up, saw that my face was suitably interrogative and continued.

"Ye mind them little houses on the hill over the lake of Fermoyle? That's one of the oldest villages in Connemara. Men was livin' an' dyin' there before Cromwell came to Ireland. But what I'm going to tell you wasn't in his time, no, nor for a hundred years afther. In them days there was a great hirin' fair at Headfort in October, an' the whole village travelled to it, the boys an' the girls to bind themselves for the year, an' the men to trade their wool and the women with their socks and the bits of cloth they had woven. 'Twas a long journey roun' the Corrib an' across the river at Maam, but they made it in a day – they were hardy in them times – an' nex' day they started back with their meal an' salt for the winter. No one was left behind in the village but th' oul' women and the young childer.

"Now in the town of Bal in the country of Roscommon there

were two men an' they were robbers, the worst in the world. All the people in Roscommon knowed them, so they lit out an' left them places an' they came to Connemara. They did terrible mischief for no one could get a hoult of them. Presently they heard tell of Fermoyle, an' how all the people left it for the fair, an' they made a plan. They hid in the hills up by Shanapheasteen an' watched the men an' women goin' off to the fair, an they didn't move till all of them had crossed the hills beyant Clogher. Then they crep' into the village. They frighted th' oul' women an' imprisoned them, an' they giv' the childer a skelpin' that scatthered them over the mountains, an' then they started to look for the money. God knows there was little of that, but what there was they took. While they was lookin' they found a keg of poteen an' they had a few drinks. They had all the time in the world, for the people wouldn't be back till the night of the morrow, so they had more drinks an' then they fell asleep.

"Now, as the people were on their way to the fair, God sent a terrible storm on the Maam Turks the like of which ye never saw. For two hours an' more it lashted, an' it was like the flood of Noah. When they got to Joyce's river there was no crossin' it, and not a boat on the lake, for they were all away at the fair. They do say that some of the young ones got over by swimmin' and' leppin' an' draggin'. I couldn't rightly say. But the mosht of them gev' up and set back for Fermoyle. T'was dark when they got home an' they were wet and jaded an' sorrowful. They found the women locked up an' screechin', an' the money gone, an' then they found the two robbers drunk an' the money in their pockets.

"There weren't no polis in them days – ye know that yourself, Sir – an' by rights they should have taken them to the sheriff in Galway to be hanged, but Galway is a matther of thirty miles and they were wore out an' not in the besht of humour. 'Batther thim,' said one of the women, 'batther thim.' So they took shtones an' they batthered thim, an' no loss. The nex' day they considered where to bury thim for they didn't want it talked of. They took the corpses over the hill an' roun' the lake to where there was a great rock shtandin' up an' only a couple of little ones to shtop it fallin'. Ye would think ye could push it over yourself. They med a grave under it, an' into it they put the corpses, an' then they tried to topple over the shtone. Faith it wasn't too easy, but they got a bit of a tree an' they dug away at the small shtones an' they toppled it at the latther end, an' that, Sir, is how the lake came by its name. Carrick is a shtone in Irish, an' Kill is a church or a graveyard. The gravestone of the men of Bal, that's what the name does be signifying. Ye may see the shtone yerself any time ye do be fishing the lake."

There are at least two thousand great stones round the shores of Carrick which might have been up-ended in the way Jamesie described, and my Irish-speaking friends throw doubt on his etymology. Jamesie would not have worried. "Ye can be too particular, Sir, an' that's a fact".

Carrick is about the same area as Shanawona and, as with Shanawona, a good part of the centre is too deep to fish; but it has excellent drifts along the reeds by the northern shore and indeed all the shores fish well. Jamesie's "big lump of a rock," and another rock further up the lake of which also he told me, are reliable spots for salmon. Jamesie might romance on other subjects but his fishing information was nearly infallible. Only one of the many places which he described as holding salmon failed for years to come up to his description – and then on the last day I fished Clogher, long after his death, I caught one and rose another within a foot of the mark he had given me.

Carrick never flattered me. My best day was twenty-two and of these eleven came out of the long pool. At one time this pool was exceptional for salmon and large trout – I have known a five pound trout taken out of it on a grasshopper – but of late years it seems to have fallen off. Like Fermoyle, Carrick had the advantage of being in good grouse country, and if it proved dour, a walk round the shores with a gun generally produced something. Carrick was usually fished in double harness with Derreen, neither lake having sufficient water for a full day's fishing. The two were separated by rather more than a mile of hillocks and bog, a perfect garden of heather – Connemara heather, its great goblets like inverted brandy glasses, cross-leaved heath with each branch ending in a cluster of oval pink pearls, the white and royal purple of the bell heather, and the ling whose colours ran from white and lilac through every shade of rose, amaranth, and crimson.

About a quarter of a mile from the lodge and sufficiently below it to be under direct observation from the drawing-room window, Derreen spread its five acres or so of sheltered water. Squatting on a boggy level, with a bottom of weeds and bog, invaded by reeds and water lilies, without a rock to break the surface, it had all the featureless monotony which I have mentioned as characteristic of the first class pool. A big river pool it really is, but I have known no other lake so closely packed with fish. The far end, a narrow neck between the entrance of the main river and the Shanapheasteen brook, which comes in some forty yards down, is where the salmon tend most to congregate, but there is no square yard of water where you may not come across one, and at the close of the season Derreen always heads the other lakes in the number of salmon caught. It is equally prolific in white trout.

Being so small and so close to the house there was a tendency to overfish it. Nearly every day it was thoroughly combed on the way to and back from Carrick, and, if the nights were fine in July, some one was pretty sure to slip out after dinner when a few sedges were about. Even the numbers of fish which it contained did not allow it to stand up to this, and it would turn sulky till a good south-east breeze or an injection of fresh water restored its good humour. Of what it could do when in humour the following is a sample. There had been a long drought followed by heavy rain which washed all the dry grass and scurf of the bog into the river, and for twenty-four hours so filled the lakes with floating debris as to make it impossible to move a fly through the water without festooning it. I watched the trout shooting up the falls, released from their imprisonment in the lower lakes, and promised myself a couple of salmon next day. When the next day came the level was still so high that it seemed best to concentrate on the river pools and fish the butts of the lakes from the shore, and I told my boatman that I would not meet him at Derreen till three o'clock.

I got no salmon, for the Fermoyle salmon had gone up, and, owing to the delaying basins of Clonadoon and Muckanagh, those from Glenicmurrin had not yet started to run; so I arrived at Derreen disappointed, with only seven white trout in my bag. Shortly after three we were afloat on the lake, and just after six we left it. In those three hours I got thirty-three fish, averaging one and a quarter pounds, making forty for the day. The fish were still rising when I left, but I had as many as I wanted. We had to fetch a sack to carry them back.

Derreen, owing to its small size, has never earned the "cordon bleu" which is bestowed on lakes which have produced fifty fish in a day to a single boat. I often wonder whether, if I had gone out earlier, I might not have gained that distinction for it. But it has achieved one charming recognition. When a daughter was born to Sir Edward Stracey (who succeeded Molly Shepherd as owner of Fermoyle) he christened her "Derreen".

22

THE LAKES OF THE PLAIN

Glenicmurrin, Clonadoon, Muckanagh, Rusheen, Fermoyle, the lakes of the plain, the lakes of July when white trout fishing is at its best. Fermoyle, Muckanagh, and of course Glenicmurrin, have earned the cordon bleu, while of the lakes of the plateau only Carrick has this distinction. I have fished them all except Clonadoon, though not in July. It will be sufficient to deal with Fermoyle, the largest lake after Glenicmurrin, and the best known.

For a lake to rank as first class, it should have a good river pool adjacent, a good butt which can be fished from the shore, and a variety of water to prevent monotony and stimulate expectation. Fermoyle has them all, and in addition some of the loveliest scenery in Connemara. Far to the west, over the windy bog, rise the pale blue peaks of the Twelve Pins, and to the north-west the long scarp of the upland dips sharply to the Screeb valley. On the shoulder of Fermoyle hill the cluster of cottages which gives it the name huddles together, grey steadings almost invisible among the grey rocks. Over all washes the soft clear air of Connemara.

The L-shaped pool immediately above the butt is a chancy affair which often produces nothing, and then nobly redeems itself, as on a day when, arriving from Dublin at 4 p.m., I heard with interest from John Spellman that there had been a small flood that morning. I asked if it had been large enough to get fish over the falls and he said no, but that a few had made unsuccessful attempts. When this happens the defeated fish tail back again to the lake, but it crossed my mind that some might have stayed in the pool.

There was time to unpack and get an hour's fishing before

188

dinner. My guess had been correct and the hour produced thirteen fish from the pool, mostly harvesters, but with three or four good fish.

The butt is long, gradually widening between steep banks, and with the luxury of piers to fish from. In late June and July, if the water is high and a west wind is driving the waves against the stream, it is perhaps the best cast in the fishery for salmon, and at all times is likely to produce a couple of trout to a man who can throw a line long enough to cover it where it widens out.

Fermoyle was the lake to which novices in white trout fishing were usually sent to learn their new craft, and I was sometimes chosen for the role of instructor. It was an excellent text book out of which to teach the different types of water which are most productive of fish. Broadly speaking there are four. They are the areas round the inflow of the main river and any subsidiary spawning stream, the light shallow, the shelve, and the deep shallow.

The light shallow has a depth ranging around four feet, and there must be some cover for the trout if it is to fish well. Such cover is provided by patches of reeds and rushes, by weed growing in the bottom where it is boggy, and by the jumbled masses of boulders which in many places form the floor of the lakes. The light shallow is free-rising, for the fish can see the flies easily and have not far to come to take them, but they are usually on the small side, three-quarters of a pound to a pound. Often it will save a poor day but it will rarely provide a good one.

About a third of Fermoyle lake, lying south-west, west, and north-west of the big island, is a typical light shallow, paved and studded with boulders to such an extent that in low water parts of it cannot be navigated. The river flows out of it in two exits, and in July or early August, newly arrived trout hang about in this area for some time before pushing on to deeper water. This may seem to contradict what I have said earlier, that trout coming into a lake on a flood tend to swim against the pulse of the current till they reach the river entrance and congregate there, spreading backwards along the shore where the flood drops. In Fermoyle the entrance and exit of the river are far apart, there is a big area over which the flood can expand, and the island is an obstruction to any direct flow. Consequently, even in a flood, there is less inducement for the fish to pass on. But the main

reason for their tendency to delay in the western bay is that
Fermoyle can be reached from the sea in any normal water and
does not require the crest of a flood for the fish to reach it. They
are not driven onwards by the necessity of surmounting obstacles,
but make their way up in leisurely fashion and on arrival are
quite content to do a little unhurried exploration, first in the
western bay and then along the shores, till they find a place they
fancy. For the smaller fish that place may be the rock-strewn
western shallow.

The shelve is any part of a lake where the bottom dips more
or less steeply from a depth of four or five feet down to a depth
which is no longer fishable. Such a shelve may be close to the
shore and best fished from the land, as on the north bank of
Shanawona, or it may lie in a circle round a deep hole, as in
parts of Clogher, or, as in Fermoyle, it may form a belt a little
distance out from the mouths of shallow bays. The southern shore
of Fermoyle is scooped into a number of such bays divided by
rocky points. Salmon stand at the points (salmon will lie in
shallower water than big trout and isolated rocks seem to have a
fascination for them) while the trout lie across the mouths of the
bays and on the shelve. The attraction of a shelve to fish is the
opportunity which it gives them to choose the exact depth which,
in prevailing conditions of water and temperature, they find most
congenial. On a shelve trout are rather less easy to move than on
a light shallow, but the average weight will be greater. On the
whole it is best, if the wind suits, to fish a shelve so that you
cross it drifting from shallow to deep in the direction of the dip.
This may require a series of short parallel drifts, but at least you
are sure of crossing the line of optimum depth for the day.

The deep shallow – an area where the depth is from eight to
eleven feet – is the most tantalizing part of any lake. Here are
the greatest number of big trout, here if anywhere you may hope
to average two pounds, here you are continually faced with
frustration and disappointment. The casual passage of a fly is not
sufficient to bring a fish to the surface from such a depth. Only
when the mood is on them, and they start to move about nearer
the surface, are you likely to take more than the occasional fish;
and in the deep shallow the mood is usually short lived. I cannot
remember any take in such water that lasted for more than an
hour.

There are two deep shallows in Fermoyle, one off the east coast of the island and one stretching southwards from the jaws of the butt, but the classical deep shallow is in Clogher, a diagonal belt crossing the lake from the mouth of the Black River to the main exit channel. Here, I am told, on the day of the Clogher record, big fish were on the prowl all morning, and the basket, in size though not in numbers, was the finest ever brought back to the lodge.

Because deep shallows are so uncertain it is a mistake to waste time on them. Arrange your drifts so that every now and then you cross a portion of such water, and, if there is any sign of interest, concentrate on the deep shallow till interest has ceased.

Fermoyle, though I have had good days on it, never quite won my heart. It is associated with no new discovery nor any particularly noteworthy experience. For all its charm it lacks personality. But, then, I never fished it in July when it is at its best and so I probably do it less than justice. To others it is *the* lake of the fishery.

23

ALEC AND DELPHI

"I wonder if you are right in that" said Alec. It was after dinner at Delphi lodge and the talk had somehow strayed into the successful decypherment of the Linear B script. "There are still harder nuts to crack" I had said. "There is Linear A and the Phaestos disc. I don't think anyone has made the attempt, for the material is insufficient."

Alec crossed the room to a huge cupboard and opened its doors. It was crammed to overflowing with a jumbled mass of papers among which Alec began to scrabble agitatedly like a dog at a rabbit hole. The pile of papers round him on the floor grew larger but at last he found what he wanted and handed it to me with a grin. It was a discourse read before the Royal Irish Academy as far back as 1912 and was – an attempt to trans- literate the Phaestos disc.

That was Alec all over. You never knew when you had him. His mind was like a bran dip, you could not guess what would come out next. He specialised in out of the way and esoteric knowledge. By pure accident I discovered that he was an acknow- ledged authority on Elizabethan mathematics, and T. R. Henn, our Cambridge literary don, was continually being taken aback by his acquaintance with the more obscure crannies and by-paths of English poetry. He could demonstrate the mysteries of the Mobius rings to a bemused room-full, who scented black magic, or intrigue them by recounting the more scandalous incidents of Irish history which the text book writers discreetly ignored.

His appearance, like everything else about him, was deceptive. Six foot tall, big boned, immensely strong, with a tousle of corn coloured hair framing a ruddy countenance, when first you met him your thoughts went to a Viking leaping with a war cry from the bow of a long ship. The picture of the rude barbarian faded when he opened his mouth. His voice was high pitched, soft, sometimes hardly audible, the words carefully chosen and precise. They could be blistering, they were often humorous with a humour nicely compounded of kindliness and mischief, but they were never commonplace or inconsiderable. He was a talker, not a chatterer.

What was such a polymath doing in charge of a fishing lodge whose entrance gate bore the mysterious word Delphi in Greek capital letters? And why Delphi?

Why Delphi? Only a pleasant conceit born of early nineteenth century romanticism. The second Marquis of Sligo fell in love with Greece and went to live there. When the demands of his Irish estates forced him to return he brought with him a hold-full of antiquities to adorn his mansion at Westport and a heart that hankered after the land he had left. The custom of the day ordained that an Irish peer should have a sporting lodge as well as a mansion. He chose a site in the mountains of south west Mayo and called it Delphi.

At first sight there is little resemblance between the favourite haunt of Apollo, perched high on a sunbaked mountain shoulder, and Delphi lodge buried in the heel of a gorge so dank that in a few years it had to be abandoned and rebuilt further down the valley where the mountains open out. Yet there are some points in common. The Doolough pass, unequalled anywhere in Ireland for desolate grandeur, has its counterparts in the mountains of Greece; the Mweelrea cliffs are not unlike the crag that beetles over the Pierian spring; when the lodge was built there were still eagles on Mweelrea. The name was accepted and spread to cover the whole district. Delphi it is to this day.

The Marquis soon tired of Delphi and for the nineteenth and the better part of the twentieth centuries the lodge and fishery were let to tenants who kept the fishing for their families and a few friends. Delphi was off the beaten tracks – for long there was no road to connect it with Louisburgh the nearest town of any size – and it remained but little known. When the first edition of this book was published I was ignorant of its existence and unaware of the idiosyncracies which distinguish its fishing from that of all the other western white trout lakes.

Alec Wallace had been an accountant in Dublin. Accountancy can be an arid profession with no scope for adventure and Alec had adventure in his bones. At Old Head, two miles from Louisburgh, stood a large old house which had once been used as an hotel. Now it was almost derelict, without electricity or any adequate water supply, the glass gone out of many of its windows. Alec had an idea and with Alec to have an idea was to act. Like Rabbit in *Winnie the Pooh* he never waited for things to turn up but always went and fetched them. He bought the house and lands, descended on it with a collection of fifty craftsmen, himself as foreman, and, incredibly, within three weeks a new hotel was ready. More incredibly, in three days after opening it was full.

Old Head was run more like a country house than a hotel. No public bar, no music or dancing, no advertisement; only first class food and wines, great comfort and illimitable peace. To it gravitated a remarkable collection of talents. I have seen Alec sit down to dinner with two Nobel prize winners while at other tables were a third Nobel winner, the Poet Laureate, and a famous woman historian. Fellows of the Royal Society were two-a-penny. The company was not only select but selected. Alec was in his element.

It was some years before the current lease of Delphi ran out. When it did, and the tenant did not want to renew, Alec was smitten by another idea. He leased Delphi and for good measure, for he never did anything by halves, leased also Tawnyard lake on the Eriff system and the Bunowen river which flows into the sea at Louisburgh. If Old Heads verged on an academy, Delphi was a select fishing club, the qualification for which was that members should be reasonably competent fishermen and know how to behave on and off the water.

Delphi Lodge was a big rambling house built round three sides of a square, rather dilapidated, not very comfortable or well furnished, insufficient in bathrooms. Not one of these things mattered for the old house inhaled kindness and welcome. The regular frequenters were a mixed grill, a couple of university professors, a group of high-up civil servants from Northern Ireland, some businessmen and the whole gamut of the professions. Despite many points of possible friction (for fishermen have been known to be jealous and both sides of the northern divide were represented), I never heard a snarl or a spit. Whether it was the influence of Alec or of the house I know not, but everybody was on good terms with everybody else and friendships were formed which lasted till death. That is, maybe, a slight exaggeration. There was the very odd pebble – two young guards officers who tried to throw around their very inconsiderable weight and a woman whose aggressive self-assurance was only matched by her ignorance – but these were swallows of only one season and when they applied for future bookings Alec was always unaccountably full up.

Alec was not really interested in making money. It was sometimes months after leaving before it was possible to extract an account. At Delphi there was not a bar of any kind, only a press filled with every kind of drink and a child's exercise book for guests to enter their consumption. In the to and fro of conversation there must have been many quite honest forgettings. What really interested him was to be able to play the host. He was lavishly generous with his fishing. The first time I met him he invited me for a week to Delphi as his guest and my last two days at Delphi were at his invitation. Hearing that I was staying with a friend some thirty miles away he asked us both over to fish. On each day we got two fresh run salmon apiece and of the three of us Alec was perhaps the most delighted. There were often one or two anglers at Delphi who would have found it difficult to meet the standard charges and I suspect Alec of making reduced terms.

The surroundings of Delphi are a contrast to the rolling granite hills and stretches of flat bog, blanketed with heather and purple moor grass, which cradled the lakes of Iar Conacht where I had learned my white trout fishing. Here the mountains tower steeply to the sky, heads in the clouds and feet dipping into the water. Along the south west shore of Doolough stretches the massif of Mweelrea with its triple summits rising to over 2600 feet. The opposing shore is ramparted by the line of the Sheefry mountains and the bulk of Ben Gorm, only a hundred feet lower. Bed rock is an Ordovician slate, inhospitable to vegetation, A few patches of dark green on the lower slopes show where bracken has managed to get a footing but above are only fans of fallen scree and a bare scumbling of wiry grass through which uncouth bosses of rock protrude like arthritic joints. Somehow the black-faced mountain sheep manage to scramble a living, often so high up as to be indistinguishable from boulders until they move. Cold and rain and scanty sustenance take their toll. Even for the sure-footed there are concealed perils.

At the lower end of Doolough the Mweelrea cliffs drop bare and almost vertical to the water save for one small outward sloping plateau, hardly larger than a billiard table, where there is a growth of unusually green grass. Noticing this on the first occasion when I fished the lake I asked the boatman if there was a hidden spring. He did not bother to look up but answered "That is what we call the prison. There does be some water coming down by cracks in the rock." "The prison?" I queried. "Yes, sir. A sheep can get into it but he can't get out. They say that a goat did once, but a sheep never." "What becomes of them." "They get along for a bit picking at the grass that is there, but when that is gone the hunger grips them and they become feeble and one night they lose their holt and fall down and are killed. There is a heap of bones below there at the foot of the rock."

I was to see the truth of his account. Next year when I arrived there was a sheep in the prison. It had only been there four days and was still lively, moving about the narrow space and pulling up the remains of the grass. My stay was for ten days and I could see her gradually growing weaker as the supply of grass disappeared. Now she was nearly always lying down, but she was still there when I left. Then came a night of rain and gale. In the morning there was no sheep in the prison but, far below, a bundle of bloodstained wool and flesh at which the grey crows and the ravens were tearing.

It was easy to see how the trap worked. Eight feet above the plateau ran a narrow ledge along which an active sheep could make his way and an eight foot drop is nothing to a sheep lured on by the sight of that patch of grass. With a good run she might even manage to scramble back, but the plateau is so narrow that there is no room for a run and eight feet is too much for a standing jump. The prison is a sentence of death.

No one has ever tried a rescue. With modern apparatus of pitons and pulleys the cliff could easily be climbed and a first-class rock climber could possibly dispense with these aids. Mayo men are not first-class rock climbers and even if the plateau was reached there would remain the dangerous task of lowering a frightened and struggling sheep those hundred feet to safety.

How does the fishing at Delphi compare with that of Fermoyle and the Iar Conacht lakes in general? Delphi is not so well stocked for there is a shortage of good spawning beds, and numbers will be fewer, but the fish will be bigger. At Fermoyle only two fish of five pounds were recorded but at Delphi there were records of several fish just over or under ten pounds and nearly every year an eight pounder was brought in. My own best were two fish of six pounds but in my comparatively few and short visits to Delphi I must have taken more fish of 3 lbs and upwards than in the numerous years when I fished at Fermoyle. There could be many days at a time when the marble slab on which the catch was displayed showed an unhandsome thrift of silver but then would come a change in the weather and the slab would be piled with good trout and a salmon or two beside them.

The fishing has deteriorated steadily since the 19th century. No continuous record of the Delphi bags exists but figures for odd days can be collected from various sources. Seymour Bush, Master of the Rolls, visited Delphi in 1849 for nine days in August and kept a note of the catch. On four days there were four rods fishing, on the others there were five, making a total of 41 rod days. They caught in all 962 white trout, the best being $10\frac{3}{4}$ lbs, and two salmon. That makes an average of over 24 fish per rod per day. On one day a single rod caught 66 fish. In August 1924 two rods fished Doolough and Glencullen for four days catching 167 trout, nearly 21 fish per rod per day. My friend, Noll Gogarty, fished for two days in 1956 and 1957. His diary shows the total catch each day for himself and his companion. Here are the entries:

1956 Sept. 6th 26 sea trout. Total weight 31 lbs.
(Best $5\frac{1}{2}$ lbs – one salmon)
Sept. 7th 18 sea trout. Total weight 22 lbs.
1957 Sept. 20th 16 sea trout. Total weight 32 lbs.
(Best 4 lbs)
Sept. 21st 27 sea trout. Total weight 47 lbs.
(Best $5\frac{1}{2}$ lbs and $5\frac{1}{4}$ lbs)

Noll was probably the best, certainly the most experienced of Delphi fishermen. In three successive years at the end of the sixties we fished together for 10 days every September yet I cannot remember more than one day when we reached double figures. That is a measure of the decline. This steady falling off in the quality of the sea trout fishing was not confined to Delphi. Unfortunately it has been general in our western lakes.

There was always a good sprinkling of salmon in the river and lakes, mostly summer fish of about 8 lbs but with a few larger fish, up to 20 lbs in spring. I must have landed some 15 or 16, the best being 13½ lbs.

Delphi differs from all the other western fisheries in the greater height of its waves and the greater clarity of its water. These peculiarities are due to geography and geology. Doolough, the main lake, fills a trough between two mountain ranges down which the funnelled gusts can rave, piling up waves of such a height and steepness as make it too dangerous for a boat to venture out. On most days the wind blows straight up or down the lough but let it shift a couple of points and the squalls, ricochetting from the cliffs, produce small water spouts which scud across the lake to collapse in a deluge when they touch the shore. I have seen as many as six of these wind-devils (the local name) on the surface at the same time. Should a boat get in their way it can be twisted round and swamped. T. R. Henn had a narrow escape from such a disaster. In such conditions fishing is impossible but even in a very moderate wind the waves on Doolough are foam crested and larger than any you are likely to meet in the smaller lakes of Connemara.

The clarity of the water is due to the nature of the watershed. The water in most of our western lakes comes from rain which has fallen on many square miles of bog, supplemented by seepings from the bog itself. It is more or less deeply stained and has some colloidal matter in suspension so that vision of the fish through the water is very limited. The Delphi watershed is small and inordinately steep. After a few hours heavy rain the mountain sides are a silver filigree of cascading streams. But here the rain has fallen on and the water is cascading over bare rock, naked scree and clean grass. There is nothing to stain it and very little matter in suspension. I have never seen the river which drains the lakes anything which could be called turbid, at most a smoky colour, and the day after a rainfall the water in Doolough will be as clear as in a limestone stream.

In the appendix I have attempted to analyse the effect of high waves and coloured water on the vision of fish. Here it is sufficient to say that at Delphi you will need flies larger than those commonly used in Connemara with one or two making a brave show of tinsel and that you will have to cast further and strip your flies more quickly. At Fermoyle most fishing was done with sizes 11 to 9 (O.S.) while a rough day in Doolough will call for a tail fly as large as a 6 (O.S.) or even a 5. A Delphi speciality was the "Goats Toe" a fly which looks like a small tarantula. The body is of bronze peacock hurl wound over red wool, the tail red wool, the hackle taken from a peacock breast feather. It is tied large and used as a top dropper. Often it is oiled or even greased and is kept tripping along the surface. Fished in this way it can be very deadly. Another popular fly was the Delphi Silver, an all tinsel body with two black hackles, tied in the manner of a salmon grub fly, and a couple of Jungle Cock at the tail.

In an endeavour to add length to the cast and get better control over the working of the flies many anglers stood up to fish. I have seen them standing on the seats and once even on a plank laid across the thwarts. Standing is a dangerous habit and unnecessary. There is, however, a good deal to be said for using a longer rod if you can get one sufficiently light. Once I did own a light twelve foot split cane, in two pieces, which was ideal for boat work. The long joints made it awkward to fit into the car which I was then driving so stupidly I sold it and have ever since regretted.

Major (now Sir Edmond) Philipson Stow introduced to Delphi the Scottish method of dapping large artificial flies. This is one degree less desolating than dapping the natural, for there is scope for more skill. The natural is of such delicacy that it cannot be moved through the water and must float with the wind. Only a single line of water is fished. The artificials are of tougher material and so can be moved from side to side in a big arc, covering a considerable belt. This requires a nicety of touch to keep the fly skimming the surface without allowing it to be whisked away by the wind. The method does undoubtedly bring up the big fish and Sir Edmond made some remarkable bags. The proportion of fish caught to fish risen is small. Many fish miss the skipping fly and even if it is taken the correct timing of the strike is difficult. Pattern or colour of fly does not seem to make much difference; it is the movement and the disturbance of the water that attracts the fish. Dapping flies are usually aesthetic horrors, bottle brushes the size of a small plum or misbegotten creatures sprouting tufts of squirrel fur like errant ears. It is wise to carry a number, for the fly soon becomes water-logged and must be changed. In the evening used flies must be thoroughly dried on the hearth, dipped in whatever is your favourite flotant and left to be ready for the morning. I was induced to give a trial to this method and have often watched it in action at the hands of experts like Sir Edmond or Noll Gogarty but I could not get to like it. Dapping tackle is too strong and clumsy, dapping rods too stiff and insensitive to allow any feeling of intimate contact with the fish.

The Delphi system consists of three lakes and a mile of river. Highest of the lakes is Glencullen, roughly triangular in shape, rather less than a mile long and nearly half a mile wide. Two ancient crannogs lie near the eastern shore. It is a shallow lake, fishable all over, with one good stretch for salmon, and in the past had a high reputation. In two successive August days of 1924 the boat caught forty good trout each day. Those times were past and it never gave me anything more than a very moderate catch.

A short distance to the south and connected by a small stream lies Doolough, two miles long by half a mile wide. Doolough in Gaelic means the dark lake or, more poetically, the lake of shadow. The name is apt. Mweelrea is so lofty and so near that even in midsummer the south western shore is deep in shadow after one o'clock and in winter hardly any part of the lake gets a glimpse of the sun. Doolough is deep along the centre and fishing is confined to a narrow belt touching each of the long shores and two shallower shelfs at each end. Most of the big trout come out of Doolough and there are a number of well known lies for salmon. Certain spots always held an element of excitement. Would the salmon move over the Sunken Rock or off Fishermans Point? Would the large trout be stirring in Fishermans Bay? Given a moderate south east or north west breeze and a high sky Doolough could give a memorable day. There was, however, an element of monotony in the fishing, a long unbroken drift down one shore in the morning and the opposite shore in the afternoon. Inducements to rest an arm were many. The magnificent scenery culminating in a savage glacier coomb where the strata stuck out like skeleton ribs, never palled. Ravens and an occasional peregrine circled overhead. Once there came an osprey. The eye wandered to the scattered sheep, looking no larger than flies, seeking a living on the highest slopes, or was caught by a blue streak like the flight of a kingfisher, which was Alec scorching recklessly along the road cut out of the lakeside rock as he shuttled between lodge and hotel. The voice of my companion came gently chiding. "You won't catch any fish by star-gazing."

Half a mile further down the river was Finlough – in Gaelic

the fair lake or the lake of light. Again the name was apt for here the mountains had slid apart and there was nothing to obstruct the sun. Finlough was a shallow and rather weedy lake, an irregular oval, half a mile by a quarter. It is a happy lake, always interesting, for even in a calm it fishes well to the dry fly. The best patterns for this were the Daddy-long-legs, a large red or grey sedge and, unaccountably, the claret bumble. Left to float motionless the dry fly was not effective. It had to be twitched along the surface in short intermittent jerks.

Finlough gave me my best sea trout, a fish of rather over six pounds, firmly hooked at the base of the dorsal fin. Over a fish so hooked there is little control. He is not in the least incommoded and there is no bit in his mouth with which to steer him. The moment after he was hooked he made upwind on a forty yard dash. Sea trout, unlike salmon, do not allow you a few seconds to collect your wits and a big sea trout runs faster than any salmon. Having finished his burst he turned broadside on and rested. A trout rod or even a salmon rod cannot drag a large fish, hooked halfway between head and tail, broadside through the water. The correct tactics are to row up wind of the fish and drift down, taking in line as you go. That fish would have no such nonsense. Every time the boat drew level with him he was off in another up-wind dash, again to rest broadside on. As he tired from running the spurts grew shorter, but he was still able to put himself up-wind and lie there recuperating. It became clear that he would have to be netted from his down-wind side. At last it was done. The boatman stole the boat up to him while Noll crouched in the extreme bow. There he was, still broadside on, about a foot under water. I held as hard as I dared. The boatman ceased rowing and Noll standing up and stretching out till he looked bound to fall in, slipped the long handled net under him, drew him nearer and lifted him in. That was the toughest fight I had with any fish, trout or salmon. No doubt a purist would have put that fish back, for he was foul hooked. I did not.

Finlough was a good lake for salmon. In 1927 it gave eight in a single day including one of 22 pounds. A small patch, about ten yards by three, where the stream from Doolough began to peter out, was the best spot in the fishery for a salmon. Any day when the wind blew against the stream you might expect one and if there was falling water it was nearly a certainty. One morning conditions looked perfect. There had been heavy rain during the previous evening but now there was a high mixed sky and the glass was shooting up. The lucky pair to whom the roster assigned Finlough for that day were betting how many fish they would collect. At lunch they were disconsolate. Not one fish, salmon or trout, had risen except a couple of finnock, too small to keep. One of them talked about going after mackerel in the sea; at least he would be sure to bring back something. I offered to exchange my beat on Doolough for the afternoon and the offer was at once accepted. This was not nobility of character on my part but a hunch bred of experience. Some time that day salmon were bound to move.

They did. Almost at my first cast in the favourite spot one took, and then a second and a third, and a fourth which got away because the dropper was caught in a patch of debris brought down by the flood. Then the lake closed up again and not another fish moved.

Shortly below Finlough the fishable part of the river begins, a merry stream which can be covered anywhere with a trout rod. Mostly it is a collection of short pools broken by falls and weirs. Only one pool is deep and long enough to hold a resident population of salmon but nearly all have a lodge or two where the fish can rest on their way to the lakes. It gave me half a dozen salmon and should have given more. The clarity of the water was such that a salmon could be seen coming for the fly long before he reached it and this betrayed me into striking too soon. It could hold big trout. Alec once got an eight pounder and an angler who fished before Alec (and who was not always veracious) boasted of catching a large number of five pounders. I never got a trout of any size. It should have given good night fishing and in July or August there were always some whose energies were not exhausted by the day and who went out again when the sun had sunk. I never heard of much success.

Besides Delphi, Alec rented Tawnyard and the Bunowen River. Tawnyard discharges into the Erriff. With its wooded islands it is a very lovely lake with a more gentle beauty than Doolough. Like Finlough it fishes well to the dry fly. There is one peculiarity. Owing to some configuration of the surrounding hills it is plagued with contrary winds. I have known the wind to be at my back when I lifted the flies and in my teeth when I started the forward drive. Often when the cast was just settling down it would be whisked sideways over the line of my companion.

One incident is worth recording. After a poor day Noll and I were having a late tea before a final drift over a sandy bay to where the boat was kept. A few medium sized sedges were floating out from the shore and I mentioned that the old Irish Orange Grouse was supposed to be a sedge pattern and that I had done well with it on the sand in Corrib. "Try one now" said Noll. I changed my tail fly for an Orange Grouse which I had recently tied with a rather prominent tag of fluorescent green silk. Before we had drifted a hundred yards I had three trout of five pounds, three pounds and two pounds. This encouraged me to experiment further with fluorescent materials, but without success. Indeed I think that, unless used with economy, they can have an adverse effect.

The Bunowen was purely a spate river. I have taken one salmon and a couple of sea trout in low water but it was not worth fishing except in a spate. Even in a spate, timing had to be exact. If you got your timing right the sport was magnificent. At Old Head was a photograph of a local solicitor with sixteen salmon and a good sea trout at his feet, all caught in an hour and three quarters out of the famous Carr's pool where the fish rest after tackling a fierce weir. Other anglers have caught fifteen or sixteen salmon in the course of a day and Alec once took six out of another pool in forty minutes, after which he grew bored and went away.

To illustrate how important timing can be the experience of one day is illuminating. I arrived at Carr's pool about eleven to find the river in nice order. There had been rain in the night but now it was fine. Over the Sheefry hills black clouds had gathered, warning of a new downpour. Before one I had three salmon but by now the river had risen two inches and was still rising rapidly. The first two inches of a rise can be good but after that fishing is at an end so I went off to Old Head for what turned out to be a prolonged lunch. After lunch I started to go back to the lodge and stopped to have a look at Carr's pool on the way. I was surprised to find it again falling. The first rise had been due to a heavy shower which had preceded the main downfall. A three pound trout came at once followed by a big salmon, a sulky fish who would not run but kept boring in the deep part of the pool till finally the hook came away. By the time he escaped the main flood had come down and the water was visibly climbing up the banks. Finish!

For fourteen years Alec managed the two establishments at Delphi and Old Head, shuttling twice a day at a reprehensible speed over the ten miles that separated them. At both ends of his journey there were always people waiting and looking out for him. It was accepted that he was able to fix anything from a broken switch to a broken engagement. Whenever he appeared there was a slight and pleasurable increase in tension, a kind of suppressed excitement. He stimulated, encouraged, commiserated, teased, mocked, sympathised, as the mood took him. Ideas sprouted in his mind as an August field sprouts mushrooms. The sea trout in Poland were giants? Ova were procured from Poland, hatched and introduced as fry into the waters of Delphi. Lobsters hung around rocky reefs and there were still some reefs uncharted in the Killaries which could be pin-pointed by an echo-sounder? An echo-sounder appeared in his sea-going boat. A new wing might be built on the hotel. It was. But at last the fishing leases came to an end and the rents demanded for renewal were exorbitant. Alec was getting tired of hotel keeping and the demands of the Tourist Board ran counter to the methods he favoured. Besides he had engendered a new idea. Old Head was sold, a Land Rover bought and Alec was off to Afghanistan with a few stops on the way to inspect early mathematical manuscripts. Another little Eden had vanished.

ENVOI

The old man working by the roadside looked up and said something in Irish to his companion as I passed. Having no Gaelic I asked my ghillie to translate, which with a little embarrassment he did. "He says, 'There goes the last of the ould lot and he's sticking it out well.' "

"The last of the old lot" – well it was true, though I had not realised it. Only John Spellman and I could look back on Fermoyle for thirty years. "Memory fades, must the remembered perishing be?" When John and I crumbled who would remember? No one. I should have liked to write more of Sherry and Molly Shepherd, of Sir Edward and Lady Stracey and the hospitality they showed to me when they were owners of Fermoyle; of the good fishermen, good shots and good companions who made up their house parties; of Jack Meldon, who introduced me to the fishery, and who was, at varying times, the best bat, the best cue, the best shot and the best rod in Ireland; of Paddy Mor with the immense shoulders and uncertain temper; of old Pat who died at eighty-six still thinking of fish and snipe, still planning improvements to the fishery he had made; of Michael Walsh who never stepped into a boat without bringing luck. I am tempted to tell of the magician of Fermoyle (though that was only one of Jamesie's tales); of the house abandoned when the roof was ready because it had been built across a fairy pass; of the lad who described to me how, as a boy, he had been taken away by the fairies and returned by them because he would not eat or drink, none the worse save that he was deaf and dumb for a fortnight – indeed rather the better, for the fairies had given him the whisper and the touch for a sick cow; of the fears and hauntings of that wild upland, and the great grey boulders that play grandmother's steps with you as night closes in. But this book, as my publisher reminds me, is already too long. And so I can only say a last farewell to all those who fished the lakes and tramped the mountain with me, and who now have gone their ways. Fermoyle remains, Fermoyle – grey boulders and flood.

And not only Fermoyle. The pleasant company who used to assemble at Delphi lodge are dispersed and the greater number are dead, but the morning mists still swirl and boil in the great coomb of Mweelrea; the Slaney waters still murmur down the Fairy Seat though all those who fished the bank opposite have gone. They are there for new generations to enjoy.

"For what we have received may the Lord make us truly thankful."

REQUIESCAM

Bear my body, when I die,
Far from men, and let it lie
   By a salmon river.
Where the larches troop their ranks
And, above the granite banks
   Silver birches shiver.

Stay not, stranger, passing by,
For decorous lament or sigh
   Where I rest beside you.
Go, my brother, cast your line,
With a craft that once was mine,
   And good luck betide you.

There, who knows, I still may ply
O'er the stream a phantom fly
   For a midnight capture,
And, if heaven attends my wish,
Bring to bank a ghostly fish
   In a ghostly rapture.

APPENDIX

THE EFFECT OF (i) WAVES AND (ii) DEEPLY STAINED WATER ON A FISH'S VISION OF A FLY: AND SOME PRACTICAL CONSIDERATIONS ARISING THEREFROM*

Some years ago when writing about Fermoyle, a Connemara white trout fishery which I had known intimately for a quarter of a century, I ventured some general observations as to the most characteristic form of rise, the best way of working the flies, the sizes to use and the features common to the most successful patterns. I went further and said that my remarks, with minor modifications, would apply to any sea-trout fishery from Donegal to Galway. With all these fisheries except one, I had rather more than a nodding acquaintance. Rashly I had assumed that the exception (the Delphi fishery in South Mayo) would conform to the general pattern. Two years afterwards I visited Delphi, to discover how wrong I was. I had said that the most usual form of rise was the hairpin, straight up, over and down, but here the trout often came slashing at the fly in a long slanting rush which might be visible for ten feet, and which by its pace when first visible, showed that the fish must have glimpsed the fly at an appreciably greater distance. The sizes I had recommended for normal conditions were 11 to 9, and 7 in a high wind. At Delphi 8 and 7 were normal and 6, and even 5 could be used if the waves were high. Instead of the moderate length of line and slow, even draw which Connemara required, a long line stripped back as rapidly as possible gave the best results at Delphi. Finally, while in Connemara the most successful patterns were sombre, black and claret being the favourites, with little show of tinsel, and colour added only in the form of translucent hackles and picked-out fur, Delphi demanded some lighter and brighter flies with a brave show of tinsel.

* Reprinted by kind permission from the *Flyfishers' Journal.*

What was the explanation? It was natural to look for differences in the characteristics of the two fisheries, and three were at once apparent. The waters in Delphi were bigger, the water was unstained by peat, and the surface of the bottom was pale in colour and so capable of reflecting more light than the boggy bottoms of the Connemara lakes.

The difference in the behaviour of the fish seemed likely to be due to some difference in the way they saw the fly, and the way they saw the fly would be affected by the differences in their surrounding. But exactly how? No doubt the books would provide the answer. I was fairly familiar with the diagrams of a fish's vision, based on the accepted laws of optics, where an object in

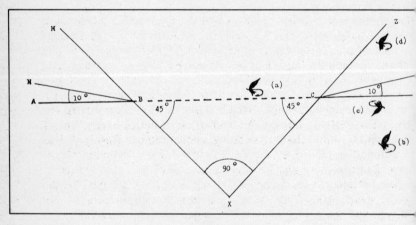

DIAGRAM 1

one medium (water or air) is seen by an eye in another medium (air or water), and I turned to the printed page to refresh my memory. The diagrams were there all right, but they were little to the purpose, for the conditions they supposed depended on water whose surface was level and unbroken, and whose clarity was nearly infinite. Such conditions might be approximate in a tank, and relevant where a fish wanted to inspect a fly as closely as a diamond dealer would a suspect jewel, but in a lake or a rough stream where the surface was disturbed, the visibility limited by colour in the water and where fish often take with a lightning dash, there would have to be many qualifications before the diagrams were of any assistance.

Let us make a start with the standard diagram, very slightly modified. This is Diagram 1. ABCD represents the surface of the water. X is a fish lying two feet below the surface. BCX represents his cone of vision within which he can see not only objects in the water, but objects on the surface and above it. Owing to the bending of light rays when they enter the water from the air, the fish can also, so to speak, see round the corner at the edge of his cone, and objects in the areas NBM and YCZ such as the fly shown at (A), in the air, would be visible to him in a blurred and distorted form; but these objects would be up in the air, and as we are concerned only with the angler's flies when they are on the surface (dry fly and dap) or under the surface (wet fly), this area can, for present purposes, be left out of account.

If the fish sees the area BC as a window, how does he see the surface AB and CD surrounding the window? The answer is that he sees that surface as a mirror, reflecting the underwater world, just as a man looking out over a calm lake sees the surface as a mirror reflecting the overwater world.

The fish, then, can see an angler's fly in three ways: (a) If it is on the surface he can see it within the area BC, in the same way as we would see a fly held over our heads in the air. If it is on the surface outside that area he cannot see it at all. A fly so seen is shown in the diagram at (a).

(b) If it is underwater, he can see it anywhere, within the area of the window or outside it. In water ideally clear the distance at which he can see it depends only on his powers of vision and the size of the fly. The anatomists tell us that a fish is shortsighted, but from observations of the distance at which a salmon can be alarmed by a mere wave of the hand, I would suggest that his vision is sufficient to enable him to pick up a moving object of reasonable size at a distance of up to 20 yards. No water is ideally clear, and if it is stained or turbid the range of vision will be cut down proportionately just as our own over-water vision is cut down by haze or fog. A fly seen underwater is shown in the diagram at (b).

(c) There is a third way in which a fish may see a fly. As the surface of the water outside his window is for him a mirror reflecting the underwater world, he can see a mirror-image of the fly (b) reflected as an upside-down fly at (c). This could perhaps induce him to look around for and find the real fly (b) which he had not previously noticed.

Though these are the only ways in which he can actually *see* a fly, there is another way in which he can become *aware of its presence* in the neighbourhood. If something be dragged along in the skin of the water, as when a big top-dropper or an artificial dapping fly is made to skim along the surface, this will be seen by the fish as a distortion of his mirror which will indicate that on the surface there is something moving, therefore probably alive and possibly edible. If he is moved to investigate, a few strokes of his tail will bring the moving object within his cone of vision. I doubt if the importance of this mirror-distortion in alerting fish has been adequately realized.

So much for the laws of optics in ideal conditions, which are never fully realized in lake or stream fishing where the surface is usually disturbed and the water of restricted clarity. I should perhaps explain that there is one apparent error in Diagram 1. The laws of optics decree that the angle of the point of the cone should be not 90° but 97°, and the angles at the base should be not 45° but 41½°. I have made the alterations for two reasons. The vision round the extreme edge of the cone is so distorted and so subject to chromatic aberration that I think this marginal vision should be neglected and the cone of practical vision reduced to 90°. There is moreover a practical advantage in taking the working angles to be 90° and 45°. It means that the diameter of the base of the cone of vision is always exactly double the depth at which the fish is lying. It means also that however the slant of the surface may be altered by wave motion, the fish may be assumed to see everything on the surface if a line from his eye to the floating object makes an angle of 45° or more with the plane of the surface at that point. This angle is easy to visualize, to calculate and to draw, and for purposes of really effective vision is, I believe, more correct than the theoretical 41½°.

The complicated nature of a fish's underwater vision may be more easily realized if we compare it with the analogous vision of a man standing on a high rock in the middle of a calm lake. If he looks down he can see through the adjacent water, observe the stones on the bottom and spot any fish moving. The area of the circle of water into which he can see is limited to a diameter of about twice the height of his eye above the water; this is the counterpart of the fish's window. Outside this circle the man cannot see anything underwater. The surface of the lake becomes a reflecting mirror: this is the counterpart of the fish's under-water mirror. Now suppose a cormorant appears. As long as it is in the air (that is, in the same medium as the man's eye) the distance at which he can see it is determined only by his own powers of vision, the size of the bird and the absence of haze or fog: this corresponds to the fish's vision of a fly when it is underwater (that is, in the same medium as his eye.) The cormorant now dives. If his dive is close to the rock his progress is visible to the man in his cone of underwater vision: if further out, the bird disappears beneath the mirror surface. Just so is the fly on or above the surface visible to the fish as long as it is within his window, but invisible when on or above the mirror area surrounding the window.

The man may not have been looking in the direction from which the cormorant was coming. The first signal of its existence may be its reflection in the surface mirror: the man lifts his eyes and picks up the bird in the air. This is the counterpart of the underwater reflection which calls the attention of a fish to the existence of a fly, and one may reasonably suppose, enables him to look round and find the fly in its real position.

Finally, suppose that the man has not seen the approach, or the dive, or the reflection, of the cormorant. It has stolen up on him from behind, and is swimming underwater, close enough to the surface to distort the mirror. The man knows that something alive is moving there. That is how a fish becomes aware, by the distortion of his underwater mirror, that something which may

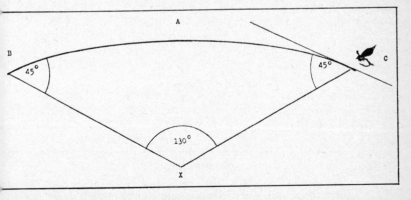

DIAGRAM 2

be of interest is likely to greet him if he goes in for a closer look.

So much for what happens in ideal conditions of calm and clear water. In practice there will be larger or smaller waves on the surface, more or less colour in the water. Consider first what will be the effect of waves, a matter of importance to anyone fishing a dryfly or a dap. Imagine a lake covered with big, rolling waves, two feet from crest to trough, such as may be encountered in our big Irish lakes. Diagrams 2 and 3 (drawn to the same scale as Diagram 1) show the effect of such waves. X is a trout two feet below the normal surface of the lake, which means that he is three feet under the surface when the crest of a wave is above him (Diagram 2) and only one foot below when a trough is over him (Diagram 3). We have seen that a fish can see anything on the surface when the angle which is made by a line from his eye to the surface plane at the point at which the object is floating, is 45° or more. Now see Diagram 2. If we draw a tangent to the curve of the imagined wave at the points B and C, a line from the trout's eye to the tangent at B or C will make an angle of 45° and everything on the surface between B and C will be within the window, and the angle at the apex of the cone has expanded to 130°. Diagram 3 shows the position where the fish is under the trough. The points where a line drawn from the fish's eye would meet the surface plane at an angle of 45° are again indicated at B and C and only objects between B and C

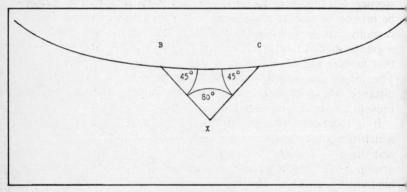

DIAGRAM 3

are within the window. The base of the cone of vision in Diagram 1 is 4 feet, in Diagram 2 is approximately 9 feet and in Diagram

3 is only $1\frac{3}{4}$ feet. These striking differences arise from the combination of two factors, the difference in the curvature of the surface (in one case concave and in the other convex) and the differing depth of the fish below the surface.

The waves are rolling by continuously, now a crest, now a trough, and as they do so, the area of the fish's vision is expanding, contracting, expanding like the iris diaphragm of a camera. When he is under a crest, the fish can see the fly at double the distance at which he could see it if the surface is calm and level, but he can see it only momentarily: it disappears when the trough arrives, to reappear with the next crest. It seems probable – though this is no more than conjecture – that these glimpses may be sufficient to induce the fish to go for the fly and go for it quickly in an upward dive. As he gets nearer to it, it will come within the narrower cone which exists even when he is under a trough. My own observation has led me to the conclusion that, where there are considerable waves, a fish does go for a fly from a greater distance and on a long slant, followed by a kind of porpoise roll as he takes it. This is more noticeable in clear than in coloured water because the fish is seeing the fly *through* water, and if the water is sufficiently coloured he will not be able to see through it as far as the theoretical edge of his window.

It can be objected that these diagrams are theoretical and unreal, and in a sense this is true. Waves may be shorter, lower, steeper, than those in the imaginary diagrams. Their surface may be broken by smaller waves which alter the angle of vision. What remains true in any conditions is that the fish can see the fly at a greater distance if there are waves than if there are none, but that he sees the distant fly only in a series of repeated glimpses. The longer vision would account for the dash from a greater distance, the fact that it may be seen only in glimpses would prevent too critical an initial inspection.

It is something of a relief to turn to the simpler conditions which prevail when the fly is under water. As both the fish's eye and the fly are in the same medium, there are no complications arising from the refraction of light when passing from one medium to another. The effect of waves is comparatively unimportant. Looking down at the bottom of a lake when there is a strong sun and waves, the passage of the waves is shown on the bottom by moving shadows, and this means that the illumination of the underwater fly will vary somewhat in intensity as waves come and go. This may to some extent impair the distinctness of detail of the fly as seen by the fish. Otherwise waves may be neglected.

The important factors are the size and distance of the fly, the nature of the illumination, the colour and turbidity of the water. That a large fly can be seen more easily than a small, a near than a distant, requires no elaboration. The nature of the illumination, as well as its intensity, is vital. An underwater fly is illuminated by rays of light coming from every direction, direct from the sky at various angles, and reflected from the bottom and the surrounding vegetation, also at various angles. Of these rays, those coming from the sky are much the strongest, but an appreciable amount of light can be reflected from a pale coloured bottom. All fishes are darker in colour on top than underneath, a form of camouflage, for the light underside, illuminated by feebler rays, appears to the eye of a predator as being much the same in tone as the dark upper side which is illuminated by stronger rays, and so the fish is less conspicuous.

The rays which hit and illuminate the fly may reach the eye of the fish in two ways. They may be *reflected* from the surface of the fly in greater or less degree where the fly is constructed of opaque materials, and in proportion to the reflecting power of those materials. They may also *pass through* the fly in so far as it is constructed of translucent materials. If all the materials are opaque and the greater part of the rays come from the far side of the fly, properly speaking the fly is not seen at all: what is seen is the interruption of the rays by the materials of the fly. It appears as a black silhouette.

These facts are more readily appreciated if we imagine a chess board in which one set of squares is made of opaque but brightly coloured enamels, and the other set of richly coloured stained glass. If you put this board on the ground and look down on it, the enamels will shine back at you in all their colour and the coloured glass will be no more than a dowdy inconspicuousness: the board is below you, no appreciable light is striking up from the ground, and you see it only where the materials reflect light from above. Now hold the board directly above your head. The opaque enamels become a colourless gloom, but the squares of stained glass flash into brilliance. Again the light coming from below is negligible. The opaque enamels have nothing to reflect. The strong light coming from the zenith is unable to pass through the opaque portions, but it is transmitted directly through the coloured glass. If all the squares were opaque, the chess board would be seen only as a silhouette.

A fly is constructed of various materials; opaque and non-reflecting as in a body of black silk, opaque and highly reflecting as in a body of flat tinsel, opaque and reflecting in some parts but not in others as with jungle cock cheeks, partially translucent and partially reflecting as with good quality hackles, picked-out seal's fur or golden pheasant toppings; almost entirely translucent as in the body materials of some of Dunne's dry fly patterns. Most wing and body materials are mainly opaque and reflect light in a greater or less degree according to whether they are pale or dark in tone.

Translate all this into practical terms, taking first the case where the water is clear and the bottom light, as at Delphi. The fish can see the fly a long distance sideways through the water, and the larger the fly the greater the distance. He can also see it for a great portion of its travel as it is dragged through the water, and a rapidly travelling fly is more likely to attract his attention than one moving slowly. Because the light from the sky penetrates easily through the clear water, and there is also a considerable amount of reflection from the bottom, he will be able to see the light reflected from the tinsel and the brighter colours. A large fly, a rapidly travelling fly, a good deal of tinsel and brightness would seem to be indicated: and this corresponds with experience. If the water is clear, the fish is not confined to seeing the fly when it is more or less above him, but can see it laterally from a considerable distance, and so rises will not be confined to the up-and-down type but will include the long, oblique dash. This is also what we find in practice.

The considerations are very different where the water is deeply coloured and the bottom dark and non-reflecting. These are the typical conditions of Connemara. The rays of light can penetrate only a very limited distance through the water, the distance being directly proportional to their intensity and the extent to which the water is coloured. Rays striking downwards from the sky and meeting the water at angles not departing much from a right angle are the strongest and can penetrate the furthest, their power of penetration gradually diminishing as their angle of incidence grows less. Compared with these rays coming direct from the sky, the power of rays reflected from the underwater fly is negligible. If I may speculate from recollections of my own efforts to see a fly through deeply stained water, I would doubt if a fish lying three or four feet below the surface could see a fly, even a large fly, sideways at a distance of more than three feet. But he would see a circle of light above him where the stronger rays from the sky were able to penetrate the water and reach his eye, and he would be able to see an object moving within that circle. He would not see the object by reflected light, for the dark bottom would not give any light to its undersurface, and nearly all the light would be coming from the far side of the object. It would appear to him chiefly as a silhouette, and the darker and more opaque the object the better the silhouette. If there were translucent materials, especially round the edge of the object, he could see the colours by *transmitted* light. We may take the analogy of a man trying to see something in twilight, perhaps trying to thread gut through the eye of a fly. He will hold the fly above his head to get it silhouetted against the sky.

What would we expect to be the result of these considerations in practice? Tinsels and other materials which show by reflection would be at a discount. What we would aim at would be a dark fly for a silhouette, with translucent hackles and picked-out seal's fur to provide some element of colour. This is in fact the type of fly which does best in Connemara. It need not be large, for no matter what the size, it would not be seen for any great distance laterally, while a comparatively small fly can be seen from below silhouetted against the sky. It would be a mistake to strip the fly too rapidly if it is visible to the fish only for a small part of its travel: better to move it slowly so as to leave it longer in the area immediately above the fish. As the distance over which it would be moved would not be large, there would be no need to cast and recover a long line. Finally we would expect nearly all the rises to be of the up-and-down type where the fish had seen the fly immediately above him, and not the long slant which occurs when the fish has seen the fly laterally from a distance. Again experience seems to correspond with the theory.

None of these conclusions can be pushed to extremes. They represent tendencies rather than hard and fast axioms. Large lakes may have only small waves; the extent of staining in Connemara and other turf-fed water varies widely according to the conditions. Fish can be taken with a silver-bodied fly in Connemara or with an all-black fly at Delphi. The experience of other

anglers may confirm or refute my own. I put the theories forward
as a target for attack.

Water	Date of Capture	Weight in lbs. ozs.		Length in inches	Age in years *
L. Corrib	28/7/59	21	6	36.0	11+
R. Shannon	22/2/57	20	0	33.0	11+
Lr. L. Erne	26/9/59	16	7	33.0	7+
L. Mask	26/3/59	15	0	33.0	—
L. Mask	24/3/59	14	12	31.0	—
L. Melvin	5/9/58	14	0	29.5	—
Lr. L. Erne	25/4/59	14	0	31.0	—
L. Mask	30/3/58	13	8	31.0	8
L. Mask	8/9/59	13	6	32.0	—
L. Mask	22/7/58	13	0	30.5	8+
L. Mask	14/8/58	12	6	32.8	8+
L. Mask	25/3/59	12	4	32.2	6+
Lr. L. Erne	10/8/58	12	3	31.0	—
L. Corrib	27/2/58	12	0	31.0	9
L. Corrib	31/5/58	12	0	34.0	6+
L. Mask	29/8/58	12	0	31.5	—
L. Erne	13/8/58	11	10	29.5	6+
L. Mask	30/5/58	11	4	29.0	7+
Lr. L. Erne	18/9/58	11	2	28.0	8+
L. Erne	13/8/58	11	0	29.5	8+
L. Conn	29/9/59	11	0	30.0	7+
L. Corrib	14/9/58	10	13½	32.0	10+
L. Carra	11/8/57	10	13	29.0	5+
Up. Lk. Killarney	16/6/57	10	13	28.5	10+
R. Shannon	18/8/58	10	12	29.0	8+
L. Mask	18/3/58	10	12	29.5	8
L. Corrib	16/6/57	10	8¼	29.0	8+
Lr. L. Erne	15/8/59	10	8	27.5	7+
L. Corrib	19/4/59	10	6	32.0	7+
Up. Lk. Killarney	30/2/58	10	2	30.0	11+
L. Corrib	26/5/59	10	0	—	10+
L. Corrib	19/8/59	10	0	29.0	6+
L. Corrib	17/5/59	9	12	29.5	8+
L. Rea	21/6/59	9	10	29.0	—
L. Mask	26/5/59	9	8	—	7+
L. Corrib	26/5/59	9	6	—	10+
L. Corrib	22/5/59	9	4	28.5	9+
L. Mask	22/8/59	8	13	28.0	7+
L. Mask	20/7/59	8	4	27.0	5+

* The + sign indicates part of a year.

LARGE BROWN TROUT CAUGHT ON ROD AND LINE, 1957–1959

Table compiled by Arthur E. J. Went, D.Sc.,
and reproduced by permission of *Irish Angling and Shooting News*

Index

221